BUTTERFLY

From daughter to mother

Danielle Lacy

To Kari —
I hope this book
makes you smile and
reflect! Cheers to the moms in heaven!
Tiffany Lacy 2019

Cover Photography Copyright © 2013 by Danielle Lacy
Cover Design by Matthew Lacy
Editing by Kim Catanzarite
ISBN: 978-1-7335753-9-3
Publishing: My Three Roses

Contact: www.DanielleLacy.com

I dedicate BUTTERFLY *to my mother,*
Mona Debra Mason
who, clearly by an accident, taught me perseverance!

I thank my mother for working closely with me for six months discussing our lives and the topics of this book.

I thank my father for his complete support and willingness to answer a thousand questions during the writing of this memoir.

I thank my new husband, Matt, for living these memories with me and for rereading the book ten times so I could have it perfect.

I thank my beautiful children for having my back and trusting that what I wrote always had their best interest in mind.

I thank my readers Lori, Roseanne, Selbs, Remi, Jaimie, Sam, and Megan for helping me keep this book on track.

I thank my friends and family for always believing I could write a book or at least keeping their doubts to themselves!

I thank every character in the book that made a positive difference in my life and agreed to let me include them in this book.

I also thank all of the characters that my editor slashed…sorry you didn't make the final cut! You still impacted my life!

And most of all I thank my editor, Kim, who started this journey with me and saw it through to the end.

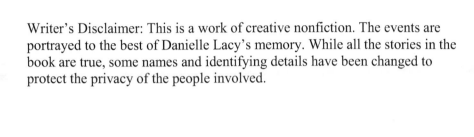

Writer's Disclaimer: This is a work of creative nonfiction. The events are portrayed to the best of Danielle Lacy's memory. While all the stories in the book are true, some names and identifying details have been changed to protect the privacy of the people involved.

PROLOGUE

"**D**anny, I need you to come home." The sound of Dad's voice was like no other sound I had ever heard. He seemed so far away as he uttered these words on the other side of the phone. My eyes shot open as I stared at the ceiling, fully awake. I hurried out of bed, nauseous as I attempted to hold my emotions together.

I drove home down Jackson Road to Oak Shade Road in complete silence, zombie-like, holding onto the steering wheel tightly. The drive felt monotonous on most days but today it was different. I was on auto pilot, barely able to catch my breath through each loud sob, while desperately trying to pay attention to the road. At six in the morning, the road was empty, and I was thankful.

I fought to recollect every word my mother said as I walked out of our home the prior night, during what I now realized was our last conversation. I pictured her face and what it felt like to kiss her skinny cheek as I said, "Goodbye, I will see you in the morning." I stepped away from her bed and felt her tiny hand grab onto mine. Smiling, she said something she had never said before.

"Danielle, I am so proud you are *my daughter,* and if given the chance I would have picked you as my friend."

I smiled back and chuckled, "I *know* Mom! I love you too."

As I drove, I heard these words in my head. Tree after tree flew past at sixty miles per hour, in a forty-five, while I imagined how I would react to a police officer if one pulled me over. "My mother just died, Sir," was all I could think to say in the hope that he would help me drive ninety miles an hour to get back to my mother's side. I dismissed this thought as memories of Mom barged into my head. "The rain is coming, Danielle. We need to get out there before the lightning."

I ran outside, at five years old, barefoot, waiting for the storm to come. I couldn't wait for the puddles to form so that we could splash our feet in them. The storm would rush in and Mom would raise her face to the sky and feel the rain as the drops washed her body. She looked like an angel as her dark hair became slick and wet, and her makeup smeared. I laughed as we soaked ourselves and danced with our arms reaching for the sky.

Once the thunder started, we would rush inside and change out of our wet clothes to curl up on the couch. "I'm making you beautiful, Momma," I said as I wiped her smeared makeup away from her eyes. Curling into a resting position against her, I hugged her tighter. "And you will always be beautiful, my doodle bug," she replied.

Wishing I could just be home already tore me apart inside. I wanted to regret leaving my mother's side but I couldn't because Mom wanted me out of her house that night. She wanted time alone with Dad, and with both of my kids gone for the weekend, Mom willed that I "skedaddle" too.

Earlier that night she'd said, "Find yourself a good man!" and smacked my butt, laughing. Normally I would roll my eyes and yell "Mom!" in return, but that day I smiled knowing some things never change. I was thirty-seven years old, and I know that she truly had only one wish for me: to be happy, because happiness had been elusive lately.

"Make sure you clean up after yourself," Mom yelled to me as I walked out the last night I saw her. It was something she always said when I was a kid. I laughed at how unbelievably simple those words truly were and how, as a teenager, I lost my mind when she said them… even if *I left my sneakers at the entranceway.* As a teenager, I freaked out when Mom mentioned one more chore that I'd forgotten to do before I left the house.

"Really? Mom! Stop. I'll get to it when I get home," I would yell upstairs, knowing Mom was happily cuddling in her bed at three in the afternoon. It seems so trivial now that shoes could cause so much hardship between two people, but as a teen they had the power to set our home on fire. Unfortunately for me, I was the gasoline and she was the open flame.

At that moment, I regretted the many years we wasted arguing over the silliest five-second issues, especially when there were many painful serious issues to argue about.

I felt myself glorifying my recently deceased mother. After all, why hold onto the past? The last six months, we were the perfect mother and daughter—loving even. But it hadn't always been that way, and I was wondering why. *Where had we gone wrong?*

The emptiness set in. Mom was gone. Still searching I questioned our past. Our relationship had many ups and downs—but wasn't that normal?

It seemed strange to think, that much of my life all I ever wanted was for *Mom to be "normal"* and now all I wanted was for *Mom to be "alive."*

Tears welled up, I was losing control. Forcefully, I blinked them away. The thirty-minute drive seemed like an hour. As I wiped the tears from my cheek, I caught a glimpse of a police car safely hidden among the pine trees. My heart began to race, pounding out of my chest. *I am going to actually get pulled over.* I shook my head at the irony. I slammed on my brakes and slowed down just enough. *Two more minutes to home.*

I turned into the development I grew up in, losing the cop from my line of sight. I sighed with relief. Pulling up to my childhood home I felt proud of Dad, because forty years ago he bought Mom her dream home. My parents moved to Tabernacle, New Jersey, so Mom (a Northeast Philadelphia girl) could have a farm and own horses.

I climbed out of the car, "I miss you already," I whispered to the wind. I walked toward the house while staring at the barn with the fence that held mom's horses over thirty years ago.

I missed the days when I rode horses with Mom on the dirt roads. She put me in front of her on our western saddle and told me to grab the reigns.

Whenever I thought I might fall off, I let go of the reigns and dramatically screamed, "I am falling off. I'm slipppppping. I'm *gonna* get my head stepped on by the horse!" She grabbed my hand, pulled me back in front of her, and shoved my hands back to the safety of the horn of the saddle.

"You're going to lose the horse, Danielle." Mom would yell at me when I let go of the reigns. Not wanting Mom's horses to run away, I grabbed the reigns and pulled fast. Sometimes I yanked the horse's mouth and it would stop short. Mom didn't mind and laughed when I started to slide off the saddle. She let me ride with her until I was eight and I started to complain that I wanted to ride alone. Mom was not letting anyone ride her horses without her, even if she was watching. So, I stopped riding horses.

Mom controlled the horse anyway so it didn't matter if I let go, but still she would say, "You can't ever let go of the reigns Danielle. The horse *will* run away and you need to *always* be in control."

Part 1:
Youth and Innocence

Chapter 1
1986- Life is "easy" as a kid

I survived my childhood never quite understanding why I had to keep my room clean. I tried to tell my missed-her-calling-as-a-drill-sergeant mom "My stuffed animals aren't done playing yet." She would frown at me, and I frowned right back. How could she not know that the dust would get mad when I forced it to leave it's perfectly covered counter space? That my clothes didn't want to be smashed in the drawers when they were happy living freely on my floor? That my necklaces enjoyed hanging in a tangle together! And my earrings, which I couldn't wear because they were fake and turned my ears bright red, were happy linked together as they were. Even my blankets liked to wrestle with the bed, and the remote control sometimes played hide-and-go-seek.

Everything, in my nine-year-old opinion, was as it should be.

At night with the lights off, I jumped across the red-and-black shag carpet, careful not to get my leg stuck in a laundry pile before hopping onto my bed. Reaching over to grab my book and flashlight, I curled up in my blankets, hiding down as far as I could while tucking the blankets around me to form an air bubble inside the dark cave. I would finally have time to read.

Each night my reading was interrupted when I heard Mom or Dad coming down the hall for their last goodnight-lights-out-routine. When such "emergencies" occurred, I quickly lay flat, as if hiding from a

1

bear. I shut off my flashlight and breathed only as much as necessary. The door-knob turned and I lay flatter than I thought possible. Pretending to be asleep would hopefully prevent the yelling about how I "*forgot* to clean my room again." Hopefully the barriers of clothing still stood tall as a blockade to the door. If not, I prayed the mine-field of laundry and sticky, filthy food plates would stop my parents' advance. I held my breath, hoping the door would close again so I could go back to reading.

On this particular night, something went horribly wrong. After the door cracked open, there was a bright, bright light. *Was I spotted?* I worked hard not to breathe. I didn't want to face getting yelled at because I didn't clean my room. I lay in my bed knowing fake sleep would only get me so far, that tonight I had to feign death. I prayed the bathroom would make a noise and distract the invader. Someone struggled in an effort to push the door past a layer of shoes blocking the way.

"How can you live like this?"

My mother!

"You're such a pig. Someday your husband will deal with you, Danielle."

I leaped into standing position on my bed. "Husband, husband...He will love me as I am!"

"Yeah, okay!" She laughed as if she knew something I didn't know.

I reached for her to come closer as I fell less than gracefully onto my unkempt bed. She wouldn't venture through the mess to kiss me goodnight but it was always worth the effort of asking. This was the risk I took for not doing as I was told. As I emitted a round of fake, gargantuan snores, I peeked one eye open and caught a glance of my annoyed yet-stunningly-beautiful mom. Dressed like a skinny dark, pink teddy bear in her fluffy robe with her brown permed hair and perfectly set makeup, including blue eyeliner to accent her dark brown eyes, she was flawless. She closed the door, waving goodbye, and said "Ha! Don't let the bed bugs bite, Danielle."

I returned to my book under my blankets. Finding out what happened to Margaret in my Judy Blume book was much more important than dwelling on Mom's snide remark about bugs. Soon after Mom, Dad would come to kiss me goodnight. My mess didn't bother him. He always said, "As long as I can close the door, I don't care!"

"I'll pick a husband like you Daddy!" I said proudly of my patient father. He'd climb over the piles of clothing, sit on my bed, and give me my last kiss of the night. I pet his long red hair and giggled as his red beard brushed against my cheek. After he left, I turned my flashlight back on and read until I was too tired to read anymore, usually an hour. Heavy-eyed, I switched off the flashlight, happy that my messiness had survived another day.

Falling asleep was the easiest part of my childhood. I loved the feeling of blankets wrapped around me. The nighttime quiet of the house brought me peace. I could hear Mom and Dad chatting in their bedroom behind a locked door and, I would drift off, comforted by the fact that they were close by should a real emergency occur.

Sometimes I pondered why they locked their door. *What if there was a fire?* We never did put up those safety ladders I considered essential, despite my begging for months after our school had an assembly for fire safety. Dad said, "We can jump just fine with minor injuries." I protested this decision by following him around for the next several days.

"Dad, we are on the second floor." "The teacher said we need to have fire safety," I argued. "Are you disagreeing with my teacher? Isn't a ladder and no injuries a better plan?" Dad didn't seem to think so and I trusted him. So, we never got our safety ladders.

Waking up, I watched and waited until Chad, the long-haired, head-banging, Metallica-shirt-wearing teenager that lived in our home, walked out the door. In my nine-year-old opinion it was better to keep a nine-year-old girl and her thirteen-year-old brother separated as much as possible. We had a love-hate relationship like most siblings, but the mornings came with more hate than love.

Once he left, I'd walk into the kitchen to get some cereal. I preferred the sugary cereals that my friends' parents bought but apparently, they were "bad for you." So I was often stuck chewing on some "Yummy, healthy, and cheaper," version of Raisin Bran. Realizing it was all we had, I learned to deal with it. It was a blessing on the Sundays, once or twice a month, when Uncle George, Mom and Dad's friend, rode his horses over and offered us bagels, cream cheese, and lox.

Monday was the best school morning ever when we would have bagels left over. Whenever I woke up and all of the bagels were gone, I knew Mom was the culprit. Sometimes she woke up in the middle of the night and ate all of the best bagels! The next morning the sight of the lonely crumbs of a cinnamon raisin bagel crushed me. God forbid we had any fancy cakes left-over from my grandparents' visit. Mom hid them in her room— even if they needed to stay refrigerated. Looking in the trashcan at seven in the morning and seeing a half-eaten piece of key lime pie never failed to depress me.

Cooking on weekday mornings was not an option despite my constant begging. I knew that I would be great at making eggs or French toast, after years of watching Dad cook them on Sundays. However, I wasn't allowed to touch the oven until I turned twelve. Because, "If anyone is going to burn the house down, it will be *her!*" (Meaning me) Mom's words.

As it turns out, I would come close to burning the house down only once. And, truly, it wasn't my fault that the curling iron didn't shut itself off that morning. I remember leaving the house for school like I did every other week day. I got on the bus and freaked when I realized the curling iron *might* still be on. I relaxed, however, when I reasoned that the curling iron must have an automatic overheat shutoff that would prevent it from burning the towel it rested on. By the time I arrived at school I had forgotten all about the curling iron and was happily fear-of-fire free for an almost eight-hour school day.

Meanwhile, Mom noticed a strange burning smell four hours after I left for school – when she finally woke up and got out of bed. She thought it was the dryer in the basement. "The smell grew stronger and didn't go away," Mom lectured when I came home. She "walked down the hall and noticed the towel smoking in the bathroom."

4

All I could think was, what kind of curling iron engineer doesn't include an automatic overheat shutoff? I attempted to lead the conversation with this argument, but Mom shut me down fast. "You woke me up and I thought our house was on fire, Danielle," she said. "This is no time to act cute."

Defending my long-term cuteness wouldn't be effective either so I sat back and listened to Mom being "very mom mad." She sat me on the couch, and I respectfully acknowledged her lecture for two hours. Okay, maybe not two hours and maybe not too respectfully but it seemed like a very long time, all the more so as I considered all the afternoon television I was missing. I knew the curling iron situation was serious when *she* sacrificed watching *Days of Our Lives* to lecture me.

What I kept thinking as the lecture continued on and on, was that the simple sentence, "Please don't leave the curling iron on again," would have been enough. Apparently she thought otherwise. When she finally stopped talking, I offered these last words, "Mom, we really should get those fire safety ladders. *This* could have been really dangerous for you."

Worry-wart parents should have trusted that I would never burn down our house on purpose. Doing so would cause me personal devastation, and I would never purposely devastate myself. My parents knew that I loved everything in my room and in my house. Actually, I loved everything so much that Mom always said, "You're going to grow up to be a hoarder." To which I responded, "I don't know what that means, but I will aspire to be the best at it, Mom!" I grew up thinking it meant I loved my stuff too much. When I realized what she meant, I couldn't believe Mom had compared me to a hoarder. I *never* stacked newspapers in my bedroom. All I had was a zoo of stuffed animals and a FEMA-worthy clothing mess, and sometimes plates didn't make it to the sink, but that's all.

I openly admit that I had an obsession with stuffed animals. I am still secretly attached to some of these now thirty-six-year-old friends. For instance, I still have my Piggy. Piggy is an adorable pink pig that my grandmother and grandfather, on my mom's side, gave me when I was two. We were so close that she even came to my three-year-old ballet recital at Fay Schanne Dance Studio. Piggy stuck to me like glue while we danced on stage in front of a gazillion people. She was an amazing dancer, and she wasn't mad when I dropped her in front of everyone. I was, however, very embarrassed, and it may have even ended any hope for a future dancing career.

Growing up Piggy and I loved to play with her best friend, Mr. Bear. Mr. Bear is a brown teddy bear that Uncle George gave me for my fifth birthday. He once was amazingly soft. That is, until one day, when I was eight-years-old, standing outside of my house, holding onto the door. My best friend Stephanie ran out the door in such a hurry that she smacked my arm, the one that was holding Mr. Bear. "Mr. Bearrrrrrr!" I screamed as he flew out of my hand, somersaulted in the air, and landed on the wet, dirt-covered ground. I ran outside, snatched him off the ground and brushed him off, yelling at Stephanie for being such a rude friend.

In her defense, she was running late to get home to her dad and she had to go all the way up the hill. Steph was "not allowed to be late" according to her dad, Norman. Norman was a single dad raising twin daughters. He wasn't around much during the week, due to work but on the weekends we would rake leaves, clean the twins' bedrooms, and bother Norm until he forced us to go back to bother my parents at my house. I wouldn't see Steph for a week if she broke the "never late" rule.

Feeling less sad for Steph and much more concerned about Mr. Bear, I cried staring at his fur, which was covered in mud. I stormed back into my house, thinking, *"How could she ruin my bear?"* His face was all sorts of dirty from the muddy walkway, and I couldn't oust the leaf stuck in his fur. This was unacceptable to me— I felt like Steph had just ruined my life. I needed to fix the problem right away. So, like any good owner of a pet bear, I decided to wash the poor thing.

Dad was at work when I called him, and he didn't seem to care about Mr. Bear's serious facial injuries. I tried to explain how "Mr. Bear could have lost an eye!" but received no empathy from Dad, who said, "I can't be bothered with this at work, and please, next time, bother Mom." *Bother?* This emergency should not be considered a

6

bother. I pushed this aside knowing I would sit my parents down later and discuss emergencies, *yet again*.

Mom did not encourage me to wash Mr. Bear. She sat in her room and listened to me complain and cry before finally shouting, "YES, just wash the damn bear and don't disturb me about it again!" I assured her that I would clean up my mess. She laughed, but at least she had said yes. Mr. Bear had never been washed before so when I put him in the sink, he looked rather sad.

Mr. Bear's long wet silk hair had become slicked back on his forehead and for the first time it looked as though my poor bear's eyes were popping out of his head. After scrubbing him from head to toe, all of the dirt came off. His long, wet fur was tangled and no longer silky. Now I needed to dry him; he was dripping water from the stuffing inside of his head and there was no way I could chance him growing mold. To stop the impending brain trauma I needed the quickest way to dry a bear's innards. So I threw him in the dryer and waited.

I did not ask Mom if I could use the dryer. She had specifically asked me to not bother her about the bear again. Technically, I was not allowed to operate the dryer. For a brief period when I was seven I had been allowed to do my own laundry but this privilege was revoked just as fast as it was given. I still feel bad about the kitten in the dryer. Kittens naturally want to curl up wherever they comfortably can. And so it was on the day Mom asked me to close and turn on the dryer because she had forgotten. I went into our creepy basement, closed the dryer, and hit the button. I didn't even make it to the steps when I heard a loud banging, as if there was a sneaker inside the dryer. I rushed back, opened it, and pulled out the roughed up kitten. Too young to realize this was a tale better left untold, I brought the kitten to Mom to make sure it was okay. Mom acted as if I'd tried to kill the sneaky barn escapee. After that, she never asked me to turn on the dryer. But, I was pretty confident that putting Mr. Bear inside wasn't going to be a concern so I took the risk.

Thirty minutes later the dryer beeped, and as I approached, I smelled a horrible smell. Mom screamed from her room and then stomped to the top of the stairs, "Danielle, *now* what is burning?" I

7

ran and opened the dryer and what I saw next broke my heart. Mr. Bear was unrecognizable.

He had no hair … well, he had hair; however, what was once silky amazing hair had become burnt and smelly. Every single hair on Mr. Bear had shriveled into a kinky tight curl. I grabbed him and stormed into my room, angrier than ever at Stephanie. This was all her fault! I curled up in bed with Mr. Bear, and cried. Mom didn't yell at me this time because I guess she felt bad for me and Mr. Bear. She came to me, and while patting his head, she sadly confirmed, "There is nothing left to do to help him. You did your best. I'm sorry." And then she walked away.

My friendship with Stephanie eventually recovered. Mr. Bear, however, did not.

Truly, I never had any reason to burn the house down, but I can see why my parents were concerned. I guess mandating soggy raisin cereal instead of allowing me to operate the oven was a solid risk-control measure. To save my parents from living in constant fear, I would suffer through the revolting taste.

Chapter 2

Friends, Mom & the bus

All the kids in the great town of Tabernacle took the bus to school, including me. It should have been easy to eat, get dressed, and get on the bus, but once in a while I ran into some trouble.

In the mornings, I'd push my bedroom door open as far as I could to create a place to stand while I experienced a daily panic to find something, *anything,* to wear. I'd grab two shoes and throw them into the hall, two socks, (rarely matching) and throw them into the hall, then search for a pair of pants, shirt, and underwear, thanking God whenever I came across a laundry basket containing clean (though unfolded) laundry.

I rustled up the mess in the hallway and peeked in on Mom. The rising and falling of the blanket and her heavy breathing behind the cracked-open door meant she was dead asleep. Sometimes I tried to sneak into her room to use her makeup and hair supplies. I'd ask but she always said, "No!" She hated when I helped myself in this way, so I had to be very careful not to wake her. If she faced away from the door, I stood a chance of getting in and out unscathed. But if she spotted me, it would be "Off with your head!" mimicking *Alice in*

Wonderland's Queen of Hearts. And, I wouldn't just get in trouble for trying to get to the make-up drawer; I would get a lecture for waking her up so early in the morning. This would lead to my explanation that "it isn't my fault the school bus comes so early." I honestly believed she should take it up with the school principal.

One time that lecture led to me missing the bus and oh lord, I thought my mom was going to have a coronary attack. She drove me to school in complete anger after she washed her face, put on her makeup, picked out an outfit to wear, and went through her entire morning routine. I couldn't just wake my mom up and then expect her to jump at any emergency. Mom was not going to leave the house until she was good and ready. If I missed the bus, I was LATE. There was no chance that I was going to make it without my mom having to sign me in. Twenty minutes passed while I waited for Mom to accomplish her morning routine. "Mom pllleeeaasse move faster. Please! I am going to be soooooo late." I chased her around begging her to move faster. She would ignore my pleas for speed until she *finally* in complete anger mode drove me in. She was livid that I made her *rush*. Again, *not my fault that school starts so early!*

On the few days I was out the door early, I ran up the hill to Jen and Steph's bus stop. The crazy rush out of my house coincided with my hands full of miscellaneous school stuff, and seldom did I make it up the hill without something falling to the ground. For this reason, I sometimes opted to sit on top of the fence that kept our horses penned up. I would focus on staying centered on the top of the fence pole while shoving items back into my book bag. I called this *reorganizing*.

Tabernacle was very quiet in the morning. If I stayed completely still while sitting on that fence, I could watch the deer across the street. If I was really lucky on any given day, the deer would join the horses in the pen while I secretly observed. The horses never seemed to mind the deer intrusion on their grass. They would join the deer as they ate their breakfast, paying no attention to each other or the intruder who sat quietly on the fence.

One morning as I waited for the bus to take me to school, I heard someone (or a few someone's) making a raucous noise two streets away. My peaceful morning turned into hysterical laughter as Jen,

Steph, and Lauren made it to the top of my hill and continued running down, full speed ahead. Their book bags were bouncing around their bodies, arms flailing, school papers floating above the gravel and dirt street. All of them were amused with their craziness while yelling my name. "Danielle! We're coming!"

I'd scream back, "I see you there!" Laughing, I jumped off of the fence, grabbed my bags, and waited for them to reach my bus stop. It was hard to tell from the bottom of the hill who was in the lead. Dark hair was flying everywhere so I knew it was definitely one of the twins. Those girls were both blessed with long, thick brown hair and the most amazing Aladdin-like-brown eyes. They had a darker complexion compared to me and it was impossible to tell who was who from far way.

Whenever we met random strangers, we told them we were cousins. Some people believed us; others would get mad and argue. I think the fact that I had freckles, light skin, and red hair was a dead giveaway to our fib.

As the twins sped toward me, it dawned on me that, although they look so much alike, they are completely different. Steph was in the lead. I could hear her yelling "Danielle, Danielle, the bus is coming!" Jen, who is quieter than Steph, trailed behind, but she was still ahead of a laughing Lauren. This seemed very apropos since Jen followed Steph—unless Steph made her mad and then WHAM, Jen always won the fight!

One time they were so angry at each other that I feared somebody may end up bald after the brawl. They wrestled each other to the ground, screaming and flailing their arms, both trying to stop the other from pulling out her hair. They would continue to fight until the other started to cry and screamed, "I'mmm telllll-innng Daddddddy." As you can imagine, the fun ended whenever this happened.

I was smart enough to know not to fight with either of them, especially Jen. One time I got mad at Jen and without being invited to the fight, Steph took Jen's side. I was stuck with both twins mad at me. From then on, whenever one of them annoyed me, I reminded myself *"Don't do it. You don't want both of them mad at you."* It was never worth it, even when I knew I was one hundred percent right. I needed to make good choices when it came to fights or the weekend would be lonely. When the twins were mad at you, the street got boring very fast. But, at least I still had Lauren when this happened.

That morning at the bus stop, in the natural order of things, Lauren trailed behind the twins. Her normally pale white skin had turned solid red from the race down the hill. Her eyes appeared a deeper blue next to her red cheeks. The color looked good on Lauren, since she's about a half-shade away from albino. She's also incredibly funny, a pairing that sort of makes for a strange friend who ventures into strange behaviors pretty often. I can't put my finger on the specifics of her level of weirdness, but I can say that it's as though she doesn't live in the same reality as the rest of us. She laughs when no one is laughing, rarely gets angry (even when she should), and just bounces from one friends' house to another friend's house to play.

None of us hung out at Lauren's too often, and I'm sure she liked it that way. As far as friendly environments go, Lauren's house was the least friendly of all. Her mom invited me to hang out as long as I agreed to go to church with Lauren on Sunday mornings. Lauren always begged me to come and save her from the "boredom" of Sunday school— and Lauren's mom felt it was her duty to give me, "the atheist" the religious and value training that my parents were failing to instill. I often agreed to go just so Lauren could have some company. Outside of church, her parents and siblings came across as indifferent to everyone. As I grew older my parents said it was just "better if Lauren came to our house." I agreed. I considered Lauren very lucky because my mom took a special liking to her. Mom protected Lauren—from what I never knew.

On the weekend, we were forced to pick up Lauren at her house or she couldn't come out. The twins and I stood outside while one of us was sacrificed as the door knocker. The door knocker had to quickly escape before having another lesson in Godly ways from Lauren's mom. I was the oldest, so they normally sacrificed me. I learned to *be in a hurry* even when I was not in a hurry at all. I often wondered if lying about being *in a hurry* was a sin to Lauren's mom's god.

We got a lucky break when we were spotted from down the street by our friend Ryan. We heard him yelling from his driveway as we stood at Lauren's and we ran to his home next. Technically that means we were indeed in a hurry! Ryan was the world's cutest boy and Lauren was so lucky that he lived across the street and down a few houses from her on Summit Drive. Lauren thought that they were best friends but Mom always said, "Ryan loves you, Danielle."

One time he gave me a blue and silver pinwheel headband. As a young girl, this was huge and I had it displayed on my dresser so everyone knew Ryan loved me. Together, we were adventurous! One time we conducted an experiment of chewing a piece of gum for over a month. Every night I stuck it on the side of the dresser and every morning I would put it back in my mouth and chew it. One day, Dad walked in and saw the gum as he bent down to say goodnight and to kiss my cheek. I was so nervous. There was a gigantic mound of gum staring Dad in the face. He looked at me with you-know-I know eyes and said, "Move that before your mom sees it."

"But, Daaaaddd. I am in a contest with Ryan. Do you want to make me lose?" His silence and stare told me the gum had to go. Breaking the silence, he rustled my hair, and said, "Get rid of that gum" and left the room.

I considered finding a new hiding spot for the gum. I thought long and hard before deciding it indeed had to be thrown out. I found this to be especially disappointing because Ryan and I had embarked on this gum marathon together, and now I ruined it. Every time I visited Ryan he would tease me with his gum-chewing endurance. Dad ruined my attempt at the "most days chewing a piece of gum" Guinness World Record and I truly believed Ryan was going to win. He never did set the record for gum chewing, though I wish he could have.

Truly lucky that the girls came to my bus stop, I could get on with no anxiety. I under all conditions did not like getting on a bus *alone*. I couldn't handle the feeling of trying to find a seat. When I walked down the isle of a crowded bus and there were people on all sides of me and I wasn't sure a seat was going to be open, I would begin to panic. All I could think was, "I hope there is a seat available! I hope someone saved me a seat! Please don't let me sit all alone!"

When I brought up this fear to my parents and brother, my brother, Chad, would say, sarcastically, "Maybe you should get a friend." As if

13

that ever helped. "You're rude and *I* have friends." I would quickly defend myself. Mom always shrugged it off and said, "I don't care if I sit alone," while Dad said, "I'd rather not talk to other people on a bus, or an elevator or anywhere. Actually I'd just rather not talk to people." Well, we were nothing alike on this point because I did care, and I liked to talk too.

Much of my childhood was spent making sure I had a friend on the bus. That was the issue of grade school, making sure you always had someone to sit with, walk with, eat with, and so on. Being the kid who no one wanted to be around was a silly yet huge fear of mine. I was devastated whenever I was met with a "seat taken" comment and indeed the seat was not taken.

The bus ride home from school was never as rough as the bus ride to school. By the end of the day, everyone was tired. The kids would fight less, yell less, and bother me less, except when we had a substitute. Those days, for some reason, were out of control. The kids never sat in the right areas with other kids from their grade. The third graders took over the back of the bus. The substitute driver kept yelling for everyone to "sit down NOW."

I would sit in my seat near the window, hunched down with a notepad, avoiding being called "Dansmell" (a name stolen from one of the characters in the Garbage Pail Kids), for the thousandth time. I could kill my parents at that moment for such a terrible name. Didn't they even think of all the bad nicknames before condemning me to "Dansmell?" My brother, Chad, was lucky. Nothing that rhymed with Chad made an impact. "Bad Chad" was the worst nickname he had to withstand, and it actually fit him because everyone *for some reason* was afraid of my brother.

I would like to point out that in no point in my life did I actually smell. I made sure of that. There was nothing worse than a horrible nickname that is actually appropriate. By fifth grade, I began introducing myself as Danny. This took some serious work. Every time someone said "Danielle" I had to either say, "No it's Danny" or ignore them until they said "Danny." This led to more torment for half of the year, until I convinced all my teachers of the change and the rest of my classmates got the memo. Eventually Danielle was extinguished, except by family and my closest friends, and I had forced the name Danny on everyone at school. I had to fight hard to get people to stop calling me Danielle, but at the time the fight was worth it. With the successful launch of Danny, "Dansmell" died.

In order to survive the bus and to avoid the bus chaos, I would lean on my knees against the seat in front of me and use my legs as a desk. I placed my journal on my legs and pulled out my #2 pencil. For some reason, the school made us use #2 pencils only. I often wondered how the #1 and #3 pencil felt about that. I wanted to know why the #2 pencil was so important. As a second-born child, I would often yell at my brother saying, "If the #2 pencil is the best then I am too!" He didn't care.

I would write in my diary about my day, the plans I had for upcoming days, or a list of something that I wanted to be doing. The lists often looked like this:

> Go play with Jen and Steph and Lauren
> Get McDonalds and ice cream
> Have a sleepover
> Climb through the rain gutters with Ryan

One amazing Friday, I walked in through the front door of my house, and kicked off my shoes (paying strict attention to the SHOES OFF sign) as I walked in. I dropped my book-bag and ran upstairs. Hearing Mom stirring in her room I did my normal yell down the hall, "I'm home Mom." Mom yelled back "Put your stuff in your room." I rolled my eyes, annoyed by this greeting, and acted like I didn't hear her— even though every day it was the same greeting, *if* she was awake. I figured I had enough time to watch at least one episode of *Care Bears* before she would come out of her room to see if I'd done as she told me. Every day I was excited to grab a snack, a blanket, and the big black remote box. I would then jump on the couch, clicking row by row until I came across one of the best TV shows ever, *Care Bears*. Loudly, I would sing the theme song.

Care Bears Countdown 4-3-2-1
Who's that comin' from somewhere up in the sky?
Movin' fast and bright as a firefly
Just when ya think that trouble's gonna pounce
Who's gonna be there when it really counts?
Do the Care Bears Countdown

Interrupted by a bang on the door, I ignored the bang and continued to sing with my show. Another blasted bang. I screamed "Commmmmmme innnnnnnnnn" as loud as I could from the top of the steps. Realizing I just doomed myself to chores because I surely interrupted Moms resting I, like lightning jumped up out of my seat with my cozy blanket and ran down the steps yelling, "Hold on, I'm coming." I expected one of the twins or Lauren to be standing there, but when I opened the door I was shocked. It was Dad's sister, my favorite aunt, Aunt Barb!

Chapter 3
It takes a village

W hen Aunt Barb walked through the door, I assumed she was visiting for the weekend, rushing I said, "Hello, I missed you," gave her a half hug, and rushed back up the stairs. I pointed to the bedroom where Mom rested and went into the living room to resume watching the *Care Bears*.

Aunt Barb walked back to Mom and Dad's room. I recall the familiar sound of the door closing behind her. This was the norm when Aunt Barb paid a visit. The adults went into the bedroom and closed the door. As used to being excluded from the adult world as I was, I didn't pay it any mind. I only cared when I was trying to interrupt a conversation so someone could watch me cartwheel, sing, dance, draw, or do something else.

I'll never forget one time when I was seven-years-old my Aunt Barb must have said something that angered Mom in a serious way. I had never seen my mother so livid, and believe you me, I made Mom livid daily. Mom followed Aunt Barb into the kitchen screaming at her. Unfortunately, I was not in a good spot for this fight, as I'd been making myself a snack. Stuck between the two of them, I tried to mind my own business as Mom kept yelling and Aunt Barb stood by and listened.

I was just happy that it wasn't *me* getting yelled at. So I grabbed my snack and ignored Mom while she lectured someone else in the family. I wondered if Aunt Barb would get the spoon for whatever she had done wrong. She kept talking back to Mom and when I did that the spoon was threatened. Luckily, I never was bad enough to feel the spoon but, my aunt seemed like she needed it! Talking back to Mom was not a good option. The thing Mom hated more than being woken up in the morning or from a nap was not being heard. When she complained about my failure in hearing, Dad in an extremely frustrated tone said, "Danielle, Can't you just learn to shut your mouth?"

Not wanting to be involved in any of this, as soon as I had everything I wanted for my snack, I wiggled out from under Mom, intending to get out of the kitchen. At this exact moment, Mom yelled, "Leave *my* home." Shocked, I looked up to see how Aunt Barb felt about this. I opened my mouth to protest this demand at the same time Mom made a fist and threw a punch at Aunt Barbs' face. It was as if real life slow motion took over the moment. I watched in shock yelling "Nooooo Moooommmm!" The room became silent and chaos reigned the second Mom tripped over my body, and her fist crashed into the plant window. The glass from the window clattered to the kitchen floor. Mom had taken out the plant window with one punch.

As Mom wailed, her hand oozed blood, dripping over the floor where I stood. Glass shards scattered everywhere. Dad ran in from outside. I started to cry and Mom tried to console me with *her* blood dripping everywhere. My clothes became saturated in gross hand blood. Shocked, I just stood there. Aunt Barb tried to console Mom who was still yelling for her to "get out!" My brother, on my father's command, grabbed me by the arm and shoved me out of the room. "My snack!" I yelled. He pushed me out. Ugh, he thought he was in charge— but at least he had to stay with me. I didn't want him to be a part of the action if I couldn't be.

I heard Dad yell, "Oh, what the hell? What is wrong with you two?" and I tried to go back to them. But everyone else kept yelling "Stay out Danielle. You're not helping, Danielle. You're always in the way." I had no idea what I was supposed to be doing, but apparently everything I was doing was the wrong choice. The fight to get past my brother to rescue Mom's wounded hand challenged me. He guarded the kitchen as delegated and unfortunately he was fantastic at his job. My family watched as I pushed toward them— with no support. Eventually I managed to crawl between his legs as he grabbed my shirt. I flailed my arms at him and attempted to scratch him. Dad witnessed what was happening and glared at me. I stopped flailing and played dead until Chad stepped back over me and assumed guard position. "Why do you have to be so annoying, Danielle?" he said. I stuck out my tongue and responded, "Don't talk to me, Chad."

Someone must have called 911 because the ambulance showed up shortly after the fight. Dad led Mom outside and Aunt Barb followed. I stared out the window, listening as hard as I could to the paramedic men. This infuriated my family and I was instructed with their eyes to "Stop staring and get away from the window."

I heard Dad tell the paramedics that Mom slipped and put her hand through the window. I assumed Dad had no idea what had happened, and I really wanted to make sure everyone knew the truth. My brother, however, stood between me and the door leading outside. I watched as Mom climbed into the ambulance, was driven away, and disappeared from my sight.

Aunt Barb and Dad came back into the house to grab some personal items for her and to talk to me. They both explained that Mom had *slipped*. I'm not sure who they thought they were fooling, but even as a kid you know if your mom is trying to kill your aunt, and you remember it clearly. Dad and Aunt Barb followed the ambulance while my brother stayed home with me. No one in the family spoke of the fight again. Even as I got older, Mom refused to address this story. She never understood that I just wanted to know her side of the story.

I had a different type of relationship with Aunt Barb than I had with Mom. Aunt Barb, ten years younger than Mom, was only fifteen when I was born. She had more energy to hang out with me than Mom did, especially as I got older. She was absolutely adorable, with her curly blonde hair that was originally redder than mine. She dyed it and always told me "Never dye your hair, Danielle."

The list of what we had in common was never ending. We both loved traveling, the beach, skiing, shopping, and most of all gymnastics. She was a gymnast when she was in high school, so whenever we spent time together, we worked on my back walkover, my cartwheel, and my back handspring (which scared me to death).

One Friday, two years after the fight, Aunt Barb came over, she walked back to Mom's bedroom, but soon yelled out, "Hey, Danielle, are you ready to go?" Apparently, I had forgotten or was never told that Mom made plans for me to go away with her for the weekend.

I would come to love my time away from home. It was a monthly vacation, sometimes twice a month. I was excited to learn I was going to Aunt Barb's house. I never minded changing my weekend to-do list! I jumped up fast, grabbed my list, called my friends to let them all know I would be away again for the weekend, and joyfully headed to my room to pack my bag.

Another awesome thing about going away: I owned the coolest Strawberry Shortcake suitcase. It unfortunately was never big enough to hold all of my stuff. I crammed in my clothes, my coin pouch, Piggy. Piggy never fit. I sat on the suitcase, pushed everything flat and still couldn't zipper that darn thing. After five minutes of struggling, I decided to attach piggy to the outside of my bag. Then I brought my bags to the bottom of the steps and screamed "I'm all ready!" Hearing the *Care Bears* in the living room, I'd jump back on the couch to squeeze in a few more seconds of the show. On the good days, Mom and Aunt Barb would talk forever, and I'd watch the whole episode wondering to myself whether or not Care-A-Lot would be a peaceful place to live. Aunt Barb walked back in the room and yelled, "Ready? Let's go!"

I walked over to Mom and dramatically said, "Remember me; I will miss you terribly while I am having so much fun!" Mom brushed her fingers through my long hair and said: "Be good, please. I don't want to have to come pick you up in Pennsylvania." At this, I was highly insulted! I would never have to be picked up. Okay, one time, *one* time I had to be picked up but it wasn't my fault. Aunt Barb was mad at me because, I spent an entire day "annoying" her. There was truly no forgiveness for simple mistakes around here!

I hugged Mom and asked for her to say bye to Daddy for me. I smirked at my brother and then yelled to Mom, "and feel free to sell Chad while I am gone!" I promised that no one would need to pick me up *again* while secretly wishing a teenager sale would happen while I was gone.

Aunt Barb rustled me out to the car, dragging my bags behind me. I leaped into the front seat—I loved driving with her! She allowed me full control of the radio. I was *never* allowed full control of the radio in my parents' cars. Mom wanted to listen to her country and Dad listened to Metallica's screaming. My brother had taken a liking to the screaming. But I thought it was just horrible. "Can't we just listen to Pat Benatar?" I would ask. To which I would get back a universal "No." Sometimes when their music became too much for me, I put on my headset, plugged it into my Walkman, and sang as loud as I could, "*Hell, hell is for children!*" This made everyone around me pretty angry after about one minute. I stopped after two.

Driving with Aunt Barb I would turn the dial through all of the channels and back. Sometimes there was nothing on the radio, just people talking. "Goodness, what could they possibly all have to talk about?" I'd say. Aunt Barb soon became very annoyed at my constant changing of the stations. When that would happen, I refrained from making eye contact with her, and continued switching station, because I knew if I looked up I'd find her glaring at me. She let me keep switching, but the moment I took my hand off of the radio – Wham! She seized control. Then I was stuck listening to the Rolling Stones or something equally unsatisfying. I ended up learning all the words to *her* songs. The "if you can't beat them join them" philosophy came in handy at a young age. After all, "You can't always get what you wa-ant." Right, Mick?

During most visits Aunt Barb would take me to Wendy's either on the way home or on Saturday morning. I had the liberty to do *whatever I wanted* because she was the manager there. My Wendy visits ranked high on my list of "the most fun I ever had." The other workers liked me and let me tour the entire restaurant, made me whatever food I wanted to eat, and then fed me Frosties. Once I was done with my restaurant tour, I would sit and draw for hours while she took care of managerial things. I rarely got bored (Aunt Barb would not tolerate boredom) so when I would get fussy, another Frosty would show up. I must have eaten three hundred Frosty desserts over the course of the time she worked there. Reminiscing makes me, crave a chocolate Frosty right now.

In order to get to her house in Philadelphia, we had to cross the dreaded Burlington Bristol Bridge. I always found this bridge to be very frightening. I swear it shakes when you drive across it. As a child, I felt that the cars were too crammed together, and I saw too well for my liking, inside the windows of the opposing traffic. I wondered why there wasn't a gigantic wall on the bridge separating the coming and going lanes. I was pretty sure that the other drivers and passengers wondered the same things, as we all lived in fear of a collision that flings us over the side. As an adult, I still loathe this bridge.

It took fifteen minutes from the point that we crossed the scariest bridge ever, to the point that we pulled up to Aunt Barb's boyfriends' house, where she now resided. We dropped all of my stuff into my bedroom for the weekend, and I unpacked everything, making myself at home. I could hear Aunt Barb on the telephone with a friend, laughing in the living room down the hall from my weekend bedroom.

After that, anything could happen. Aunt Barb was always in a hurry to rush me back out of the house, throwing me back into the car. We constantly had somewhere to be: a party to plan, an event to attend, or a friends' kid's birthday to attend.

One time my Uncle Jack, the guy dating Aunt Barb, gave her money to buy me some toys for the weekend. We had enough money to buy either one Cabbage Patch Kid or three Barbies. At the store, I paced back and forth, between the Barbie aisle and the Cabbages. It was a very hard decision. An aisle over, Aunt Barb was yelling, "Hurry up, we need to get dinner." I grabbed the three Barbie boxes and ran to the checkout. And I never regretted that decision.

The minute I picked them, I knew the twins and Lauren were going to love these new Barbies. I prayed my older neighbor friend named

Candice would play too. She was two years older and she had more Barbies and dolls than anyone. Her mom would pick me up to go to Candice's recitals with her. One time she amazed me when she was an actress in the King and I. Every time I went over to her house she tried to teach me how to sing and play Bette Midler's "The Rose" on her piano. Candice was gonna love my Punk Rock Barbies who sang in a band. Could Barbie get any cooler? I couldn't wait to rip those boxes open! Aunt Barb said, "Danielle, you need to wait until we get to dinner." I thought I would die waiting.

Dinner usually meant meeting up with Aunt Barb's friends. Aunt Barb had friends from all walks of life. I remember clearly that she especially liked long-haired, loud people in bands. Dinner at a bar was always fun! I loved watching the bands set up their equipment. One time the drummer gave me his drumsticks. I couldn't understand why Aunt Barb took them away lightning fast. Okay, so I'd been banging on the tables. "Isn't that what drumsticks are for?" I asked. Apparently not. Aunt Barb gave the drumsticks back to the drummer, letting him know that I wouldn't stop banging on everything. Couldn't she see that I was making music with the band? Twenty years later, at twenty-nine, I was drumming again, and my good friend Pat sadly informed me that "I have no drumming ability and should probably stop trying." He was laughing when he said but I realized that day that maybe Aunt Barb was right to take away my drumsticks.

Even without the drumsticks, I beamed happiness those nights when I got to watch the band set up. I would sit for hours just watching everyone. On this day, I opened my Barbie boxes and set up their stage on our table. I was so excited when Aunt Barb's friends walked over to say hello to me, and I introduced them to my new amazing Barbies. Ever since I could remember, Aunt Barb introduced me the same way, "This is my daughter, Danielle," she said. She said that she told everyone I was her daughter because I was the closest thing to her baby that she lost. I never told my parents that everyone in Aunt Barb's world thought I was her child. It never came up and I had no idea that this kind of story could affect someone as they got older. Confusion set in my adulthood where I began quietly questioning who my mom was. Was it Aunt Barb or Mom? As a child I didn't realize

Mom would be mad that this was happening. I was just happy that everyone wanted to play Barbie's with me, and I liked that I wasn't considered a baby. Being the only kid in a bar after 8 p.m. on a Friday night was awesome. When the band finally started to play, the bar suddenly filled up with people dancing, drinking, and smoking. That's when I made my way to the dance floor. I danced and danced carefully avoiding a cigarette burn, alcohol dripping on my head, and drunk people wanting to dance with me. I danced and danced until I was too tired to dance anymore. I fell asleep with my head on the table plenty of times. Aunt Barb carried me to the car so I could sleep more comfortably. I spread out on the back seat and fell back to sleep until eventually Aunt Barb returned to the car, drove us back to Uncle Jack's, and put me in my bed. I'm glad her boyfriend gave me my own bedroom. I liked Uncle Jack. I also liked that dancing on the dance floor until I passed out was a normal pastime on those weekends without my family.

The next morning, I woke up feeling gloomy that my weekend was already half over. Aunt Barb and I only had twenty-four more hours together. Looking at my Smurf watch only instilled panic. Realizing it was past ten in the morning and that I'd overslept resulted in a strange sense of urgency to hurry up and have fun. I ran down the hallway stopping outside the kitchen to smell the bacon and eggs cooking. It smelled incredible.

"You hungry kid?" Uncle Jack would ask. I shouted "YES!" at least thirty times before I grabbed my plate.

Uncle Jack's eggs were the best eggs on the planet. First, he cooked the bacon, and then he removed the bacon from the pan and used the bacon grease to cook the eggs. Oh my goodness, it was heavenly. Every bite tasted like bacon. The smell was to die for. The taste shocked my taste buds, and made me so happy. Then he added two pieces of toast with butter melted on top. I sat on the living room couch with my plateful of greatness and ate every last speck of bacon grease before turning my attention to the T.V. I fussed with the remote control, driving everyone crazy, as I flipped through in search of one of my favorite shows. When I found one, I immediately began to sing the theme song.

> *Dance your cares away,*
> *Worry's for another day.*
> *Let the music play,*
> *Down at Fraggle Rock.*

I sang along to the end and let everyone know how much I loved *Fraggle Rock*. I loved being at Aunt Barb's because I had full control of the TV. No one yelled, "I don't want to watch your baby show. Ewww turn this off. We are playing Atari," and all of the other annoying things a big brother yells while you try to watch *Strawberry Shortcake* and any other fun show. But I especially hated when he would interrupt *Fraggle Rock*. Something about watching puppets move flawlessly on the TV screen impressed me. *How did they do that?*

As soon as I was finished eating, Aunt Barb would use her just-finished-eating-radar to yell to me, "Please come clear your plate and help me, Danielle." Every Saturday when I stayed at Aunt Barb's, we cleaned. I didn't mind helping her clean her house because I never wanted to leave. So many times I begged her to "Please, let me stay 'til Monday." One time, I begged for about twenty minutes and Aunt Barb yelled: "Danielle, if you ask me to stay 'til Monday again, I won't take you for a month!" I let out one more "Please!" and she stomped out of the room, picked up the phone, and dialed Mom. "No, no," I screamed. "I don't want to go home. Stop. Don't call her."

"Go to your room," she screamed even louder.

I sulked with my head down all the way to my room. Anger, filled my body as I lay with my face smothered in the pillow. I couldn't help but think, *Okay, okay, Jeez. No one needs to get so mad just because I want to be with my awesome aunt.*

Infuriated, my parents drove to Aunt Barbs. I didn't get to say a single word. No one hugged me to say hello, and no one hugged me to say goodbye. Mom was not excited to see me and I sat in the back of the car in complete silence. Driving back over the Bristol Bridge I imagined we were flung off the bridge saving me from an entire hour-long lecture on how "I wasted her day." I heeded Aunt Barb's warnings from that day forward and Mom reminded me of that day *every* time I went back to Aunt Barb's. Instead of begging this time, I went back to cleaning the kitchen, which included the greasy, horrible, bacon pan. It's hard to believe something that tasted so scrumptious looked so gross afterward.

I believe I was nine years old when I decided that I loved Saturdays almost as much as Fridays. After we cleaned up our breakfast at Aunt Barb's, we began prepping dinner. Uncle Jack cooked dinner on the grill, and we were in charge of making the different salads, prepping the meat with seasoning, and making sure we had everything we needed for the dinner. We made potato salad, a green salad, pasta salad, and fruit salad. Aunt Barb let me do all the cutting of the vegetables and the fruit. I was not allowed to use sharp knives at home. Remember that fear of a fire? Well, apparently the fear of me cutting my finger off was equally as scary to Mom. Although, in my defense, I have never cut off a finger and I use knives regularly as an adult.

Saturday nights were calmer with Aunt Barb. She would often decide to just snuggle on the couch and watch movies together. This was fine with me. I loved watching movies, shows, or anything that had to do with a television.

On Sunday morning, my vacation time ended and life went back to normal. I returned to New Jersey and would have to deal with school, teachers, my brother, my dogs, my cats, and of course, Mom. Actually, now that I look back, it wasn't all that bad.

Chapter 4
Parents cry too

"Y ou are going to be okay. I am right here." The sirens screamed loudly as they rushed through the town, down the dirt road, hitting the concrete and then sped up even faster. Pain engulfed my entire face as the blood dripped down my neck and settled in my already red enough hair. The white neck brace to keep me from moving my head, forced down on my shoulders causing a neck pain and throbbing. My eyes burned with tears I couldn't wipe away because, my hands were being held down to not touch my face.

"Close your eyes and rest baby." Mom said quietly. I listened to her as I kept trying to figure out what had even happened. "Everything is going to be okay, I love you," she repeated until the ambulance doors opened and the bright sun light peered through directly on the rolling bed I was lying on. Quickly I was taken from the ambulance on the bed through a hallway, Mom followed as fast as she could. Lights were above my head. Light, after light, after light, I tried to count the lights as we passed them into the elevator.

"This won't hurt honey. You'll be okay soon." Mom sweetly stated as she stood over me. I noticed her eyes had welled up with tears waiting to pour out onto my open wound. The doctor's shooed Mom away and all I felt was her hand slip from my grip as I tried to hold her tighter. Feeling her hand offered relief and they had taken that away. I wiggled and screamed, "Mom, Mom, *Mom.*" A moment later, while both of my arms were being restrained and the doctor was trying to talk to me, a new pain set in. My chin began to throb in agony. I couldn't move my neck, and directly in front of me the doctor was holding the largest needle I had ever seen. He shoved that needle into my chin. I screamed louder for Mom. I heard her shaky, broken voice from a room over. She was gone, and all I could see were doctor faces, unknown doctor faces.

I calmed down with just enough time to breathe before I could scream again, and I felt another stab to my chin. Dying, I was dying. The shower had officially taken a victim.

An hour before the ambulance I was in my house, bored, and waiting for something to do. Taking a bath was a normal pastime for me so it wasn't abnormal for me to be in there for an hour or two. Mom loved bath time because it gave her time to do whatever she wanted—uninterrupted. I filled the bathtub with water and soaked in the silence. After an hour, I stood up and reached for the shampoo. It bothered me that it was on the top shelf that I was unable to reach because Mom had just cleaned our bathroom and must have rearranged things. I yelled for her help once, unanswered, before I carefully balanced myself on the edge of the soapy bathtub and reached to grab the shampoo. As I lifted my arm, my foot began to slide. Slipping back I splashed into the full tub, smacking my chin and face on the edge as I came down. Instantly, blood poured from my open wound, turning the tub water a solid red.

Panic struck, I screamed for Mom to help me. Annoyed that I probably needed soap or something, yet I was carrying on as if I were dying, she forced the door open. "What?" she yelled. As soon as she saw me sitting in the blood filled water, her attitude changed. "Oh, Danielle!" she cried out.

Immediately, Mom grabbed the towel and wrapped my face in it. "Put your hand here Danielle." I wasn't listening. I was crying louder. "You *need* to stop crying. We *need* to get you dressed." I was hysterical and helping was not an option. Mom forced me to sit on the toilet while she carefully put a shirt over my wet head, injured chin and the gigantic towel that was holding my chin together. She slipped my shorts on me without underwear— while I briefly protested.

"Keep the pressure on your chin, Danielle," she said again. I wanted to look in the mirror to see what was happening—she wouldn't let me.

The pain struck again and I knew my chin was in trouble. I could sense Moms uncertainty as she tried to figure out what to do next. She called 911 and moments later, barely dressed and soaking wet I was forced to lay down on a gurney inside an ambulance. An hour later, Mom was forced to watch behind a wall through a small window as they restrained me, and I aggressively fought to be free from the grips of strangers.

Enormous amounts of pain shocked me with every stitch. "You shouldn't be able to feel it" they kept insisting, but I did feel it. They placed thirteen stitches in my chin. Six were deep in my skin and seven were placed on the outside. The moment they finished, they brought Mom back to me. Her eyes were swollen and red as she fought back her tears.

The pain from the chin injury lasted for *weeks*. Even so, visitors' stopped coming by to see me and chin-injury sympathy ended fast.

During my healing time, I was beyond excited when Uncle Hanky, Dad's younger brother came to visit. I wasn't sure if he would be moving in, staying for a few months, or just visiting Dad for the day. He often appeared out of the blue and moved into his room in the basement. Dad would tell him it was fine and to ignore *anything* Mom complained about.

My uncle knew the drill well and did as instructed.

Uncle Hanky always welcomed me into his basement space and encouraged me to hang out. I guess Mom didn't realize I loved having my uncle around—or maybe that didn't matter to her. I never understood why she was against him or anyone living with us. "Mom really likes her alone time, Danny." Dad would say to me.

Uncle Hanky was fabulous. He used to pick me up like I was a guitar. My stomach would be the strings and he would toss me around as if he was playing in a rock band. I laughed and laughed, screaming "Do it again!" He would do it until his arms couldn't hold me

29

anymore. Then he would let me sit in his room and watch him sort through his albums.

I only owned tapes at this point, and the albums in my house were not to be touched— except when I was with my Uncle Hanky. He used to play The Doors a lot, and *just for me* he played Pac-Man Fever. I loved playing Pac-Man!

Once, during the winter, my Uncle Hanky, Chad, and I built a gigantic snow igloo. It was so cold outside, but it didn't matter. We worked on that igloo all day, and we didn't stop until it was done. I thought we would be done once I could crawl inside but Uncle Hanky made it big enough for Chad to get inside too. We all fit in the igloo. It was humongous. There was never a more perfect igloo ever created. When Uncle Hanky was around, Chad was so much nicer to me—I loved Chad then. Uncle Hanky didn't stand for anything but kindness between my brother and me. Chad adored his uncle in a totally different way than I did. He was much closer to him in an older-kid way.

Mom became very annoyed when visitors stayed longer than a weekend. My poor dad would listen to her complain at night when no one was supposed to be listening. She didn't want Aunt Barb to live with us, and now she didn't want Uncle Hanky with us. She was very angry that Dad was spending *their* money to help everyone. Dad believed that he was doing what he was supposed to do as the oldest sibling. He happily took care of his family without questioning. He helped financially support his mom when she needed it, and he jumped to the rescue when his siblings needed it. My father was very proud of my uncle. He truly loved his brother. Uncle Hanky joined the Army shortly following the Vietnam War. He studied engineering in the military and was hoping to someday to have a career like Dad, who was determined to get him on his feet fast.

While living with us, one night my uncle borrowed Mom and Dad's truck to go hang out with Aunt Barb and one of their friends. Mom and Dad fought every day about my uncle living in our home, and the fact that they were now lending out one of *their* vehicles angered Mom even more. She was afraid something might happen to their truck. I didn't mind if Uncle Hanky was forced to stay home, because he was my play date. Dad let his brother borrow the truck and hours later the police called.

Uncle Hanky and Aunt Barb had been involved in a car crash. Dad rushed out of the home and I waited for him to call or return home. It was late, and Mom put me to sleep before I had the chance to find out what happened. The next morning, Dad told me and Chad that Uncle Hanky didn't survive the car accident, but Aunt Barb was there and she was as good as could be expected, considering— she had witnessed her brother's death.

Gloomy days followed the death of my favorite uncle. For a while, Dad blamed Mom for Uncle Hanky no longer being with us. Once, in anger, he yelled out "maybe if you stopped making him feel unwelcome, he wouldn't have been out that day." I felt sad knowing that he felt that way, but everyone knew it wasn't her fault—didn't they? Sometimes Mom fought fights she shouldn't have fought. It was hard for her to just relax if she thought Dad was giving away anything that should belong to her or us. Money was the hardest for her to give up because she always feared we wouldn't have enough. She certainly wished Uncle Hanky didn't die that day, but even her apology couldn't take back the nagging she done days earlier.

It broke my heart to lose Uncle Hanky. And Dad experienced pain like I had never seen before. The loss of his favorite sibling broke him. He became quiet. Laughter, momentarily, became a thing of the past.

Losing Uncle Hanky caused Aunt Barb to cry, every time I saw her. She said to me once, "You're never the same after someone you love is taken from you."

Two years after my Uncle's untimely death, I was in for yet another painful experience. Mom and Dad kept walking over to hug me while I watched my TV shows. I found it strange that my parents were acting like zombies. I kept asking, "What's the matter?" "Why are you so sad?" "Did I do something wrong?"

Mom just hugged me with tears in her eyes and kept saying, "Everything is okay, and I love you." She acted strangely over-the-top loving— as if she were hiding something from me, and Dad was even stranger. He looked like he had been crying. I had never actually seen Dad cry, but his eyes were blood-shot and he kept walking past me as if I wasn't even there. My brother was "out." All I knew was that everyone in my home was acting bizarre, and I didn't have my brother to fight with because he wasn't home.

People I had never met before kept stopping over, and everyone was dressed in black. They came in, stared at me on the couch, and said, "Hello" and "I'm so sorry." Then they walked over to our fireplace and put their hands on the special vase Dad had placed on the fireplace and strictly warned *me* not to touch. I decided it must be very rare and probably from an Egyptian pyramid. It looked like it was worth a gazillion dollars. Oddly enough, I did as I was told and stayed far away from the rare, enticing artifact even though Mom and Dad didn't care if complete strangers touched it. It was torture, and I made sure *they* knew it.

Sandy, Mom's best friend had been over all day. The two of them hid in the bedroom, and I could hear them crying, for a long time. Dad decided to take over the television in the living room. Once the visitors slowed, I cuddled up on the couch with piggy and my blanket, and I let Dad change the channels without a fight. He always watched wrestling while I snuggled in his arms. Whenever something exciting happened in the show, I attempted to beat him up. He let me be the strongest wrestler – and I enjoyed winning. That day, we sat and watched Hulk Hogan challenge King Kong Bundy to a match. My father didn't cheer, boo, or do anything else. I found it hard to wrestle with a man in a suit who had been crying and isn't cheering on the King Kong.

All the lingering strangers, my parents, and the Egyptian Artifact left when my Aunt Barb showed up. It was just me and my aunt hanging out. Normally this would have been so much fun, but I wasn't feeling very happy and she wasn't either, so we just sat quietly in front of the TV. Aunt Barb watched all of my favorite shows with no argument.

I was feeling terrible inside. I didn't know why. I was pretty sure that the flu bug had gotten me. My parents and brother came home late that night, but I was already in bed when I heard the door open and close. When I listened hard enough, I heard the faint sound of crying again. I fell asleep to that sound.

In the middle of the night, I woke up in complete darkness to an uneasy feeling. I felt like someone was in my room. I could sense someone near me, reaching for me, hugging me. I opened my eyes and clear as day I saw a blue bubble-like thing floating near me. I jumped out of my bed, screaming and crying, while I banged on my parents' bedroom door. I screamed louder and louder until Mom opened it.

She came out, I was hyperventilating. I kept trying to tell her what happened, but I couldn't even begin to describe the moment. I was crying and confused. Mom hugged me tight and calmed me down. Dad let Mom handle it, and Chad came out of his room to see what the fuss was all about. I explained that I thought there was a ghost in my room, and it was in the shape of a blue bubble.

As soon as my brother heard the word blue bubble he began laughing and headed back to his bedroom. I started to cry and begged Mom to believe me. She hugged me tighter without saying a word and took me back to my bedroom. She crawled into my little bed with me, and we both fell back asleep.

I woke up to the rays of the morning sun shining on my face through my window. I studied my sleeping mother's face. She looked like she had been crying all night. I'll never forget the look on Mom's heartbreaking face when she looked up at me staring at her. She wasn't mad I woke her up this time. Instead, she took my hand and escorted me to the living room. Dad had already left for work and my brother was still sleeping. I hopped up on the couch and got ready to turn on the television. Mom lifted the Egyptian artifact that had been safely returned to our fireplace mantle and walked toward me. I was thrilled that I was about to see what it was, finally!

Mom held it in her arms and sat with me on the couch. She then started to tell me a story. She explained that the Egyptian artifact was actually called an "urn." Already uninterested, I began to turn on the TV to watch my Saturday cartoons. Mom stopped me and continued, "It's holding your friend Ryan's ashes."

I stared at my mother. I didn't know what ashes meant. I especially didn't understand what "holding Ryan's ashes" could mean. The only Ryan I knew was a little boy, my neighbor friend, Lauren's across-the-street neighbor who I often played with.

Mom explained that these were his ashes because he had been cremated, and I wasn't going to be able to see him again. I felt a lump in my throat and became focused on the fact that just a few days before, I was at Ryan's house, when his mom, Sandy, babysat me. Mom was thinking about working at a music store so she had an interview. I could picture the day just like any other day. Sandy gave us our lunch, which usually meant hotdogs and chips, and Ryan and I set off for our regular "ditch our stupid brothers" picnic.

Behind Ryan's house, acres of trees made up a forest. A wooden fence blocked the yard and the pool, which we weren't allowed near. Ryan lived with his grandfather, who liked snapping turtles. He collected the mean little turtles and put them in the pool all winter long, and then cleared them out when swim season started again. We stayed away from the pool for fear that the snapping turtles could get us. They grew to be huge, and I read once that one bite from a snapper could snap a finger in two. Liking our fingers, Ryan and I decided to agree on this situation and leave those turtles alone.

So we escaped outside of the gate and entered into yet another gated area. Our parents told us not to venture as far as the next fence line. I didn't understand why our parents didn't want us to have any fun. As long as my brother, Chad, or Ryan's brother, Jason, didn't catch us we were free. All we had to do was make it outside the wooden fence. If they caught us, they would hang us on the fence and make us confess.

We decided that we knew better than our parents or our stupid brothers, and we climbed over the steel fence. We headed down into the meadow on the other side. We ran as fast as we could before we reached the large, white drain pipes. We climbed inside with our lunches and decided to see how far we could go before it became too dark to see. We laughed as we stepped into puddles of rotten, smelly water. We screamed to hear the echo of the pipes. We ate cobwebs when we weren't careful. We went farther and farther until it became so dark that we had to turn back.

Sandy saw us as we came back through the safe fence line and yelled at us for getting so dirty. We just laughed at each other and ran inside to clean up. We didn't get in trouble, which made it a good day.

When I was leaving, Ryan gave me a pinwheel headband with two blue and silver pinwheels that he had won at the county fair. I wore it all the way home, where I placed it on the mantle for display.

When Mom finally found the words, she said, "Danielle, Ryan died three days ago."

My heart began to pound in my chest. I didn't understand–died? "We were just playing the other day." Inside my head, I was begging for this to not be true. "Mom, we were laughing and playing. We were riding our bikes. We were fighting with Jason and Chad." I didn't understand what was happening.

I wanted to go over to Ryan's house and see my friend. I didn't understand the urn thing. It was so miniature in size, and they were saying my friend was inside of it. Why? Why did this have to happen?

It broke my heart to listen to Mom explain the most unimaginable situation that I have ever heard. I begged for her to tell me what happened. I begged and begged. I could feel her heart break as she began to tell me.

"Baby, Ryan loved fishing, he had been fishing for the turtles by the edge of the pool."

My heart started to race. *He knew we weren't allowed near the pool.*

"He was using a stick and fishing line to capture the mean snapping turtles with hotdogs," Mom said. "He must not have been paying attention, and he became tangled in the fishing line and fell into the freezing cold deep end of the pool. His jacket and winter clothing pulled him down and he couldn't swim under the weight of it all."

Mom cried as she spoke.

"When they found him, he had been attacked by the snapping turtles and not much remained." Mom looked at me as tears streamed down her face.

Ryan was gone.

I ran to the bathroom to throw up. *Nothing* came out. My heart was breaking and I could feel it happening. I cried and cried. No one could calm me down. I hyperventilated. Mom must have called Dad and asked him to come home. *He did.* Dad never took a day off of work or came home early without a solid reason. Mom must have begged him.

Dad walked in the door, hugged Mom and scooped me up in his arms. I could tell he had been crying too. He led me to the car and we went for a ride. I didn't ask where we were going. I stopped sobbing and sat in silence until we reached McDonald's, which always helped when I was sad. He ordered the Happy Meal just for the toy. I barely ate my food, and Dad didn't order anything at all for himself. The toy did bring me a quick smile, which of course dissipated when I remembered what happened and became angry again. I wanted to yell at Ryan for doing this. I didn't want him to be gone. I wanted to play outside with him for hours. Who was going to torture my brother with me now? I hated what had happened. I blamed everyone for not protecting my friend. *Where was everyone when he needed help?* How could he be gone? First my uncle and now my best friend, I wallowed in sadness.

The car ride from McDonalds to our development, ten minutes away— was the longest car ride ever. We passed Ryan's house on the way home. Ryan's mom, Sandy, was at our house picking up the urn when we returned. I hugged her tight— she cried. I said a weird and awkward goodbye to Ryan through the metal artifact. After that, Sandy disappeared forever with her son, Jason, leaving the house and the grandfather behind.

No one ever talked about my blue bubble again but I know, to this day, it was my best friend saying "goodbye."

****

The few years following Ryan and Uncle Hanky's death flew by quickly. Death had become something we needed to get used to— because it became an epidemic in my family. Every time I turned around, we were dealing with more stress, death, and sadness. By the time I turned eleven, I had lost the most influential members of my family, and both of my parents had no parents. I was invited to funeral after funeral. Sometimes I wished I wasn't. I was glad that I hadn't been invited to Ryan's or Uncle Hanky's.

The family on Dad's side was still suffering the loss of my uncle when Dad's mom became sick. Dad put her in an apartment and financially helped her stay there. Mom never wanted to visit my grandmother, Dad's mom, when she was alive. I remember Dad sometimes snuck me over there, and she was very nice to me. I don't remember many stories with her in them, but I do remember that she always said she loved me and that I looked just like my daddy. The day she passed away I was roller-skating on the back concrete patio, and, my mother screamed out the window to me: "Your grandmother died," as if this were just normal, everyday news. I immediately began to cry. Then Mom yelled, "Don't cry. It was your dad's mom." I cried anyway.

Her reaction confused me. I wanted to know what happened, how she died. No one told me anything, and I wasn't afraid to keep asking. Sometime in my thirties, I found out that Mom and Grandmother *hated* each other. They had a terrible fight one day, before I was born and in anger my grandmother called Mom a "dirty Jew." My mother wanted nothing to do with her from that day on— understandably.

Unfortunately for Dad they never repaired their differences and the family was torn in two. Sneaking me over to see my grandmother was Dad's only option.

After my grandmother passed away Dad gave me her high school class ring. The engraving on the ring was barely readable, but it didn't matter to me. I wore that ring and was grateful that I had gotten something from my grandmother.

One night shortly after the death of Dad's Mom, Mom was driving home from a friend's house. The winter roads between Tabernacle and Medford were unsafe when any amount of snow thinly covered the streets. The snow-drifts rushed across the farm-lands and settled on the black asphalt, and then the roads slicked over with a layer of black ice that the tires of your vehicle couldn't grip. Black ice is impossible to spot under a layer of snow and drifting snow-banks. The day Mom was driving home from her friend's house, her car hit some black ice and she lost control of her car and rear-ended the car in front of her. Her head hit the steering wheel upon impact. Other than minimal damage to both cars, and a headache (in my mom's case) everyone walked away from the accident safely. The doctor visits began days later, as Mom was having medical issues.

Months after the accident, Mom started having severe headaches and after numerous doctor appointments Mom woke up and her entire body was shaking uncontrollably. She had no idea what was happening, but she couldn't stop. Dad came home from work that day and took her back to the doctor. Both Mom and Dad believed when Mom hit her head in the car accident, it must have caused this new issue: seizures. The car insurance company refused to take responsibility for the seizures, and the doctors couldn't be one hundred percent sure the accident caused it. They started to discuss a possible chemical imbalance, and prescribed medication for Epilepsy. In an attempt to control the seizures, Mom began to sleep more. The more she slept, the further she drifted away from me, and the more resentful I became.

I couldn't understand the seizures and blamed the world for hurting Mom. Mom became distant and medicated, and she shook often. It felt as though the epileptic medication was causing a whole new set of Mom crises that weren't there before. Too much medicine and Mom would sleep more than before; not enough medicine and she would shake for hours. It was unbearable to watch. I hid myself away when Chad or Dad were home. I didn't want to deal with any more medical problems.

In the midst of an argument, I recall telling Mom, "I will never be as sick as you." Her response was, "I pray you never are, Danielle."

Shortly after the accident and all the doctor visits, Mom's mom became sick, and we visited her at her apartment, more often than ever before. I didn't understand at the time that she had cancer, and it was attacking her brain. When we went to visit, everyone would just say, "You're grandmother is very sick, dear." Usually this was followed with a list of how I needed to be quiet around her, refrain from asking too many questions, and do nothing to upset her. After we found out she was sick, we started to go to my grandparents' apartment every weekend to visit them. I remember the smell of twenty different foods while walking down the hall to my grandparents' apartment. Inside, it was the most beautiful home I had ever seen. They had phenomenal antique furniture, porcelain elephants I could sit on, gold mirrors bigger than I was. I was not allowed to touch anything unless I asked my grandmother or Mom. I was used to this, so it wasn't that bad. Mom and I fought over what I should wear every time I went to visit my wealthy grandparents. She insisted I wear a dress, even though she wore her comfy jeans. Mom said "You can be a caterpillar at home, Danielle, but out of respect, you must be a beautiful butterfly when we visit my parents."

On those days, I looked like royalty. By the end of a grandparent visit, I was pleased to take off my black and white, tight, plastic saddle shoes and matching stockings, and fall asleep in the car for the hour-long car ride home. Dad would carry me into the house and place me in my bed, dress and all. Mom would tuck me in and say goodnight while shutting off my light.

The dress rule obviously didn't apply to Mom. I remember Grandfather yelling at her because she was always dressed like a "slob", according to his standards. My mom's sisters said that Mom was rebelling and had been since she was a child. I couldn't get Mom to talk much about her childhood, though I diligently tried.

One time during our sick visit, Grandmother suddenly became angry and since I was in the room with Dad, she yelled at me. She had never yelled at me before. Everyone told me "not to be sad, because she was very sick," but to be honest it made me feel horrible inside.

Mom had a hard time seeing my grandmother in her bed. Everyone thought having Grandmother in the comfort of her own home was best for her. Every time Mom had to face her dying mother, she had an epileptic seizure. She stayed in the living room, trying to control the seizures and Dad and I went in and helped whoever needed help. My grandfather couldn't physically move my grandmother without Dad's help—so he helped. Dad was friendly with the nurses, and in return, they were nice to me. We spent hours with the family on visiting weekends and it was very emotional.

My grandmother soon died and I attended the funeral. This was my second funeral and I was *only* eleven years old. I clearly remember how Mom and Dad made me go up and kiss my grandmother. Even as a young child, I knew this was UNFAIR! Dead kissing is so odd.

Afterward, my Grandfather seemed depressed, but soon he started to travel to his Florida house more often. He began a new life, met a woman, went on expensive vacations, and eighteen months later he died too, of a heart attack.

The last memories I have of my two grandmothers and my grandfather are breathless, motionless, grand-parents in open caskets. We sat Shiva for Mom's family, had Irish wakes for Dad's, hugged family members we had never before met, made promises to strangers that we would hang out soon, and we ate and ate and ate. Apparently, when you lose someone you love, eating makes it all better. Since I always loved food, I became very good at this part.

After the death of both of my grandparents, my family on Mom's side no longer celebrated holidays and we were no longer partaking in anything Jewish. I desperately missed my grandparents and my older cousins. I missed our Matzo bread with a $1 bill attached at the holidays. I missed going through my cousin Jeff's boxes of jewelry from other countries, and how he always let me keep *anything* I wanted. All of my cousins were ten years older than me, so by the time I was eleven, they were in college, living in different parts of the county, or married and preoccupied. The only time I was able to see Aunt Shelly, Mom's sister, was when she took me to her beach house for a weekend trip to swim in the ocean, shop for adorable clothes and eat the most fabulous dinners. Other than those last few visits, we all just went our separate ways.

At first I thought I was being punished for misbehaving when I visited Aunt Shelly, but she assured me that "Everyone is just busy now, dear." That made more sense since I tried hard to abide by her rules, be kind to her friends, and never interrupt her conversations. That was all she cared about and anything else was "party on!"

Mom and her two sisters, Aunt Marlene and Aunt Shelly seemed completely different in personality; however, they all sounded alike and they looked similar, with brown eyes, brown hair, and darker complexions. None of my physical characteristics came from Mom's side of the family. My freckles never got darker, just tanner. They multiplied and my face turned red. My hair color comes from Dad's Irish side. My brother Chad, on the other hand, looks just like Mom except for his hazel eyes, which remind me of our beloved Uncle Hanky's.

A few weeks following the final funeral for Grandfather, Mom's family cleared out my grandparents' beautiful apartment and all of the items went to their three daughters. My grandfather's death resulted in Mom having seizures more often than before, and she was diagnosed with situational depression. She started to sleep more than ever, and I left her alone, as Dad told me to. My brother, Chad, was extremely empathetic. He seemed to understand Mom. I didn't. I grew closer to Dad as I got older, and Mom acted like she didn't want to be bothered with me. I started to resent her lack of attention and could only get her to talk to me, or even care about me, if I were sick or had a relationship or friendship issue. Sometimes, if I was open to listening, she was really good at dispensing much-needed motherly advice.

By this time, Chad was a teenager in high school, busy with girls, newly listening to dance music, and partying with friends. Except for missing my uncle terribly, Chad seemed fine as always to me, but it was hard to tell since I annoyed him at every turn. I was even more surprised when he publicly hugged me at Grandfathers' funeral when we both read the poems we had written. This act of kindness was shortly followed by his universal statement of, "Danielle, you're too young to understand anything." To me, eleven was very old in spite of what he said.

Aunt Barb started to date her new boyfriend, Uncle Joe, who was Uncle Jack's brother. She didn't explain much about the situation. All she said was "I love Joe." For me, it was very confusing. After all, Uncle Joe looked so much like Uncle Jack. But, as a kid, swapping uncles is something I just had to accept. I really didn't have any say, and Aunt Barb seemed much happier with Uncle Joe so I didn't pitch a fit. Besides, he lived in an amazing house, and I was allowed to play with the pool table, which was the best part.

We weren't there very long when they sold this house, and Aunt Barb was pleased when he bought her a new beautiful home in Pennsylvania. I was pleased because I had my own room there too. I did, however, have to share my new room with many porcelain dolls and an entire stock-room of Aunt Barb's new business venture, Avon

41

products. I played with all of the makeup samples, and Aunt Barb sent me home with some products of my own. She said we shouldn't use our own product for fun because it would cost her money.

One night when I was thirteen-years-old Aunt Barb hosted an Avon party and all of her friends came to visit the new house. She was selling her product and drinking with her friends. I was very tired so I decided to go into her room, lie down, and watch TV. In her glass dresser I couldn't help but notice, there was another urn. This one was a box labeled Francis Mason. My Uncle Hanky now lived in this box. It saddened me to be reminded about my uncle.

The death of so many family members shook up my world— a world that was otherwise pretty stable, or at least I had thought so.

Part 2:
Bratty & Cocky

Chapter 5

Money problems? Nah!

When I was thirteen-years-old, my parents began to use the new money inherited from the estate of Mom's mom and dad. My parents didn't discuss the new money with us kids. They were keeping it a secret. They even referred to the times they locked themselves in the bedroom to talk about how they would spend the money as "business meetings." I found out about the money one night when Mom was bickering with Dad. "The new changes are going to make the house too big," she said, "and this isn't what I want to do with my money."

I wasn't fully aware of the changes that were occurring, but because of the new money, someone had decided that *I* needed braces. The day I got my braces was the same day the construction on our little split-level home began. The construction crew was adding a new garage, a new top floor, a back deck, and alterations to the front of our house to create a bigger walk-in entrance. Dad designed these plans himself and was very excited to begin construction.

Mom seemed distant, stressed, and wanting nothing to do with change. She said she didn't want to make the house bigger and didn't feel it was a smart investment for the family. She was concerned that they wouldn't have money like that again, money that meant security for her future. To Dad, having money meant things could get done in our home and that was a form of "securing the future." The more we did to the home, the more concerned Mom became. The more they did to my mouth, the more concerned I became.

Nothing prepared me for the medieval experience of having braces put on. No one warned me that it hurt so much. I sat in the chair as they shoved metal in my mouth, forced teeth in new directions, glued chunks of sculpted metal to my teeth, and then bound this torture device together with wire. I couldn't open my mouth for a week after the ordeal. The only perk to my despair came from getting to select the colored rubber bands I used as wire holders. I chose the green miniature rubber bands and stopped complaining to everyone for about thirty seconds.

Ironically, as a younger kid I had desperately wanted a retainer. It seemed to me that everyone had one, which gave it cool status. One time I took paperclips and bent them to fit over my teeth and, *voila!*, instant metal retainer. I suffered through an entire day of school with a metal paperclip stabbing at the inside of my mouth while everyone else debated whether or not it was real. Admitting it was a fake was not an option— doing so might make me look weird. The next day I simply stated that it dropped in the toilet, and my parents wouldn't let me get another one.

The orthodontist thought it was funny when I told him my paperclip retainer story. I thought he had a sense of humor until he handed me my new "face gear." I took one look and declared to all present that, "There is no way I will be wearing face gear!" I repeated myself about one hundred times, as I informed my father, then the orthodontist, then the lady helping the orthodontist and anyone else who could hear me from my position in the very uncomfortable orthodontist's chair.

When we got home, Mom met us outside the house and I once again repeated my declaration. She told me, "You are going to wear it, Danielle, because this is the only way to fix your over-bite." I never knew I had an over-bite, but if I did have one, it surely was not the social disaster that wearing face gear would be. Seeing the firmness of my anti-face-gear stand, my parents had no option but to bring out the guilt trip. After hearing their counter protests about "wasting $500 on an ungrateful child," I promised to "try" the face gear and, with a lot of moaning and groaning, put it on.

I walked through the door of my construction zone of a house, surrounded by workers, and I wanted to die. My face was aching, my head was pounding, and I had promised I would keep the face gear on. Let me explain how it worked: I put the face gear in my mouth by pushing it into place and attaching it to my braces. It forced my jaw into an unnatural position and the pain soared. What kind of sadistic invention was this? A-do-it-yourself torture chamber? Torment-to-go? It was 1990, for god's sake!

I looked in the mirror and freaked out. I looked like the biggest nerd in any 1980's movie. I was not going to wear this thing outside of my house, not ever. Not for a sleep-over, not if you paid me. I was *never* wearing this thing out of my home!

I grabbed a blanket and collapsed on the couch in the middle of the construction zone. I passed out immediately after hitting the couch and I woke up hours later. The workers had all left and the pain in my mouth had not subsided. I believe I made it worse by using the stupid night brace. One side of my face leaned on the wire and my jaw was throbbing from being pushed left for hours.

That was it. I had tried. I took the face gear off and never put it on again. A year later the dentist removed my braces because I wasn't doing what I was supposed to do, and as he said, he was "wasting my parents' money." *Fine with me.*

Looking back as an adult, I swear it was all a scam. My teeth are straight just like my mother's were, and my children's teeth are straight. I think braces were the cool, expensive thing back then, and my parents were suckered in.

The addition on the house took three months to build. Dad insisted that this was fast. Mom hated the construction zone and resulting dirt, and often freaked out about it taking "too long." It seemed fast to me. Mom's new complaint became how there was too much for her to clean now. Dad shrugged off all of her grievances and made sure to warn me "not to ever complain like that."

My brother and I liked the new addition because, as part of this project, the room at the bottom of the steps that Uncle Hanky use to stay in became our new kid living room. A few years earlier we were spoiled when Dad built us new bedrooms in the cold, concrete basement. He embedded the pillars I used to roller-skate around into the walls to our rooms. Turns out those poles were beams that held up the house, not just cool features for roller-skating girls. Mom did love when our old bedrooms upstairs became my parents' master bedroom, with my old bedroom serving mostly as Mom's closet. Dad ripped out my red shag carpet with the promise that "shag would never come back."

The new deck on the back of the house hosted all of our teenage parties and allowed our parents some privacy without having to hide in their room. I spent hours on the deck talking to my friends on our cordless phone or lying out in the sun. When not on the phone, I wrote for hours in my journal, sitting in my folding lawn chair overlooking our old mildewed barn that stood a stone's throw away.

As a matter of fact, that old barn has lived a life of its own. Before becoming a teenager, my friends and I all spent an incredible amount of time there. Despite Mom saying I "neglected" the horses because I had too much love for the kittens, the barn and I had a great relationship. It always helped me win games like tag or man hunt. Back then, I climbed up the ladder (like a fire escape ladder) faster than anyone else. No one could catch me once I ran into the barn. I would hit that ladder on the second to highest rung and, just like that, I was through the hole in the ceiling. I then ran to the side of the barn, squatted down, and leapt off of the edge of the barn like Spider-Man. I rolled into the dirt and took off from there. I was unstoppable.

Sometimes my brother asked me if I wanted to play hide-and-go-seek. He told me to go to the barn and hide. I would wait and wait, and he would never come out. He tortured me two or three times before we stopped playing hide-and-go-seek. I didn't mind hiding in the barn without someone trying to find me thanks to the always entertaining feral kittens that had taken over residency. They made great company for a non-sought-after little girl. They would crawl all over me, climbing through my legs and waiting patiently for me to pet them while showering me with more love than I could handle. If I had any work to do in the barn, I wasn't allowed to pet a single kitten until I was finished. If I did, I would never complete a task. They eventually became bored with their game of running between my legs and hid in the hay. The older cats wanted nothing to do with visitors and spent their time hissing. We had a good understanding and ignored each other.

The barn had sheltered many animals over the years. I was too young to remember the goat Dad to this day still talks about however; at one point we had two horses, a pony, and almost forty cats and kittens living in the barn at the same time. Luckily for us the cats and the horses were allies. Once in a while, by accident, a horse would step on a kitten. Of course, I hated when that happened. I remember begging Mom to "please save the kitten." Realizing the kitten had little chance of renewed life, considering it was dead, Mom took it anyway and promised to do her best to save it. Those kittens never returned to the barn again. Mom simply told me that "the kitten is being taken care of."

And that was good enough for me.

Tragedy struck one afternoon when my brother gathered hay for the horses. He reached for the hay bale at the top of the stack, ten hay bales tall. The hay-bale was too awkward for him to hold by himself; suddenly it dropped out of his hands and plummeted to the floor, landing with a loud crash. We heard a squeal from underneath the hay. My brother lifted the hay bale and found one of the kittens underneath.

I couldn't believe it. He had killed a kitten. It was an accident, but I still freaked out on him.

Distraught, I ran to the backyard, through the sharp blades of tall grass and raspberry bushes to climb the very challenging ladder to the tree fort. I stayed up there, yelling into the air at the universe for its evil doing. I blamed Chad, too, but deep inside I knew he didn't mean to hurt the baby. When I felt better, I prepared to face the world but then it occurred to me no one tried to coerce me into leaving the tree fort. *No one cared.* I cried as I acknowledged the lack of love my family showed me, until I was hungry enough and cold enough to want

48

to go home. I entered the house fuming. No one said a word to me, and I, despite my normally jabbering mouth, didn't say a word to them.

The next day I asked to stay home from school because I was so upset. Mom said, "No!" Then she reminded me of the rules: We were not allowed to stay home from school unless we had a fever or were throwing up.

I argued relentlessly, "The death of a baby, a kitten, *is* a reason to stay home." She didn't budge, and I carried my sad self to school, complaining to anyone who would listen: "You think you have it bad, I wasn't even allowed to stay home when my kitten died."

As the youngest child in the house, I was often elected to close the barn door at night. I would run outside into the barn, which was freezing half the year and sweltering heat the other half.

The horses took comfort in the barn when snow or thunderstorms hit. Winter nights were often too chilly for them to stay outside of the barn, and Mom felt calmer when every animal was safely tucked away. We didn't lock the animals in the barn very often; however, during snowstorms we closed the barn doors. If it snowed a lot, we had to dig them out very early the next morning. The horses liked to eat early, and even snowdrifts covering both sets of doors wouldn't stop that hunger.

Mom usually took care and enjoyed her horses, but as we grew older and she grew sickly, Chad and I became "the barn helpers." I never cared for that job, and as a result, Chad always handled it better than I did. I was always in a hurry— dashing outside in twenty degree weather without a winter jacket would make anyone forget to replenish the horses' water, and then the small amount left would freeze overnight. Mom was never happy when that happened. She knew it was my fault, and I knew it would annoy her. But sometimes I still forgot.

When I was six years old, my family starred in a movie that was filmed in the barn. My cousin Stacy, who went away to college, came to visit for a weekend. She had to make a film for a college class and decided to use our family as the actors. We filmed in my yard, in my house, and in the red barn. It was the scariest movie ever. Not only was there a "creature," there were chainsaws, burns, blood, and death.

At six years old, I was excited to be a part of the coolest movie ever made. Mom and Dad played the main characters and both kept laughing while they tried to act. My role was the best because I was the only person who had a speaking part. My brother was lucky because he was allowed to scream really loud over and over again. We practiced looking and acting fearful of the creature. For the gory parts, we used ketchup. We smeared it all over Mom's robe, and at one point we squirted it at the barn wall upstairs. The smell of ketchup in the barn became putrid pretty fast. We tried to wipe it off of the wood, but it sunk in and left a residue. On hot days for years to come you could smell rotted ketchup— but that was okay, because it always made me reminisce about the best horror movie ever.

In all the years of good times associated with that barn, Mom had only one rule: "Stay off my horses!" I promised I would not go near the barn if she wasn't home. And I was faithful in this situation, except for the few times that Chad and I tried to jump on Mom's rescued Polo horses just to prove we could do it!

We sat on the fence line, waiting for the exact right moment to jump on the horse and hold on for dear life. I gripped my legs against the bareback skin and held onto the mane. I lasted what seemed like a long moment, until the horse ran towards the first curve of the fence. Unable to maintain my strength against the speed, I was thrown into the corner of the pen. Once on the ground I had to think fast as my brother screamed, "Get up! Watch out for the horse! Don't just lay there!"

Our bodies sustained bruises from the rocks and roots in the pen. We could never tell our mom about the bruises so we hid them and tried again another day. I did well hiding these bruises until one day I smacked my face against a stick. When questioned, I tried every excuse in the book to explain it. And then our neighbor Ruth told Mom that she had seen me on the horse.

And that was it: I had lost my mother's trust…

Chapter 6
Babysitters? Seriously...

A fter the horse incident, Mom refused to allow me to stay home
alone during the day or at night because she didn't trust that I
would stay out of the barn or off of her horses. I couldn't
argue that she was wrong because she reminded me over and
over again, "Danielle, you lied to me." She never knew Chad
also lied because I never told her— it wasn't solidarity, but fear of him
killing me that stood in my way. This led to a constant need for
babysitters, which in the worst-case scenario, meant my brother.

When Chad babysat me, my friends and I would hide somewhere
playing Barbies and leaving him alone. At twelve years old I would
complain relentlessly about the absurdity of having anyone sit me.
Mom said, "If you can find a friend to keep you, then you won't need
to be babysat." I tried so hard to find a place to go, anywhere, with
anyone, in order to not be babysat. The way I saw it, I was saving my
brother's life and my own by making this effort.

The opening of our above-ground pool caused another area of
concern for Mom and the babysitter plan. As a young girl, I loved the
moment it would turn spring again. The first second of warm weather I
begged Dad, "Please let's open the pool early!" Nothing was more
exciting than the grand opening of the pool followed by days of
constant swimming. When Dad deemed me old enough to help, he had
me sit on the deck watching as he took off the tarp, which served as a

pool cover. He took the cover off and then siphoned the solid dark green pool water through a funnel. Dad sucked on the end of the funnel, explaining exactly what he was doing and why.

When the water didn't start pouring through the blue tube, Dad assumed it was clogged and sucked harder. He sucked so hard that the nasty pool water flushed into *his mouth*. I started laughing. I laughed so hard, I sounded like a hyena. I couldn't believe what had happened. An angry glance from my father stopped me from uttering another single chuckle. Dad looked like he was going to lose his mind. He stomped around the concrete base, spitting and yelling, "Oh Jesus Christ, Jesus f'ing Christ, what the hell?" I resumed my hyena laughter – whenever I repeated the story of how Dad drank *bug water* to all of my friends.

He cringed every time he heard me repeat the story.

After Dad finished draining the pool with the siphon, the bottom was still covered with a foot of pool water—that someone had to remove. At this point, he'd labeled me and Chad "the kids who were now old enough to work for a pool." This came in handy whenever Dad didn't feel like doing his chores anymore. With a smile on his face, he handed us a bucket and told us to climb in and "help drain *our* pool." We'd then bucket out the pool water, scrubbing the walls and picking up thousands of leaves off the filthy floor.

Bucket by bucket we got the scummy, mosquito-larvae-infested water out. The entire experience was unsanitary, and I didn't hesitate to complain openly. Before I started, I walked inside my house, slipped two plastic bags on each of my legs and hands, and then put socks on top of the bags to hold the bags in place. I climbed slowly in the pool that held the coldest, grossest, slimiest water I ever felt. I prayed that the sock and bag barrier would keep my feet safe from all horrendous watery life forms. The closer I got to the water, the more rancid the smell became— everything about cleaning the pool grossed me out.

One good thing was that skating around the pool in my sock-and-bag shoes and gloves proved very successful in knocking all of the dirt from the pool's surface. I rubbed the sides with my hand socks and squirted the hose at the grime that flowed back into the pool. Taking all day to bucket out water, scrub an area, spray the area, and bucket out the area again, was not fun at all. I worked as fast and hard as I could, knowing that the quicker this was completed, the quicker I would be swimming in my pool.

One time I climbed into the pool and as I was walking around, cleaning the bottom, I felt a log under my feet. I let out a yelp and yelled, "Ew, ew, I don't want to," catching my brothers attention. He looked over and watched as I reached into the stinky, murky waters with my sock hand. I grabbed the end of what felt like a stick attached to a log. Heavier than I expected, I pulled fast and hard. As the log emerged from the water, I stared at it. It only took seconds to realize the log was actually a soaking wet, stiff dead squirrel staring back at me.

I let loose a blood-curdling scream from my body and threw the squirrel up in the air. Then I ran through the water toward the ladder as fast as I could. Before making it back to the ladder, the flying squirrel hit the water, splashing the larvae infested water all over the back of my shirt and in my hair. Chad laughed hysterically. I spent the next ten minutes lecturing Dad, "I am not going to get that animal out. I quit!" Sensing karma from the siphoning incident, Dad found this hysterical. However, he also *understood* that I wasn't going to pick up the rotting, soggy, water-logged rodent. He grabbed a bucket, scooped it up and simply threw the squirrel across the fence line. I spent all summer telling everyone the story of the dead squirrel. It's still a favorite.

We all loved the pool, but Mom loved it the most. During the prime sun hours of twelve to two we weren't allowed to bother her while she basked in the sun. I tried to adhere to this rule, but the house was hot without air-conditioning and I wanted to be in the pool too. So I begged to be allowed to at least hang out quietly. Sometimes she would reluctantly agree and the twins, Lauren, and I would swim around the pool in whispers, pretending we were mermaids. During "Mom pool time" which meant mom, a float, a book and some strange metal reflector, we were to avoid splashing, laughing, or making a single wave. The moment someone made a wave, we were kicked out of the pool. We quietly decided what type of mermaids we would be and what we would look like. I was *always* the mermaid with a rainbow tail. We sat at the bottom of the pool having tea parties, swimming through holes further into the sea, and circling around the raft in the middle of the pool.

If my friends weren't able to play, I hung on the edge of the raft and floated around with my mom. I tried to talk to her. Every time I would talk, she would say, "Danielle, I will kick you out if you talk again." This was never much fun, and I couldn't stay quiet another minute so, I usually opted for a bike ride.

When Mom wasn't home, bike rides, pool time, and wandering the streets weren't aloud. With advance notice of Chad being my babysitter, I'd call my friends, begging for one of them to take on a stray kid so that I wouldn't have to be *baby*sat. This proved to be more challenging than I expected. Jen and Steph had started living with their mom on the weekends, which meant they were seldom around. But sometimes their mom agreed to take me for a weekend. Lauren disappeared at random intervals, especially during the summers. It was hard to hang out with her, anyway. Her parents harbored some anger toward me for an accident that had occurred, though it was clearly an *accident*.

No one could have done what happened on purpose.

One hot summer day, when we were twelve, I went to pick up Lauren from her house, a three-minute bike ride. I often rode her on the handlebars to my house. Riding someone on the handlebars is a very tough trick, but I did it like a professional. I had to keep the bike straight while holding the weight of Lauren's wiggling butt, pedal the bike, and turn without knocking her off. I managed this trick every time we hung out and didn't mind doing it. I never wanted to be the person sitting on the handlebars because it was so uncomfortable, so being the driver was fine with me.

One day, Lauren and I rode to my house and played for hours before we got bored. "Going for a bike ride," I screamed outside to Mom. Once I was settled on the bike Lauren retook her position on the handlebars and we rode around the streets looking for other kids to play with. Unfortunately, there were none to be found, so we decided to head back to my house for a swim. Lauren sat on the steering wheel as she always did. But all of a sudden she screamed, "Stop, stop!" I stopped as fast as I could. Apparently I wasn't fast enough. We'd been going down a hill and I wanted to prevent launching her off of the handlebars. When we came to a complete stop, she hopped off of the handlebars and sat right there, in the middle of the road. Lauren's skinny, bare foot had sustained severe injury when it tangled in the spokes of my front tire. I almost threw up when I saw the blood. I panicked, but she wasn't crying, not even a tear. Thinking she may be in shock I yelled, "Wait here, wait right here," I kept saying this as I ran toward my house. "Wait there, wait there," I yelled louder.

I charged through my front door, screaming, "Mom, Mom, Mom!" She was nowhere to be found. I ran out to the backyard, all the while screaming, "Mom, Mom, HELP!" I was beside myself. Mom looked up from the inflatable pool lounger, her metal sun-catcher under her chin, and replied "WHAT?" She was utterly annoyed that I had interrupted her goddess time. There were only two warm months in Jersey, and Mom used them wisely to relax in the warmth and get *extremely* tan. Even worse than interrupting her sun time, I was now forcing her to come and pretend to be a nurse. Mom always liked to say she took care of a problem, but she actually didn't like to be bothered. We were definitely bothering her this time.

"Turns out, there is nothing you can do when you chop off the bottom of your foot." Lauren told me. "N-oth-ing?!" I said, my jaw dropped in awe. Her heel looked like a cheese slicer had cut halfway through. The skin flapped up and down or open and closed, depending on your angle. It was horrible, and I swore Lauren would need a hundred stitches.

Mom and I rushed Lauren home so that her parents could take her to the hospital or a doctor, something. I couldn't believe what happened to her next. Her parents grounded her, and she didn't come out for months after that. From what her parents told us you just have to wait for this kind of injury to heal

Mom made me clean the blood off of my spokes and spinning stars. I wasn't mad at Lauren. Mom decided that no one should ride on the handlebars anymore, and I agreed.

This was my second bike accident, and it reaffirmed what I had learned when I was younger and that is "Bikes are VERY dangerous."

Back when I was eight, Santa brought me a brand-new bike. It was green, my favorite color, and it was made of plastic parts. I was so excited when the seasons changed and the weather warmed up, because I could try out my new bike that Dad had painstakingly put together in our living room. I begged and begged all winter to ride the new training wheel free bike. Finally, the first spring day arrived and I was granted the right to ride.

Excited, I bravely walked my bike to the top of the hill on Anne Drive with Jen, Steph, and Lauren watching. I climbed on and prepared for my first run down the hill. "Catch me if you can," I yelled to everyone. My new bike was much faster than anyone expected. I rode as fast as I could toward the bottom, leaning as the road curved. Speed was mine. I was going faster than I ever had on any bike, and I felt so mature, amazing, and *very cool*.

The bike started to wobble and wobble and then it wobbled a lot more. I was losing control. It felt as though the tires weren't holding up to the speed of the downhill adventure. I tried to gain control of the trembling bicycle as I screamed, "Help, help, HEEEEEEELP!" Not knowing what was happening, I heard the faint sound of my friends laughing. Moments later I was tumbling with the bike entangled around my skinny body. I smacked forcefully into the ground three times before the pain sunk in. I hit my nose, my head, my knees, my leg, my arm, my butt, and scraped up all the parts of my body not covered by clothes. I felt the pain of hitting the dirt road numerous times. All of a sudden I was doing summersaults over my new bike. I no longer heard laughter, but screaming filled the air.

"Danielle, Danielle! Are you okay?" "Get help." "We are going to be in big trouble."

The commotion stopped, and I lay on the street staring at the girls hovering over my mangled body. We all started to laugh once we realized I wasn't dead. We continued to laugh until we looked at my bike. It had landed ten feet away from me, twisted and surrounded by plastic pieces. It appeared to be un-rideable. The front tire was bent, the cute glitter strings hanging from the handlebars had jumped ship, and little green chunks of bike littered the entire hill. I felt the pain of my injuries as I witnessed the death of my new bike. The girls helped me walk the bike home. Mom assessed my bodily damages.

I was injured across my entire body, no area left unscathed. Scrapes and bruises showed proof of my accident. Mom was happy that nothing *seemed* broken. She sent my friends home and stated "Girls, Danielle needs her rest." But I didn't want rest! I needed to take a shower to wash every single last cut to "save myself from infection." I then sat on the couch Band-Aiding my injuries. One hundred Band-Aids on my body meant I was completely healed— Mom disagreed.

Everyone felt horrible about my "near-death experience" except for Chad. My brother didn't believe my injuries were real, and he informed me that his bike accident was far worse than mine. *I already knew his was worse.*

Ryan had an older brother, Jason. Unfortunately, for Ryan and I Jason and Chad were also best friends. It seemed their friendship would break the day Mom was watching Chad and Jason while they rode bikes at our house. As Chad was riding his bike past Jason (Ryan's brother), Jason picked up a handful of sand and chucked it at him. The sand landed in my brothers eyes, and he lost control of his bike. He crashed to the ground and hit his head upon impact. Mom called 911. The ambulance rushed to our house again. And Chad ended up in the emergency room for a few days.

Even more traumatizing was the fact that, Dad was in the same hospital. Dad drove a motorcycle to save gas money on his commute to Pennsylvania and back every day. He worked as an electrician at 3M, and it took over an hour daily to get there. Mom needed a car too, but paying for two cars wasn't feasible at the time. Dad was driving home from work as he did every day when a semi-truck veered into his lane. The truck hit Dad's motorcycle, destroying it, while he slid under the truck for a few feet after the impact. Dad sustained numerous internal injuries, and Mom was afraid he was going to die. He ended up spending a solid month in the hospital.

Mom forbade me to go to the hospital despite my daily freaking out. She didn't think a child of nine-years-old should be in the hospital, let alone see a severely injured dad and now brother. I begged her to, "bring me to see *my* Daddy." But Mom refused. She was afraid that seeing him hurt would scare me. It scared me more that she always had to be in charge—even when it came to Dad. I stopped fighting Mom when I realized it was fruitless. I settled for the promise of being allowed to hold his hand on the way home from the hospital. And I hoped they could afford a safer vehicle.

When we returned home, Dad spent the next two weeks healing and happily playing his video games.

Dad was rather particular about his games. I remember one time he spent an entire weekend playing Zelda. He had beaten Zelda at least five times already. I only beat it once, and only with lots of Dad's help. And I was beyond ecstatic and extremely proud of myself when I did. On this particular day, Dad was timing how fast he could beat the game. A few hours after Dad played, I went into my Zelda game and I was playing, then I was leaving the controller for some time, coming back and playing some more, asking Dad for advice while trying to navigate a map in a Zelda castle. The game ran for about two hours. My father then asked me if he could please get into his game. I stopped, saved mine and went outside. About eight minutes later, Dad began yelling and carrying on.

When Dad freaks out, he states passive-aggressive facts under his breath while pacing and waving his arms in a "What the hell!" way. Speaking to him at such moments is a horrible idea. So I didn't.

In the end, he realized that what I thought was my Zelda game was actually his. This led to two hours added to his time and a whole bunch of things I did in what I thought was my game actually being done to his game. So he had to start over.

Honestly, I still feel horrible about that even though it was an honest mistake. Mom was pissed because Dad was pissed. I begged for forgiveness. Mom didn't want to hear any of it. She came up with her own way of handling the situation: Her solution was to never let me play the video games again. I prayed, as it was happening, that Dad didn't follow her punishment on this one issue—he normally didn't. Thank goodness he remained pissed only until he caught up to where he'd been in the old game, and then everything went back to normal.

Video game deaths were nothing compared to how lucky my family was to be alive with all of these bike accidents.

For the longest time Mom allowed my brother to be my babysitter if she had anywhere to be. I complained, protested, fought back, freaked out, and begged Mom not to leave me with my horribly mean brother. I wasn't joking. As a babysitter, he offered one benefit to Mom—he came cost-free. However, it was dangerous for me to be left in that situation.

One time when I was ten-years-old, Chad and his friend Bobby locked me in a dog cage in the basement. That wasn't even the worst of it. They then used a metal baton to smack the dog cage every time I tried to unlatch the door. Having one big brother pretending to be a babysitter was annoying enough but having his friend torment me was even more upsetting. I spent an hour in a dog cage with more baton smacking, laughing, and a million threats of what would happen if I told on them.

As soon as Mom came home, I told on them. Unfortunately my complaints to Mom often fell on deaf ears. I remember her disapproving look when I complained and an even more disapproving look when I declared that "they should be in trouble." I was infuriated when they received no punishment at all. But Mom knew I was not going to stop there. I would not hesitate to bring this to the man in charge! I was so angry I walked over to the telephone on the wall and dialed my father's work number.

When Chad saw what I was doing, he ran at me. I threw the phone barely missing Mom and sprinted screaming down the hallway, into Mom's room. As I attempted to shut and lock the door with my body, he forced the door forward and lunged at me. I jumped onto the bed and ran back past him, down the hall and down the stairs. He missed me at the steps. I reached the second phone in Uncle Hanky's old room and WHAM, he power drove me into the corner of the wall. That was it: A siren came out of my mouth. "Mmmmyyyyy ribs are cracked. Take me to the hospital." I screamed.

Chad tried to help me up apologizing profusely. "Stop screaming, I'm sorry, I didn't mean to do that. Please stop."

"Donnnn't touch me!" I yelled again.

I calmed down after a few more screams. All the while, however, Mom didn't come running. She didn't stop the craziness. She didn't ask if I was okay. Instead, she merely said, "Danielle, stop being so dramatic."

The rest of the night I was so angry that I stayed in my room until I assumed everyone had fallen asleep. I checked the multiple bruises on my ribs repeatedly, feeling angry until I had no more patience for starving and snuck out to eat a bowl of cereal. Lucky enough, Dad had the same idea and it was us, just me and Dad. I complained to him whenever we got the chance to be alone. "I don't like the way Mom treats me or how Chad follows Mom's lead, Dad." He always smiled and asked, "Why do you let it bother you so much?"

Pondering that thought, I ate while reading the back of the cereal box and he ate while reading the paper. Knowing I had Dad was comforting; however he wasn't around enough to be there to really lean on.

I missed Dad when he was away and often felt like I was alone. Holding on to the moments of laughter with Dad saved me from dwelling on the arguments when he wasn't around. My plea for a new sitter, despite relieving me from the chaos of Bad Chad, ended up being a big mistake. Chad turned seventeen, and he had a *real* job. Lucky for him, he was done with babysitting. This led to one incredibly long, painful year during which Mom hired "The Devil," Lauren's sister, to watch me. It wasn't long before I began to beg for Chad again.

Lauren and I called Michelle "The Devil" for very good reasons. She was a horrible babysitter. She sat on the couch, watching TV, yelled at us to leave her alone, and made us cook our food and clean it up. I swear Mom should have left me alone rather than with this lunatic who cost us money. At least my brother could sometimes be entertaining. Lauren and I tried to tell Mom how horrible her sister was as a babysitter, but Mom called me "a constant complainer." I complained about Chad and now I complained about "The Devil." I begged and pleaded that I was old enough to stay home alone when Mom needed her hair or nails done. She never left the home nowadays otherwise. I could never understand why she didn't schedule these appointments while I was in school.

When I turned thirteen, Mom said she would let me stay home alone once I had proved I was a responsible young lady, so I was doing whatever it took. I even started saving my holiday and birthday money for my "new business." I used any money I got to buy bulk candy and sell it at school to other kids during the week days. I cannot pretend I came up with this idea all on my own. The truth is I stole it from my brother. He bought Huggies (drink containers that held the nastiest drink ever) and bulk candy, and sold it in high school. My biggest selling item was Big League Gum. I was at an advantage financially. Everyone would pay me $1.00 and my actual cost was $0.65. I took my money and I walked all the way to Sandy's Market, which was over a mile away, to buy as many snacks as I could.

I had to walk down my winding road, through the woods, across the lake, back up a dirt hill, back to blacktop and the walk for another fifteen minutes to arrive at the store. The woods that I had to cross held many memories for me. Everyone went there to play Truth or Dare and Spin the Bottle, and the teenagers were always having parties and leaving beer bottles behind. The younger kids would take the beer bottles and throw them at the trees to see them explode. I've never told anyone this; my first kiss with my childhood friend took place in those woods.

The locals called Sandy's Market the "Hindu Hut." As a child, I had no idea they did it because the owner was an Indian man. He and his family lived above the market and ran the store. The store was in a bit of disarray. The floors of the market were covered with sticky filth. As you walked into the store your sneakers became a squeaking instrument planting and peeling across the floor. The shelves were dusty yet fully stocked with new items. I had one purpose at Sandy's Market: to get my product for a cheap price and turn a profit. I was, however, always curious about the room with the black curtain and a sign written on a piece of paper that read "XXX 18 and over."

My brother had already told me that it was a "nudie thing," and I really had no idea what that might mean. One time I snuck into the eighteen and over room, and I was blown away. Everywhere I turned I saw naked people. Naked people of every race, every gender, every shape and size stared back at me. Or, should I say their parts did. I stood there and stared, mesmerized by the world around me until some man walked into the room. I looked at him with an obvious jaw drop; he looked at me with a what-the-heck glance, and before he could utter a word, I quickly walked through the black curtain. I never went into that room again.

If it wasn't for the cheap candy I would have never went to Sandy's Market. Chad didn't care that I stole his idea. Unfortunately, both of our businesses were shut down when our schools stopped allowing junk food. They said it had something to do with allergies.

Proving I could be alone solved all of my problems. I found that babysitting myself was *so* easy. *Days of Our Lives* became my entertainment and eating snacks became my pastime. I could never understand why it took my parents so long to trust me on my own. I actually started to babysit other neighborhood children around the same time. I found babysitting to be easy too. I, unlike other babysitters, played with the children and I never yelled at them. They were lucky to have me and not Lauren's neglectful sister.

Neighbors paid me three dollars an hour to babysit their children— sometimes till two in the morning. The scary part of working this late was the walk home at night. I didn't ask my parents to pick me up because they were sleeping, and I never made the parents drive me home because I felt bad making them get back into their car. Sometimes they were drunk, and I definitely *never* wanted to drive home with the dads alone—Mom's advice.

The dark roads, lined with pine trees were only lit by the hidden moon. On the nights where the clouds covered the moon, it was overwhelmingly dark. None of the street lights worked on our streets, and at two in the morning everything was pitch black. Luckily for me, the sounds of crickets and whip-poor-wills broke the uncomfortable silence in the darkness. Pretending not to be afraid, I walked through the development alone—actually I ran. I would run so fast that I'd make it home in no time. My fear was that someone would jump out of the pines and grab me or chase me. I never looked back.

Fears of the Jersey Devil ran through my head. According to childhood stories the locals told us, the Jersey Devil was real! In 1735, there was a baby born to a woman called, Mother Leeds, a Pine Barons resident who some considered a witch. Mother Leeds became unhappy when she found out that she was going to give birth to her thirteenth child. She cursed the child in frustration, calling it the Devil. Nine months later she gave birth to her new baby at home with the help of a midwife. The moment of birth, the thirteenth child grew into a creature with hooves, a goat's head, bat wings, and a forked tail. In a fit of rage, it killed the midwife, then flew up the chimney and headed into the pines to kill any children it could find outside alone, from that day forward.

Someone told me once that in the nearby woods, up the hill from my house, people had *actually* seen the Jersey Devil. Dad didn't believe any of this. He said it was all made up. I tried to let his words assure me as I ran home in fear of being mauled by the Devil himself. I know Dad said it was ridiculous and impossible, but I still worried about one big thing: "What if Dad was wrong?" I couldn't take that risk.

So I ran as if something chased me until I slammed into the front door. As soon as I reached the door, I opened and shut it as fast as I could and locked both locks. Peering outside the little glass window, panting desperate for air, I made sure that I was still alone. Next I would run up the stairs and turn on all of the outside switches controlling the bright shining light from the barn and lighting up the entire driveway. Then I'd test Mom and Dad's door to make sure Tisha, our giant Weimaraner was awake. One bark from her and a lighted home meant, I could safely fall asleep.

Around this same time, I began attending church services with some of my friends. If Dad was wrong, and there was a God, then there must be a devil, which would make the Jersey Devil plausible— and then I was screwed. Chad and I grew up atheist on my dad's side and Jewish on my mom's. It was very difficult as a child to understand what religion was when Dad talked about Darwinism, the evolution of the fruit flies, ape genealogy, and other blue prints of life. Dad's information got me in serious trouble in school. When I was a child, people still prayed in school if they were sad about a schoolmate or when someone passed away, as our principal did.

I followed all the other students and prayed with them even though I was taught I was praying to an imaginary man in the sky. I never knew who I was praying to. I just prayed. Sometimes if life was stressful, I would pray alone. I never really considered it praying. I was more reliving my day, or thinking about what I would like to see happen in the world, and putting it out there to manifest what I wanted in life.

In my lifetime I went to Sunday school, Awanas (a children's church program), sang in church choirs, went to Bible studies, sat through communions, christenings, baptisms, weddings, and I spent at least three times a year listening to a sermon with one of my friends. My parents encouraged me to go anywhere I could with my friends, including church. They were just happy that I left the house for a few hours. Dad may have enjoyed freedom for the few hours I was gone, but at night I came home and deluged him with the hundred questions the pastor asked me when I explained I was an atheist. Apparently the church looked down on atheism. I remember asking the pastor questions like, "So you don't believe we came from apes at all?" Then I would explain the scientific theory of evolution. I didn't get very far into my speech before the Sunday school teacher stopped me. Looking back I was probably a serious threat to the church classroom, explaining evolution to other eight and nine-year-olds. By the time I was thirteen, with adhering to Mom's advice, I stopped telling everyone I was an atheist. It was too much work to discuss it and to explain evolution to people who only wanted to argue with me. Not to mention, I really wanted a God too, though I never told Dad.

Chapter 7

Sometimes Mom is a little too much

By thirteen, I prayed daily to a god that *I didn't believe in* – wishing Mom's seizures would go away and that she would stop needing to sleep so much. She started to become distant more often than not, and she was less interactive than ever before. I could only dream about the days when Mom would tuck me in or snuggle with me on the couch. I found my own rides to and from sports, organized my own outings, and prepared my own meals when Chad and Dad weren't home.

During my teenage years, our main interaction became fighting. It didn't help that Mom's new favorite word had become *no*. Because she could never be certain she would be feeling okay, the answer to every plan I wanted to make was no. No, she didn't want friends coming over. No, she didn't want them sleeping over. No, she wasn't going to drive us to or from. No, I wasn't allowed to go to the high school parties, especially if Chad was going to be there. No. No. No. The less Mom was involved with me and my stuff, the happier she was. By the time I reached high school, I felt the same way about her and her stuff.

Following the car accident and Mom's diagnosis of epilepsy, the loss of both of Mom's parents leading her to a deeper depression, Mom wasn't living life the same way she used to.

And understanding illness was not my strong point— I was a terrible nurse. Mending the sick turned out, *not* to be my specialty. I was annoyed with Mom and her many health issues, and even more annoyed that, by association, they had become my issues as well.

Mom became lost to me and I was then lost to her too. School work was on me, failing was my issue, life was survived and she was distant. Resentment sunk in deeper.

Her seizures seemed to occur more as I reached eighth and ninth grade, or maybe it just seemed that way because I was the only one home to see them. No one was around as much as I was to help out with Mom's episodes. Dad started traveling for work more than ever before, and Chad was a teenager in his senior year of high school. He was too busy working a job, driving, dating, and having adult-free fun. I wished I was an adult daily.

I never knew what to expect when I came home from school. Some days, she would be sleeping, and I would leave her alone. Once in a while, she acted like Mom from when I was nine years old, and I tried to embrace those days. But other times she was either having a seizure or raging about something I did wrong or didn't do at all.

Never knowing which Mom I'd get was the most difficult part.

One afternoon when I returned home from school, Mom was passed out at the top of the steps. I saw her as soon as I walked in the front door. My first thought was that she was dead. I ran up the steps screaming "Mom!" I grabbed her and startled her awake. She must have had a seizure already, and by startling her I threw her into another one. I knew not to jolt an epileptic, but my first instinct was to wake Mom up. We always had to make sure she was safe when she had her seizures or else, as the doctor informed Dad and Dad informed me, "She could bite off her tongue." Apparently this had happened to other people, and I was not about to let that happen to her. I rushed down the stairs to grab a pillow, placed it under her head, ran back to the kitchen to get her a glass of orange juice with a straw and I sat with her making sure she was comfortable and hydrated until the seizures passed. Sometimes this could take fifteen minutes, other times an hour.

Dad trained Chad and I how to handle an extreme attack, and where to locate the emergency medication. We had to be prepared for these moments. Random black outs happened during which Mom passed out and couldn't remember anything that happened. It broke my heart to deal with her sickness and to see her this way. I never stopped wishing that she would just wake up better one day.

But, I resented having to take care of a sick mom, and over time, I disconnected from her. I didn't know how else I should feel. I didn't understand why she was getting worse. Dad was trying his best to get her properly medicated, but it took a long time to get it right. Dad and Mom went to doctor appointment after doctor appointment. Each time the doctors explained that the medication takes time to work.

Being honest with her doctors resulted in the doctors taking away her driver's license for six months. Without her driver's license, Mom suffered more than just seizures. She fell into a deeper depression, with her ailments engulfing her. Dad promised Mom he would get her driver's license back, and he would never let them take it again. This resulted in Dad and Mom lying about her seizures to the doctors. Apparently admitting she was still shaking would keep her license forever from her. She had a difficult time getting properly treated with this catch twenty-two: She could tell the doctors she needed help because she was shaking and lose her license, or she could tell the doctors she is no longer shaking, and lose her medical care. Mom quickly learned how to balance out her own epilepsy medicine and continued to monitor her own seizures without doctor assistance.

Dad had a godly level of patience for Mom. If Mom suffered new ailment, he spent months trying to find a cure. The better she felt, the happier my father became. He kept his frustrations about the continuously sick situation to himself and only discussed it with Aunt Barb. They often had conversations about her "illnesses," speculating whether they were partly over exaggerations and manipulative behaviors. Still, when Dad spoke to Mom, he acted as though every illness was truly as extreme as she said it was.

I, on the other hand, was becoming much more skeptical.

As a teenager, I often felt hopeless. Despite being annoyed at having a sick mother, I followed the rules my father set before me—mainly to stop talking back to her—and, for fear that Mom could die, I tried my hardest to do what I was supposed to do as a daughter and a student. But, that didn't negate the fact that I despised the situation. I wanted Mom to be well. I didn't want to think about losing her daily or fear coming home one day and her tongue was missing. I wanted normalcy. I just wanted her to be able to come shopping with me, to stop complaining about the ailments stemming from the epilepsy and the doctors who never figured out why the seizures started, and to stop talking about depression issues and new aches and pains from her neck to her knees to her back. Initially most of these problems went undiagnosed. And all I wanted was a "normal" mom.

I tried to talk to my brother about how I was feeling however, Chad stopped hanging out at our house as much, and strangely I found myself missing the happy moments we managed to have in our chaotic relationship. I looked forward to being a freshman while he was a senior. Mom would dismiss my sisterly whining saying, "He's a teenager and teenagers have their own lives." Chad and I recently stopped fighting nearly as much as we used to and even his girlfriends were acting sweet to me. They referred to me as "Little Mason." I missed them coming over, doing my makeup, playing with my hair, and dressing me in their old clothes. I appreciated Chad's girlfriends showing me how to be girly. Mom had never been very girly with me. The girliest I became with Mom was wearing the beautiful dresses my aunts or grandmother used to buy for me.

With Chad and his girlfriends, my fun would last until the moment I annoyed him. I tried hard to refrain from doing this, but still failed often.

When Chad found time to be around, he brought friends over, and Mom willingly hung out with them. Her kindness to his friends was granted from the comfort of her bed or, on the good days, in our living room, where she'd chat with them for hours. This drove me insane. I was so *over* having a mom confined to her bedroom yet somehow, Chad got the mom who would hang out happily on the couch.

In grade school my friends loved Mom as much as Chad's friends did. They built bonds with her prior to her illness, and the sicker she became, the more sympathetic they became. I was fine with my friends visiting with Mom, despite my lack of involvement. They often came over and headed into Mom's room like Aunt Barb did. I assumed they were looking for advice or just someone who may understand their issues. Mom would help anyone who needed it, and her kindness extended to my friends on a good day.

However, whenever Mom and I were arguing and this happened, I freaked out. "My Mom is not your friend," I yelled. "How would you like it if I hung out with your mom?" Because I had the "Mom that would listen," my friends dismissed my annoyances. Somehow everyone else was empathetic to her issues. *Why couldn't I be? What was wrong with me?* I started to think I was a horrible person who disliked my own sickly mother. No one understood. I didn't even understand.

In high school, she took her friendships with *my* friends to a new and personal level when she started talking to them about our relationship. It was one thing for my friends to ask for relationship advice or complain about their parents, but suddenly *I* was a topic of discussion. My friends would go in the room looking for advice and come out giving me advice.

The last thing I wanted was Mom telling my friends our business or *my* business. Every time a friend lectured me or knew private information—I became angrier. I wasn't able to do anything about the anger because Dad thought it was funny that I let a four-foot-eleven woman get to me. Chad knew Mom treated me differently than she did him, but he blamed my attitude. My friends wanted to talk to me about how Mom was feeling and how I should understand her better. Everyone infuriated me even more. No one could understand our relationship—not even me.

My high school best friend Samantha often became involved— she truly meant well. She genuinely thought she was helping when she told me Mom's side of things. She would come over and say, "I'm gonna go visit with your Mom!" I never cared. One day Sam came out after a visit and the next hour was spent sitting outside on my back porch listening to how "My mom wishes things were better." As I sat there, listening anger flooded into every part of my body. I responded with remarks like, "Yeah that's what she is telling you. You don't live with her. You have no idea. She's been sick and indifferent to me since I was nine. You just can't understand." Followed by, "It isn't only my fault we fight."

Like all of my other friends, Sam would say, "I am just trying to help."

I felt betrayed by Mom for acting like she wanted to be close with me and even more so for pretending my friends were her friends. And I felt betrayed by my friends for taking her side. I became defensive and protective of myself.

I coped by telling myself, *It just is what it is.* I was angry that she never wanted to do anything with me, that she slept all the time, and that when she wasn't sleeping we were arguing about something I didn't do correctly. It seemed I could do nothing correctly. Take vacuuming the floor, for instance. Even this I did wrong! The lines did not going the right way, and the floor wasn't clean unless the lines were straight. Dishes weren't finished unless the counter was washed and scrubbed. Anything that belonged to me *better* be in my room. Lecture after lecture, I resented her sickness or lack thereof depending on how empathetic I felt that day. In my mind, Mom seemed to be able to sway her illnesses. Sometimes she would be deathly ill and cancel all of her plans. Other times she would be happy as a lark and go out with her friends or get her hair and nails done.

I entered high school and made new friends, who also quickly fell in love with Mom too. Everyone truly thought she was the "coolest mom ever!" She kept everyone's secrets, even if they were about me. If I annoyed a friend, Mom would commiserate with her on how she understood. She knew all of my friends' deepest secrets. She knew about the parties they all went to and everything that happened at these parties. She was a subtle spy and they were willing sources. I never got to experience Mom's "cool side" the way all of my friends apparently did, and it infuriated me. My annoyance hit an all-time high when my friends started smoking in the bedroom with *my* Mom. I couldn't believe anyone considered this something okay to do!

Every friend I had trusted her. They all wanted to talk to her about their problems, sit next to her on the bed while sharing a cigarette, and ask for advice on relationships. She was very wise, so I understood why they would want her advice; I had benefitted from her advice on many occasions (albeit a more parental style of advice, focused, of course, on what I was doing wrong).

I finally broke the day I was grabbing snacks from the kitchen for Lauren and I. When I was finished, I went to walk into Mom's room and as I twisted the doorknob I realized that the door was locked. Hoping this was a mistake, I knocked twice. Mom yelled, "Give us a minute honey." The words rang in my ears and stayed there—I knocked harder on the door.

This was the first time I ever felt sheer craziness. I had developed a new paranoia that she was in the room talking about me—every time. This paranoia was clearly justified.

After that, I took a hard stance, telling Mom, "I don't want you to be friends with my friends." Mom would fire back with, "Your friends can make that choice."

Who was this woman? What was her problem? Why couldn't she be normal?

I finally took control of the situation by limiting the friends I invited to our house.

Mom and my relationship affected the entire family. Our fighting led to Mom and Dad bickering. Dad would say, "Why can't you just say yes to her once in a while, Mona?" And Mom would respond with, "She's going to be spoiled because of you, Joe." Eventually Mom would say "You are all of the issues Danielle." "Two women cannot live under the same roof."

My response to this was, "Then you shouldn't have had a girl, Mom!"

Dad would then yell at me, saying "Can't you ever just walk away from the fight Danny? Walk away…"

I would do as I was told and stomp down the ten steps to my room and slam my door hard enough for the neighbors and their neighbors next to them to hear. Falling back on my slammed door, my eyes welled up with tears and I sobbed. I felt like my soul poured down my cheeks. I crawled toward my bed gasping for air, putting my face down into the pillow and sobbing muffled sobs. My heart ached. I hated fighting. I asked the universe over and over, "Why is it like this?" I'd spend the next hour crying. Mom cried too. Dad just tried to survive. And when Chad was around, he blamed it all on me.

Feeling as though the people I needed the most were also the people I needed to get away from the most tore at my heart. I longed for Mom and I to be friends, but I didn't know how to change our situation, and she didn't seem to want to. In a house full of people, I was alone.

Part 3:
Young & Dumb

Chapter 8
Life can be adventurous

The older I grew, the sicker Mom got. The sicker she became, the worse my grades suffered. I spent the days at school staring out a window and disappearing into my own mind from 7:30 a.m. to 2:30 p.m. Early in eighth grade, the school and my parents gave me an IQ test to see if there was "something wrong" with me. Fortunately (or unfortunately for my student self) they found nothing wrong. I actually tested well above average. The counselor from the school turned to my parents and said, "She's just lazy." He was probably right. School wasn't my favorite thing. But neither was being at home.

I wasn't trying in school just as much as I wasn't accepting Mom's sickness.

The high school years were academically challenging, but because I was following my brother, who was a senior, at least new friendships weren't a struggle for me. Chad ran with the "popular crowd," and I spent four years trying to figure out where I belonged. His friends treated me well, so as a freshman I looked popular with senior friends. None of them, however, were real friends; actually I wasn't allowed to be "friends" with them, only Little Mason, Chad's little sister.

Chad's friends were off-limits to me but I still had a biggest crush on his hottest friend, Steve. I ignored Chad's threats to stay away and invited Steve to my freshman Valentine's Dance. The shocker is that and he said "yes". I was so excited. I told everyone we were going together. Girls in my grade didn't believe me, and I couldn't wait to prove them all wrong when I showed up with him as my date. Chad told me he didn't want me to bring Steve—I told him I was bringing him! Mom didn't have any opinion, which was unusual. Normally she would take Chad's side and enforce whatever he wanted. But in this one case, she just stayed unusually uninvolved. I thought this may be a new start for Mom and I.

The day of the dance, I put on my adorable red dress, straightened my shoulder-length hair, and had my friend do my makeup. I felt beautiful and ready to show off my date. It was time for Steve to pick me up, and I checked the clock a million times. Finally, twenty minutes later, I walked into the living room, where Chad sat and said, "Where is Steve?"

"I have no idea," he said and went back to watching his show. I started to get nervous so I called Steve's brother, Mike. "Hey, where's your brother?" I said with the utmost confidence. "We're supposed to be going to the dance together."

Mike said, "Sorry Dan, you aren't actually going with Steve to the dance."

A sickness came over me. I felt like I was going to throw up on the floor where I stood. My throat started to close, and I was holding back the tears that welled in my eyes and threatened to ruin an hour's worth of makeup. I forced myself to breathe and calm down. My personal embarrassment was not getting the best of me.

"Why not, Mike?" I said. "Why is Steve not coming?"

Mike then told me something that made me want to harm my brother in the seat he sat. "Your brother threatened to beat him up if he goes with you." In my beautiful dress, full makeup, straightened hair, and high heel shoes, I ran to my brother and launched an irate attack. "Why would you do this to me? What is wrong with you? Why do you hate me so much, Chad?"

I started to cry. My makeup smeared down my face, and I used the bottom of my dress to wipe away the tears. I didn't just want to yell at him, I wanted to injure him. I sat on the couch hyperventilating. He came near me to stop my crying. As soon as he came close enough, I swung my arms and kicked with my feet with my red high heels in the hope of connecting with his body or face, maybe even giving him a black eye. Chad pushed me off and while walking away I heard, "Don't you have a dance to go to?"

I cried and cried on the couch. I hated my brother for ruining my life. I hated Mom for being so uninvolved, Dad for being on yet another business trip. I hated my dress for having black mascara marks across its bottom, and most of all I hated Steve for being a coward and giving in to Chad.

When I finally calmed down, Steve's brother called me back and said, "My friend will go with you, if you need a date."

I said, "Yeah, whatever. I'll meet him there."

Mike's friend, who was also named Mike, was cute enough but my heart was broken. Within ten minutes, he found another date—one of my girlfriends. It was another slap in my face. I was just the person to get him into the dance. I was alone again. I tried to put on a smile to cover the fact that I hated Chad for being the worst brother in the world, Mom for just walking away, Steve for being a dang coward, and new dude Mike for leaving me. The boys at the dance seemed to feel pretty horrible for me, but not the girls I knew.

Those girls, who never thought I could get a date like Steve anyhow, laughed at how I got stood up. I ended up calling Mom and begging her to pick me up that instant. "I shouldn't have gone to the dance in the first place," I cried. I hung up the phone with Mom even more annoyed.

When I hung up the phone, I considered whether Mom knew Chad had threatened Steve. Maybe that's why she was so calm about me going. It didn't matter, and it would be impossible to prove, so I cleared all thoughts of the dance conspiracy from my mind.

I sat in a chair inside the dance while I waited for the chaperone to let me know when Mom had arrived. I couldn't have any fun. Everything just sucked. I was talking to my friends when they suddenly stared past me with shocked faces. And then I felt a tap on my shoulder. I turned around and when I realized it was my brother, I jumped into a karate position, ready to chop him in the head. I had no idea why he was at my dance after I had just declared my long-lived hate. Mom must have sent him to drive me home.

"Really! You! I'd rather walk home." I screamed. Then he did something I can honestly say never happened again in our lives. My brother apologized for what he had done. He looked me straight in the face, and said, "I'm sorry for ruining your dance. I didn't want you to go with Steve because he is a senior and my friend. Can you forgive me?"

Friends who witnessed this exchange became immediately jealous of me for the awesome brother I had. I hugged him, and he danced one song with me—yes, he *willingly* danced with me! In my heart, this was a new beginning. That song was the only song I danced to that night.

And I made a vow to myself to stay away from Chad's friends after that— unless he approved.

Chad ventured into community college the next year, and since all of his friends graduated as well, I started by, making new friends. Jen and Steph moved over to the town of Marlton with their mom and went to Cherokee High School. Lauren hopped from school to school, and dealt with her parents' struggles, and I continued to search for where I might fit in.

One night sophomore year, I went to a party with some new friends, and Chad showed up. I ran up to him and attempted to give him a hug, but he yelled, "I will call Mom if you don't leave this second." I wasn't allowed to have a life, no fun, nothing. Stupid brother! Irate I dared him to do so. Twenty minutes later Mom walked into the party. Everyone who knew her acted like it was cool that she was there— even when she escorted me to her car.

I would have argued, but Chad would have made it even worse for me and I wasn't risking that in front of a hundred high school kids. I hated Chad *again* that very moment. I drove home in silence as Mom lectured me not for being out late, not for being at a party, but for being at a party of one of Chad's graduated friends. I was allowed to do whatever I wanted as long as it didn't infringe on Prince Chad's life. I hated them both for tag teaming me yet again.

The love/hate relationship disconnected me further from both Mom and Chad. When I developed new friendships, I worked hard not to introduce them.

When I was sixteen I became friends with this awesome girl, Eliana. She came skiing with us in the Poconos, we carpooled to parties and we became really close. I was overjoyed when her family said I was invited to their shore house for a week in Surf City, Long Beach Island. I never had a friend with a shore house before so this was really cool.

On my first shore trip we decided to go to the under twenty-one club on the island. We both got dressed in the most adorable outfits. Mine was a black, tight one-piece body outfit. The shorts came to the bottom of my thighs, and the long sleeves had this awesome hippie-like flared-out material.

We did our makeup and were about to head to the dance club when Eliana asked if we should drink before we go. I never drank Vodka before, but Chad did often while yelling at me not to and it sounded like fun. I took my first swig from the bottle and choked the moment the liquor hit my taste buds. At first the flavor was terrible, burning hot and confusing, but then my throat numbed and my taste buds just stopped working. Together we drank swig by swig of the (big bottle) of Absolute Vodka until it was half full. We did our final touches of makeup and left for the club, which was walking distance from her shore house. I remember walking to the club … but not much else!

The next day I woke up and all I could see was a bright light shining in my eyes, in the hospital, with the doctor, Mom and Dad all staring at me. It took me a minute to become aware that I was on a gurney bed in the middle of the hospital floor. Luckily for me, Eliana was there too. I had thrown up in my long auburn hair and my amazing new outfit was a mess. My stomach and throat throbbed. The pain was unbearable, but it was nothing compared to the headache I experienced. Apparently, while I slept, the hospital stuck a tube down my throat and pumped activated charcoal into my stomach. This treatment dried up the alcohol and saved my life and Eliana's.

She stayed at her shore house grounded, I was driven home in silence, and Eliana and I both hoped I would be allowed to return one day. Needless to say my parents grounded me, but only for a week.

I spent my grounded week painting my furniture white while reassuring my parents I would never do something like that ever again.

It had nothing to do with the punishment. I just never wanted to feel that way again. Nursing a five-day hangover taught me well. The charcoal took a while to exit my body, so I pooped black for days. No one was worried about this but me. I was glad I was punished. I didn't want to leave the house for a week anyway.

And that is why I was allowed to go to the shore again a few weeks later. We promised to be on our best behavior, and we made good on that promise. I had decided, at that moment, this was going to be the beginning of a peaceful life stage.

While relationships with Mom and Chad were hit or miss at best, Dad and I always got along and we grew closer and closer as the years went by. The older I became, the more adventures we embarked on together. The moment I grew tall enough for the scary rides at Great Adventure, we were on our way. Dad had waited patiently for me to reach upwards of four-foot-ten while the fear that Mom's short genes may never get me there. The moment I did, we qualified for a chance to fly on the roller coasters, drop with the parachutes, and laugh with the dolphins.

My father couldn't stop talking about the Great American Scream Machine. One of the world's tallest and fastest roller coasters, reaching 68 mph, it was also one of the scariest looking. Our main focus became to ride it. This was the whole reason for going to Great Adventure: We were going to beat the beast known as the Scream Machine.

As I stood underneath it and looked up at the beast we were about to slay, fear ran through my entire body. All I knew was I was deathly afraid that I might fall out. One time, a nineteen-year-old girl was thrown to her death while riding Lightning Loops (the second looping coaster on the east coast) because she, newspapers say, "wasn't buckled properly." The ride first looped forward and then it looped back. Dad, when I was just a bit shy of the right size, snuck me on Lightning Loops one time before that girl fell out. Dad said it was just plain "stupidity" that caused the accident. This made me feel better, but I was still nervous about roller coasters in general.

We followed our Great Adventure map straight to the Scream Machine and took our place in line. We stepped slowly as we climbed the metal rail for two brutally long hours before finally making it to the top. At this point, I could see the people getting on the beast. Dad insisted we wait in the first line so we could sit in the front. Already exhausted from waiting in line for two solid hours, I didn't want to wait longer to be in the front. But I listened to Dad and followed him into row one's line.

Panic kicked in the moment the gate opened and the people that were in front of us climbed into their seats. I said, "Dad, I can't do this."

Dad glared at me with eyes that screamed you-better-be-kidding-right-now! The gate opened. Dad pushed me through. I sat in the hot, black, sticky seat.

"Dad, I can't do this. I'm scared, Dad!"

"You'll be fine." Dad yelled back.

The attendant buckled my seat. I started thinking of Lightning Loops and the poor girl who died. "I could die!" I hollered. "Let me out, let me out *now*." The confused man turned back and unbuckled my seat. Without any hesitation, I jumped out.

Dad looked at me in shock as he realized I just ruined my opportunity at the front seat of the tallest and fastest roller coaster in the world. "I'll wait right here, Dad." I shouted from the platform.

Dad was still waving at me to come back to the ride as another worker pushed me back behind the safety line. He must have seen this happen, and as the roller coaster was about to go, he waved for the man to get off.

I was shocked. "What are you doing?" I was a chicken, but that didn't mean he had to get off. I didn't want him to miss his chance at riding the beast! The disappointment I felt was punishing. We walked down the exit, past all the people waiting in line, knowing we were never going to ride the Great American Scream Machine.

I chased behind my Dad, holding my tongue so I wouldn't say something that would make matters even worse. Turns out, I didn't need to do anything. The skies turned black and seconds later the rain poured down, wetting us like drenched rats. Lightning followed, shutting down all the rides in the park. I was extremely thankful for the rain—even though I wished it had come sooner.

Though I know he was still mourning the death of the roller coaster ride, Dad let go of the silent treatment to say, "We need to get out of the rain." He wasn't openly discontent, but his fun vibe was way off. Luckily, we found an incredible spot to spend time not getting wet— The Song Booth. It was a new recording studio, karaoke style, in the middle of the park. The thrill of recording a song was almost too much to handle. We stepped into our booth while a Great Adventure guy explained that we had to pick a song and he would record our songs on a tape. I begged Dad to pick a song, any song. Finally, after listening to me sing "Straight Up" by Paula Abdul and Madonna's "Crazy for You" he picked his song. I started to laugh when the opening to "Pour Some Sugar on Me" came piping into the room. He waved at me to stop laughing and belted his song proudly. His crazy real-life singing cracked me up. We really laughed when we realized that Great Adventure was pumping our voices through the speakers, and everyone in walking distance could hear. I wondered if they were laughing as much as we were.

The rain continued, and by the time we sloshed our way to the parking lot, we were soaked down to our underwear. It had been an extremely emotional day, and in an effort not to freeze, I curled up on the seat and slept the whole way home while Dad listened to AC/DC.

As I grew older, adventures with my father became more exciting. By sixteen years old, he invited me everywhere he went. One time I went with him on an overnight fishing trip with the guys from his work. We left at six at night and came home at six the next morning. My girlfriend, Melissa, joined the trip to keep me company. She spent the entire time puking off the back of the boat and cursing me for bringing her. I wandered around the boat hoping someone would hook a fish, so I could help reel it in. It seems that in order to reel in a fish, you must be the one to catch the fish. In order to catch a fish, you must stand outside in the freezing cold while the water sprays you over and over again. For a long, long time.

I lasted one hour trying to fish before I gave up and sat inside. (Later I tried again to reel in someone else's line, but fishermen don't want you to lose their hard-earned catch so it didn't work).

Here's what I learned on that trip: Sleeping on a hard seat in a boat that is bouncing up and down isn't comfortable. Staying awake when you're exhausted is pure torment. Fishing in the dark is fun, but not when you don't catch anything. Last but not least, I don't enjoy fishing and wouldn't want to do it again.

Now playing paintball with my father was a different story. Paintballing is exciting. And I was allowed to be the only girl on the work paintball team. Dad was extremely respected in Sancoa Machine Division, and no one argued with him about bringing me along. Besides, I was very stealth-like, shot pretty straight, and took my hits like a champ.

That is, until one round when I got shot in the ear. It was THE MOST excruciating pain I have ever felt. Everything around me hummed for minutes –very long ones. I could literally hear the blood inside of my head. The initial hit turned everything black for a moment. I was afraid I was going to pass out, right there in the middle of the field, in front of both teams.

But that couldn't happen. I would not be the girl who shouldn't have played paintball with the men and then got hit in the ear and passed out. NO WAY! I fought through the pain, didn't shed a tear, and went back in the game. My ear continued to throb, and I swore everyone could tell. Dad's friends kept asking, "Are you sure you are okay? You may want to get that looked at as soon as possible." I ignored everyone declaring, I was fine, even as the pain continued. They all kept staring at me, and I kept saying, "I am just fine, thank you."

I wanted to cry as the throbbing grew more painful. I tried not to touch it for fear that it may make it worse. I fought through the pain the rest of the day and was thankful when we could leave. As soon as Dad and I reached the car, however, I checked the mirror to assess the damage. Lord, my ear had disappeared in an entangled mess of black and blue, none of which was paint.

My complaints began the second I saw my ear and continued the entire three-hour trip home. Dad just kept laughing and for months everyone at his work laughed too. My ear eventually healed, but the next time Dad took me paint-balling, I decided to wear head-gear to protect my ears.

Escapades with my father included his work parties. Since Mom often wasn't feeling well, I went to all of his friends' barbecues and any of our own family's parties. This made Mom feel left out on many occasions. I wished she could partake in all of the fun adventures, but she always seemed to get sick the morning of an event. We would try to talk her into coming, but she never did. Since she was the one continuously saying no, I found it hard to understand how she might also feel left out. That was a tough concept for me.

Dad invited Mom, Mom said "No," Dad invited me, I said, "Yes."

In my mind there was no situation, and I was definitely going. Mom, however, felt that we didn't really want her to go. It was all so confusing since I was invited after she was invited, and if she went, I could still go too. By age sixteen, I stopped trying to figure out why Mom was the way she was. I wasn't good at dealing with confusion like that. I wanted her to say yes if she meant yes and no if she meant no— and I wanted her to be happy with whatever choice she made. Creating a new issue where one wasn't needed exhausted my capacity to deal with her. Her annoyance that I went always led to another, "two women can't live under the same roof" conversation. This comment made me lose my temper. *Did she not want a daughter? What was wrong with me? What was wrong with her?*

Those days, Chad wasn't around to monitor the disagreements my mother and I had (thank god) but he also wasn't around to keep her occupied. Following my sophomore year of high school, Chad went to the local community college for a year and then one day he signed himself up for the Marines. I was sad the day he left for boot camp. We wrote letters back and forth when he was away, and these letters helped mend *some* of the damage that occurred between us during our crazy childhood. I was proud of Chad when he completed boot camp. Mom and Dad went to the ceremonies, and I stayed home by myself for four days. This was the first time they trusted me enough to do this. Mom made sure her friend Art came to check on me daily. (Guess I wasn't trusted too much!) Chad was stationed in Quantico, Virginia, and given the job in the finance section. I was very impressed with his bold move to sign up for the Marines and even more impressed that he had become involved in finances for the Marines. The only part that saddened me was that I was stuck at home, all alone, with Mom.

I gave Mom and Dad plenty of alone time while I continued my trips to visit Aunt Barb throughout my teen years. My parents let me spend a week vacation and one weekend a month with Aunt Barb. My Uncle Joe became my real uncle when he married Aunt Barb. I was lucky enough to be the only junior bridesmaid in the wedding party— but I guess that was because I was the only niece in the family.

Our visits took place at the new Pocono house. Either Mom or Dad would drive me to the Wawa on Route 206 to meet Aunt Barb. She would then drive me two more hours to the Poconos. I didn't dare complain about the longest ride ever, because Aunt Barb handled complaints badly.

My teenaged life with my aunt consisted of "dangerous fun," Mom would say. We skied, rode quads, and hung out at the bonfires at the lake. People brought their guitars and played music, no one told me I was too young to hang out. So I joined all the fun, including night swimming in the lake.

Sometimes Aunt Barb let me bring friends. My most memorable trip happened my junior year with my high school friend, Samantha. I remember swimming across the freezing cold lake, wishing we didn't commit to this swim. The dock was much further than we thought and stopping only made us more frozen. Once we reached the dock, we stayed as long as possible. We laughed, talked, and sung songs until it became dark, and we *had* to swim back. In the hours we sat on the dock, we practiced harmonizing the song "Don't Take the Girl" by Tim McGraw. And as the temperature dropped, and we dreaded the frigid water we had to swim across to get back to land, we sang as loud as we could. I don't think we would have made it back if it hadn't been for that song.

I didn't have to bring friends from home because I had plenty there. My Pocono friends ranged in age from fourteen to nineteen, and everyone treated everyone the same. We spent hours riding the quads through the game lands. One quad followed the next with hopes that the leader knew where they were going. We would navigate through mud and streams leading us up mountain-sides with the rocks tumbling behind our tires. The trails were worn down and we bounced up and down as we drove over the moguls that lined the path.

We always headed back when the sun started to set. It was very scary to be in the woods when darkness set in. I worked hard to keep the deep-rooted fear of dying in the woods, as a last case scenario, to myself. I always knew if we lost our way, we would be lost in the woods for hours. I didn't think I could handle a night in the woods, without cover, very well.

One time we were riding in the woods, and we didn't time our trip very well. We went further into the hunting game lands than we had ever gone before. We started to notice that the sun was beginning to set, and I was ready to head back to the houses. The group we were with all agreed it was time to head back, and it was unsafe to continue going further. We all jumped back on our quads and started to head down the path leading out of the woods. I drove faster than I have ever driven before. The 500 Polaris was big and bulky compared to the other quads. It was made more for leisure riding, and I had it jumping logs and splashing through unknown depths of water.

The darker the sky became, the faster I drove. The faster I drove, the scarier the woods became. The scarier the woods became, the faster I drove. It was all becoming an overwhelming vicious cycle of danger. At one point I hit a mogul and bounced straight into the air. My body was above my quad and I gripped the handlebars as tightly as I could. I felt a moment of complete fear that I may fly off the quad, but I held on and pulled my body back down, slamming into the seat. I began to lose momentum with the rest of the riders. The Pocono kids knew these woods well and had no fear of them. I ignored the panic of trying to keep up and pushed the Polaris as hard as I could.

When we finally found the entrance to the game lands, my heart started beating again. I never wanted to feel that rush or have that sense of panic again. My heart didn't stop speed pounding for hours. I never spoke of how scared I was to my aunt or uncle, and I planned to be more careful the next time I headed out with the quad.

The last thing I wanted to do was crash the quad and risk upsetting Aunt Barb. Heading into my last years of high school, I was expected to show her a higher level of maturity. I honored this as much as I could. Unfortunately, I did crash one time. This crash put me in the hospital, Aunt Barb's quad in the junk yard, and a month of a headache from the concussion I sustained. Aunt Barb was rightfully pissed at me. I truly shouldn't have tried to jump a hill with a 500 Polaris.

The older I grew, the more peculiar Aunt Barb began to act. For a while every time I visited her she kept talking about changes and new beginnings. She kept explaining how people transform and grow. I had no idea what she was babbling about, and as far as I was concerned no one needed to change or grow—except for Mom.

The happiest change that was next to take place was the fact that soon enough I would be driving to the Poconos all by myself. No one would have to meet, coordinate, or organize these trips for me. I was going to be able to visit my aunt whenever I wanted to. Unfortunately I wouldn't be able to drive until six months past my seventeenth birthday.

Most of my friends got their licenses before I got mine, because when I was sixteen I went for a ride with my friend, Mark. Mark and I met when we were twelve years old at the Evesham Skating Rink. I loved roller-skating. I thought I was amazing. I could shuffle, skate backwards, slow skate, and do twists and turns. Mark and I slow skated together, and after that we became good friends and remained in touch. I remember when we first met I would sit on my kitchen counter and talk on the phone with him for hours. My brother always tried to take the phone from me. He would get annoyed because he was missing calls or had calls to make. Everyone in my family became so much happier when call-waiting became available. No one ever missed a call again. Mark and I would fall asleep talking and wake up breathing on the phone. I'd yell, "Hello, I am hanging up now!"

Mark turned seventeen a year before I did. He was so excited about his new car. It was a 1971 Chevelle SS with a cowl-induction hood. The car was green with white dual racing stripes. This car was a beauty and, boy, was it fast. Mark was so excited, and I was so jealous. Mark's bar mitzvah really hooked him up financially. I had no money so I couldn't imagine what type of car I would be getting.

One afternoon Mark drove to Tabernacle twenty minutes from where he lived in Marlton and picked me up. We headed to Burlington County College. We drove past the fields of corn, and down the curvy roads, faster than we should have. Mark asked me if I wanted to drive when we were in BCC's parking lot. There was no one around, and a parking lot seems like a safe place to practice driving a car. I impressed him with my skills of driving around the parking lot over so much that he actually said, "Hey, you're pretty good." After that, it wasn't too hard to talk him into letting me drive home.

I drove through the school's parking lot, stopped at the stop sign, and then, as I began to pull out onto the lane heading home, I hit the gas, and we peeled out for at least thirty feet. I didn't mean to do it. Not realizing the power the car possessed, I had pushed the gas down harder than necessary. And Mark yelled at me not to do it again.

Five seconds later, a campus police officer put on his lights. I pulled over and was unable to display my driver's license because I didn't have one. He brought us to the offices of the campus security and made us sit while they called our parents. Mark glared at me. I felt really terrible for both of us, but I had no idea what would happen next. We both had to go to court to talk to the judge. Dad had to hire an attorney. Poor Mark lost his license for six months, and I was suspended before I even got mine! Need I say, this was devastating to me? Mark was so perturbed I thought for sure we would never be friends again.

Luckily, I was wrong.

Chapter 9

Anyone want two sisters?

After the court stuff settled, I practiced my driving hours with Dad so I could get my license as soon as I turned seventeen and a half. I needed a summer job and was hired at Dad's company, Sancoa, as a secretary and file clerk. Monday through Friday all summer long I drove to work with him. During our drive, the conversations revolved around politics and my lack of understanding them. Every day I asked him one hundred questions pertaining to what was happening in the world and why things happened the way they do. But one morning, my father sat in silence while we listened to the news, and he provided me with very short answers.

Our commute took thirty minutes or less, depending on whether we stopped for coffee or a newspaper. Ten minutes into the drive my father said, "You are going to meet some new family members soon." Thinking nothing of it, I replied, "The cousins in Florida? The ones Aunt Barb's always talking about?"

My father looked at me in a way that I had never seen before. It was almost as if he was afraid to continue the conversation that he had just started. He looked paler than normal and as if he were ashamed. Trying to keep my eyes on the road, I yelled, "Dad, what's up?" "You're freaking me out!"

Finally he said, "You are going to talk to someone on the phone."

At this point I knew something big was up. "Dad, who am I going to be talking to?"

This was the strangest car ride conversation ever. His response is one that I will never, ever forget. The moment he uttered these words, I became overwhelmed with a shocking flood of emotions, a brain-swirling typhoon of questions, and a sense of plunging into the surreal.

"You are going to speak to your sisters."

Wait ... what? I pulled the car over to the side of the road, carefully since I was on my driving permit, and looked at him again. "What did you just say, Dad?"

Dad explained that I have two sisters that, for me, NEVER existed until this exact moment in my life. I immediately fired off questions: Why haven't I known about this? Where did they come from? Did he cheat on Mom? Does Mom know they exist? Why hasn't he told me sooner? Did he know they were out there? Does Chad know? What the hell is happening?

He answered all of my questions as though it were a normal talk about politics. He explained that they are older than me by four and six years. He was married before my mother so, no, he didn't cheat. Mom knew about the girls; however, she didn't know they had reached out to see him. Chad didn't know any of this yet. And it had to remain a secret until Dad figured out how to tell them.

I walked into work fifteen minutes later in a state of complete shock. My father brought me into the conference room and dialed the number of my "new" sister, Joanne. We talked for twenty minutes, and all I could focus on was that she sounded like me. Joanne did most of the talking. I guessed she had time to prepare. She knew I existed for seventeen years. I knew she existed for fifteen minutes. She talked about her mom, and the fact that she had a daughter and another child on the way. She also told me about my other "new" sister, Jenny, who had a daughter, Jessica, who was then four years old.

My sister, Joanne, lived in Missouri, and my sister, Jenny, lived in Philadelphia, an hour from my home.

I had a sister that lived an hour from my home that I had never met.

We hung up the phone after scheduling a time to talk again, and I allowed it to sink in. I felt excited to meet my sisters and their children. I learned on this day that I was an aunt and I had two grown-up sisters. I was actually excited about the family getting bigger and maybe now I'd have someone to talk to when things went crazy with Mom or Chad.

And yet, all of this excitement was followed by fear. I couldn't tell Mom or Chad what was happening. Dad asked me to let him deal with that in *his* own way. He was afraid that Mom was going to freak out. After all, they had kept a secret from their kids for over seventeen years.

On the other hand, I could talk to Aunt Barb because she was aware of what was happening. Actually Aunt Barb was part of the reason the reconnection happened. She had been in contact with the girls' mother, Janice, for years. I knew that this was going to cause another war between my aunt and Mom. Maybe this was the reason they had so many issues when I was younger. Years later I found out that my other aunt, Aunt Teri, may have been the reason for the reconnection. I will never really know because both aunts take credit.

I worried about how Mom and Chad would react. Chad grew up not liking having one sister too much, and I couldn't imagine what he'd do when he learned he had two more. It took me sixteen years to get him to like me – enough. My parents had hidden this secret for over seventeen years. There must be a reason. I had a hundred more questions and no time to ask them.

The hardest part of this situation would be keeping it a secret until Dad told me otherwise.

Secrets were not my forte. I kept thinking, *I'm seventeen years old and I have two sisters that I have never met.*

My world had just experienced a major shift, and I was not sure what to do about it. I took a hour-long bath to clear my mind. My last thought before going to sleep that night was, "I could stop being Daddy's only little girl. I could lose Dad to these strangers."

It took some time to absorb the shock. I had an entirely new family that had always known I existed, yet I had no clue they were out there. I spent a massive amount of time in my own head trying to make sense of it. The only information I had was that this family of sisters existed, and for some reason, they had disappeared for a very long time. I also knew that Dad loved me, and he'd asked me to keep a secret. I followed Dad's lead and agreed to meet my new sister Jenny. It took all the power I had to not call Chad in Virginia or beg a friend to drive me to see him. I hated keeping a secret from him.

Dad, Aunt Barb, and I all drove up to Jenny's house in Pennsylvania. It seemed like it was a very long drive at the time, a drive during which I wondered what Jenny looked like, what type of person she was, and if she would like me. I was nervous that my sisters would be different than me. It took an hour and a half to get to her home.

When we arrived at Jenny's house, strangers attending her party welcomed us. I wasn't sure what the party was for, and I was very uncomfortable meeting this many strangers all at the same time. It felt as though everyone was staring at us, and that made me even more uncomfortable. I thought we were going to meet my new sister, her husband, and their child. Every time another stranger walked by I thought, "*Is that my sister?*"

A strange girl walked over and hugged Aunt Barb. She then said, "Hi, Dad!" to *my* dad. It took me a minute to let "Hi, Dad" sink in. No other girl had ever called my father, Dad, and this was a gut-wrenching moment. I held my emotions and let out a "Hi, I'm Danny." This girl hugged me and whispered, "I haven't seen you since you were a year old." My head was spinning. *She met me before? Wait. How? How is that possible?* This was the second time I was meeting my oldest sister, Jenny.

My first thought was that she was beautiful. She had long brown curly hair similar to my auburn curls and on this day she wore it half up half down. She had on a long dress with high boots up to her knees. She wore glasses which must have come from her mom since Dad didn't wear glasses. Her voice was sweet sounding. Jenny seemed nice enough. She hugged Dad and then she hugged me again. It was odd meeting someone who was your family yet you felt no connection. Instead I felt like I was meeting a stranger, a stranger who really missed my dad. It was the most unusual moment I had ever lived through. I wondered if Dad found it as weird as I did.

Jenny must have told everyone at the party who we were before we arrived. The whole thing was surreal. I never knew that these people existed, and now here I was being told I looked just like my sister. Honestly, I didn't agree. However, my sister's daughter, my niece Jessica resembled her grandfather—my dad—in an uncanny way. The shape of her face and her eyes were Mason's characteristics for sure. I fell in love with Jessica, the moment that we were introduced. She was the sweetest, most loving, and friendliest little girl I had ever met.

The day before coming out to meet them, Dad and I went shopping and bought Jessica an amazingly soft Gund bear. We named it Hanky Bear, after my Uncle Hanky, and gave it to her as her first gift ever from her new Pop-Pop. My sister remembered Uncle Hanky. It was strange that she had her own stories about a man I lost at the age of six. She also lost my uncle at six, when her family split up. And then he died six years later in the car accident, and my sister never got to say goodbye to her favorite uncle. It saddened me that my sister lost out on my family memories and that no one was talking about it.

None of us could predict the importance of Hanky Bear at that moment. Jessica fell in love with this bear and kept Hanky Bear into her adult life. Her attachment became devastating when she was living in her apartment and it caught fire with Hanky Bear caught inside. In one moment, she lost every possession that she had loved. Years later, after the fire we found photos of Hanky Bear for Jessica. They helped, but her heart still aches.

The same fire that murdered poor Hanky Bear also engulfed my grandmother's ring. Jessica ended up with my grandma's, (her great-grandmother's) high school ring, which I had originally inherited. Aunt Terry gave it to Dad to give to me after Grandma passed. It was the only item I had from Grandma at the time.

One day, after the ring had been restored, I lent it to my sister Jenny, because she said she "got nothing from the grandparents." I felt bad and decided she could wear it for a while. A few months later, Jenny lent the ring to Jessica. That's when it became Jessica's ring. I was not going to take it away from her.

And I had forgotten about the ring until the house fire. Jessica believed she had lost everything. I cried at the demise of the family heirloom. Oddly enough, a few days after the fire, my niece located the ring. It had somehow survived the fire and was completely fine. I believe the ring is meant to be with Jessica after all.

If it weren't for my niece, I wonder if I would have originally bothered with my sister as much as I did. After all, we were six years apart and had been living completely separate lives. Luckily for my sister, I really loved the idea of having an adorable five-year-old at parties, and she made the holidays fantastic. Mom had stopped loving the holidays long ago, and had to pretend until I was ten and figured out Santa wasn't real. After that Dad kept the magic alive while Mom insisted the holidays could stop being celebrated. Grandpop died a few days before Halloween—destroying Halloween. His birthday was on Christmas so Mom cried every Christmas. Easter was celebrated with baskets created by Dad and luckily Mom would enjoy the candy, but that was it. Thanksgiving was a time she was *forced* to endure Dad's family, so that was not her favorite.

I set a goal to teach my niece, Jessica, to love the holidays and I was going to be her best aunt. I didn't know any of her other aunts; however, I was going to actively work toward winning this role. I wanted to treat Jessica the way Aunt Barb had treated me. When I was able to get her, Jessica was allowed to go everywhere with me. I was so excited at seventeen to have an adorable young niece.

The next step in the introductions phase was meeting my sister, Joanne. Joanne is younger than Jenny. She is the same age as my brother, Chad. They are actually a few months apart in age. This knowledge, of course, sent my brain questioning everything we had and everything my family was. I went around asking question after question only to hit brick walls. No one was talking about the past. We were supposed to "just accept" the little we'd been told. In spite of that, I kept the pursuit of information open. Whenever given the chance to understand more, I began questioning. I have always been relentless.

By this point, Dad had explained to Mom and my brother that the sisters had reached out to him and that they wanted to see her and meet

Chad. I wasn't around for the conversation between Dad and Chad. All I know is that Chad must have taken it better than Dad expected because he agreed to come home and meet them over the Christmas break. Chad told me that he remembered two little girls when we were growing up but, Mom told him they were just neighbors that moved. Chad forgot about the little girls until the moment Dad told him that he had sisters. I'm sure Chad had as many questions as I did but he wasn't as curious as me. He accepted the situation and came home to support Mom during this holiday meeting.

Mom freaked out when she heard the news and without hesitation blamed Aunt Barb for it. Mom blamed my poor aunt for any problem that related to Dad's side of the family. Not understanding what the problem was with Dad's daughters coming back, I was convinced Mom had some extreme level of paranoia toward Dad's family.

Fuming, Mom brought me upstairs and explained that having the girls here was a terrible idea and that all they wanted was Dad's money. I didn't understand. I had met Jenny and I didn't think she wanted anything from him other than to have a dad. Mom explained to me that I didn't understand and never would. *I never did.* As someone who didn't handle change well, Mom feared my sisters coming back into the picture. I often wonder now how Mom handled the potentially life-altering secrets she was forced to keep. I can't imagine having a secret hanging over my head for that long. It must have worn on my mother's soul. That day, for the first time, I felt compassion for Mom. I even wondered if these secrets might be making her sick. Could this have been the reason Dad's mother and Mom never got along? Was the loss of these little girls that Daddy loved potentially the reason she really didn't like having a daughter – *me*?

So much in life started to make better sense after the sisters showed up.

My sister Joanne flew in from Missouri to visit us the winter of that same year for Christmas. She brought her husband and her two children. Meeting Joanne and seeing the shocking similarities between her and my grandmother blew my mind. She was definitely a Mason. She even sounded the same as Aunt Teri. Joanne's children, a two-year-old named Jenna and her little brother, Jared, became amazing additions to our holidays. Jessica was so excited to be with her cousins. The children looked nothing like each other. Jenna had crazy red hair like my father. She is the only grandchild that got the fire hair. My curly red hair was nothing compared to hers. She walked around dragging a ratty old teddy bear behind her. Jenna was a cuddle bug from the minute you met her, with a feisty attitude if you happened to annoy her. My new nephew, Jared, was a brick house, who liked to (oddly enough) head butt things. He was a happy baby with a huge smile making him so stinking cute.

Surprisingly enough, Mom held it together very well during the holidays and the arrival of our new family. Both of my sisters and their families stayed at our home for the largest Christmas we ever had. It actually couldn't have happened at a better time for me. At seventeen years old, Christmas wasn't as exciting as it had been at say, ten. The idea of having three adorable little people at our holidays closed the excitement gap.

As time went on we adjusted to our new lives. The novelty of the new relationships slowly wore off and it became normal to have sisters and new family members. My sisters and I talked as often as we could on the phone, and my niece Jessica was allowed to visit any weekend I had time. Unfortunately my sister Joanne lived in Missouri, two days away, and we couldn't see her. Flying to Missouri from Philadelphia was very expensive, so six months after I had met Joanne, Jenny and I drove out to Missouri, half way across the country. I had never taken a road trip before, so I am still impressed we made it there unscathed, without GPS navigation.

This trip taught me a skill that I may not have otherwise learned: how to drive a stick shift. I had been introduced to the stick prior, but I'd never caught on to it. Several hours into the trip, Jenny was exhausted and wanted me to drive. We did a quick lesson in the parking lot at the rest stop and I was on my way. The whole experience was a bit shaky at first, literally. Driving away from the rest stop, merging with the highway, and trying to get up to speed with the traffic were dangerous tasks. We stalled and squeaked and almost broke down more times than Jenny would have liked. By the time I got the hang of the stick, Jenny should have just drove. She was wide awake with the fear of dying and couldn't relax with an inexperienced driver.

After I'd been driving on the highway for over an hour, Jenny relaxed and fell asleep. I felt confident that I could handle the rest of the drive as long as I didn't have to slow down. A red light starting blinking on the dashboard, and I noticed that our gas tank was on empty. I woke Jenny up, and she grabbed the map and tried to figure out where we were. I kept trying to find the towns we were driving past on the map to no avail. When the signs read "now entering GARY INDIANA," our panic grew. Gary Indiana's poverty level was at an all-time high in the early nineties. It was also reported to be the murder capital of the U.S. This was not the place I wanted to stop for directions or gas. I started to sweat as we drove on, searching for a safe place to get back on track.

We ended up at a truck stop, in Gary, Indiana. I had to slow down and come to a stop. This was harder than I expected. Every time I tried to down shift, the car jolted making it hard to control. Jenny was yelling at me "Be careful!" Duh, I was being careful. Everything my parents have ever taught me about personal safety came back to me at this point. We rolled the windows to the top, locked the doors, and I pulled up to the gas station slamming the brake just in time.

Jenny, of course, had meant careful with her car.

It was unfortunate that we had to pump our own gas because in order to do it we had to get out of the car and go inside the gas station to pay. I'm from New Jersey, where self-serve gas stations are actually illegal. That said, I had no experience in pumping my own gas! My heart was racing out of my chest. All I could think was we were going to be murdered at a truck stop in Gary Indiana.

Jenny was much braver than I was, thankfully. She marched directly into the gas station, paid for the gas, pumped the gas (a lesson learned in Philly), and even asked for directions. I stayed in the car, fearing that someone may come steal me and Jenny's car. Luckily we were back on the road quickly, no longer directionally challenged, in a car with a full tank of gas and Jenny was at the wheel again.

By the time we got to Joanne's, we were sick of being in the car, frazzled from our Gary, Indiana, moment, and starving. We weren't even in the house thirty minutes before Jenny and Joanne began to fight. I have no idea what caused the fight, but apparently this was Joanne and Jenny's relationship. I never had sisters before, so everything was new for me. I spent some time hanging out with my brother-in-law at the time, Joanne's husband, Rick, while my sisters worked out their issues.

That evening, Rick took us country dancing in a real country bar. I laughed and laughed, as Rick tried to teach me a hundred new dance moves. The closest I had been to a country bar was Prospectors in New Jersey. This one was different: Everyone knew the dances and hundreds of people took over the dance floor. I, however, knew nothing of country dancing. I kept trying, though, and by the end of the dance, I would have the dance moves locked in, but then the song would end and I would be lost again. Every time a new song with new dance moves began, I messed up but kept trying.

At night, when we got the kids settled, Jenny, Joanne, and I sat in her living room looking at old photos and talking about their past. It pained me to know that my life was simple compared to the journey these girls had taken. We spoke about Dad first, and they explained from their perspective as young girls why they left Daddy. As their story unfolded I felt sick. They started with a memory of a time where their Mom and Dad were happily married. They went on family trips, saw our aunts and uncles, and loved their grandparents.

They met my grandfather, and I never had. They lived a world that didn't include me yet. Then one day, there was Mona, my mom. In their eyes, she came into the picture and took Dad away. After their mom, Janice, took them away, the girls believed their dad had a new little family with Mona, Chad, and me, and there was no more room for Jenny and Joanne. When Dad never went to find them in Delaware, they felt he didn't love them. I couldn't believe what I was hearing. My dad didn't want them?

Dad abandoning anyone was a foreign concept. He was so supportive of every member of his family and the best big brother to all of his siblings. It didn't make sense. I didn't blame them for their story; I just wished they knew our Dad. I took in all of the information that was handed to me, and I couldn't help respond with what Dad had told me. I believed that their story had holes in it.

Dad told me he had moved to Tabernacle with Mom and on weekends the girls came to their home. Dad settled with the weekend visitations and didn't mind paying support to help them when he wasn't around. For a year, they came to the Tabernacle house and spent time with Chad and me. (I was a newborn so I recollect none of this). One day, Dad went to the house they were living in because they didn't show up for visitation, and they were gone. For months, he searched for the girls after their mom moved and couldn't find them. Later Dad found out that she had moved them to Delaware with her new boyfriend, and she was starting her life over. Dad was devastated and so was his entire family. He fought with his ex to see his children, to no avail. He considered turning to the courts; however, the battle in court was going to cost Dad money our family didn't have at the time. Both Mom and Dad agreed to let their Mom raise them. No one wanted a battle. Least of all my mother, who was trying to make sure, at all expenses, her family didn't fall apart too, especially financially.

As I sat and listened to the stories, I became lost in the thought that *this situation must have caused so much grief to Dad's entire family.* Dad losing his children, the grandparents losing their grandchildren, and the aunts and uncles losing their nieces must have been unbearable. To not know where they may have gone and to hold on to the idea that these children are still out there and may show up someday, or may not, could not have been easy. No one knew for years where these kids were, so all of Dad's family, aunts, uncles, cousins, and friends stopped talking about them. They all agreed it was too painful to continue this pattern of searching, crying, and coming up short monthly, then yearly. For seventeen years of my life, everyone kept this secret from Chad and I.

Years later, it came out that Aunt Barb had been in contact with Dad's ex-wife, Janice following my Uncle Hanky's death. Unable to see the girls and for fear that she may never see them again, Aunt Barb kept this a secret. It wasn't until Aunt Barb's wedding, when I was fourteen years old, that my dad's sister, Aunt Teri, says she found the phone numbers and called them herself. This started the wheel spinning on reconnecting the family. My Mom and Dad remained none the wiser for three years after the wedding.

My entire life I believed that I was the only girl on the Mason side. I stood corrected when we found out about my sisters. My family, before I was even born, became a family of secrets stemming from loss. All secrets were covered and hidden until my sisters returned. Slowly, following many meetings with my two sisters, our past began to make more sense.

Months later I learned that once my sister Jenny called the house to speak to Henry Mason. I answered the phone and thought it was a telemarketer so I said "He is not here right now" and the person on the other end said, "Thank you" and hung up. I forgot all about the call until Jenny asked me "Do you remember…?"

The fact remained; we now had a bigger family. I now had sisters.

Chapter 10
Patience is invaluable

By the grace of God, I graduated high school in 1995. I rarely studied as much I should have and I just didn't have the drive to care. I didn't take schooling seriously because I couldn't see that far into the future. I remained unmotivated from seventh grade straight through twelfth. In high school I struggled with my grades, but I didn't misbehave. Teachers never called home, I didn't bother the rest of the class, and I did what was expected of me in the actual classroom. I just never figured out how to remain organized enough to keep homework and studying on target, and no one cared.

Graduation couldn't come soon enough, and I was excited when it proved to be financially lucrative. I received enough money to buy my first car. My Uncle George helped me to purchase a 1979 Dodge Diplomat. It was absolutely *not* my first choice of vehicle; however, Uncle George was investing five hundred dollars so he had a big say in the matter. Excited to help me, he promised the car was safe and in great shape. It came from a friend of his, and I needed his five hundred so I couldn't argue. I settled for the white Dodge Diplomat with bright red interior.

I hated driving my pimped out Diplomat. It was the least cool car a teenage girl could drive. In an attempt to make it cooler, my friends and I hung dice on the mirror as a shout-out to the "Fresh Prince of Bel

Air." Whenever the opportunity arose, I asked to drive Dad's car. The company Dad worked for bought him a big, beautiful 1995 Bonneville. One night, I drove the Bonneville to pick up an order from the pizzeria, Upper Crust, three minutes away. I rushed in to grab the pizza and rushed back out so I could get the pizza back to Dad. He said that if I picked up the pizza, I could use the car for the night. I drove back onto Route 206 from the pizzeria parking lot and reached the light where I had to make a left-hand turn onto Hawkins Road. I drifted into the turn, making sure there was no traffic, and sped up. The next thing I knew I was being told to stay still while a paramedic held scissors in his hand. It took me a moment to realize that the paramedic was cutting my pants. My initial reaction was to pull away and save the only pair of GUESS jeans I've ever owned. I pulled and my leg didn't move. It was trapped under crushed metal from the passenger side of the car. The truck that hit me drove the passenger side of Dad's car straight into the driver's side. The pizza that I had just purchased smashed into the dashboard. Cheese was everywhere.

The ambulance sped me to the hospital, where I was alone for over an hour before my parents showed up. I couldn't even look at my Dad. I felt so horrible that I had destroyed the Bonneville and I didn't have a single injury. The paramedic told me I turned in front of a truck and I must have a "guardian angel". *I didn't see a truck!* How was that possible? I had been in such a hurry that I must not have looked long enough. The Bonneville was destroyed. My father kept lying, "Don't worry. The car can be fixed."

Mom glared at me "You need to slow down, Danielle." *I knew I deserved that.*

The next day Dad went to see his Bonneville with the insurance man. When he came home, he looked rather unhappy. He waved his arm at me as if to say, "Do not speak, child!" I heeded the warning and stayed out of sight. A few hours later he explained that they deemed the Bonneville totaled and the truck that hit me was full of migrant workers on their way home from working at the farm down the road. Thankfully no one suffered injuries. I was mortified by what I had done and couldn't believe I'd been so careless. Nothing was more embarrassing than destroying my father's car, and the thought that I could have seriously hurt somebody was haunting.

My remorse and embarrassment turned to anger when I heard they sued us for damages. What damages? Their vehicle had a dented bumper, and the passengers suffered no injuries. I got a reckless driving ticket that we had to fight in court. My poor father lost his car and my insurance coverage doubled in price. The fraudulent lawsuit required many sit-downs at giant conference tables, where we talked through our lawyers about the accident. After each meeting, what came to light was that their truck suffered no damage beyond a dented bumper and none of the occupants were injured. My father grew impatient with the fact that we had to suffer through this law-suit, which threatened our house. Mom was relentless at home that I needed to move out. I was eighteen-years-old at this point and I was causing the family grief.

Dad spent many nights defending me. "She is just a kid, Mona. Accidents happen. There is nothing we can do to change it."

I truly regretted the accident and any time the family had to fix a problem I caused. I knew each one was one hundred percent my fault, but there was nothing I could do to change the past. The law suit continued and Mom's anger at both Dad and I (mainly I) sustained.

At one point, we sat at the table and listened to the wife of one of the men tell her story of alleged woe. Though she wasn't involved in the accident, she claimed to be suffering damages as well. Her husband apparently could no longer have sex with her due to the post-traumatic stress disorder he now suffered.

At that, my father lost his mind. He'd already missed several days of work and found it difficult to hold back from uttering snide remarks under his breath. "I think it has more to do with the fact that she is so ugly," he whispered to me. "Shhh, Dad." I responded. We couldn't believe the wife was trying to pin their sexual problems on my bad driving, and the husband and friends were all nodding their heads in agreement. (How did his friends know he couldn't have sex anyway? Were they witnesses?) My father's comments were enough to make me want to pee myself. I was scared to death we were going to get in trouble because we couldn't stop laughing. Relief finally came when the judge dismissed the case and everyone walked away. Now all I had to worry about was Dad trusting me to drive again.

My parents (mainly dad) never made me pay them back for the financial loss they endured. I was broke and they knew it. Following high school, I spent most of my time working as a babysitter and enjoying a summer of freedom and peace. But it wouldn't last. Dad called me on July 20, 1995, and asked me to "please come straight home after work."

I knew that something was very wrong. I ran into the house, and Dad sat me down and sadly explained, "Before you hear this from anyone else," he said, "I need to let you know." I couldn't wait to hear what he had to say. "What Dad? What?" He looked extremely torn up. The last time I had seen him like this is when he had to tell me about my sisters. "Dad!" I said.

"I'm so sorry, Danny. I hate telling you this, but Candice was found dead in her college apartment."

My heart stopped. Candice, my childhood friend, was gone. And hearing about her death flooded my mind with memories of Ryan's passing. Losing a friend meant forever, and it was unbearable to think I could never see her again. I remembered the moment Mom told me about Ryan, and I couldn't bear the loss of another person I loved. It had been years since someone in my world died. I thought I was used to death, but I wasn't. It hurt just the same.

I loved Candice. She was the older sister I never had. She taught me how to be a better friend. She helped me learn to sing and put me in my place when I acted young and ornery. She called a spade a spade, and she was an inspiration in so many ways. I pictured playing on the piano as she taught me and watching her spin on stage at her recitals. Dad went on to tell me what the newspaper said: Candice was found in her college dorm with her arms tied behind her back. She died of suffocation. *Candice was murdered.*

I couldn't believe the words Dad said. Murdered? Someone murdered a sweet, innocent girl? There was nothing Candice could have been doing to deserve such a death. She was studying to be a teacher at Alabama University. The last time we spoke, she had finally made a few friends and was excited.

The next day, I had to go to her funeral. After my grandparents' funerals, I'd sworn I would never go to another. But I knew that probably wasn't realistic. The entire town and some people I didn't know went to the funeral for Candice and waited in lines to hug her family. Everyone stood outside, talking about the injustice. To this day they have yet to find the person who killed her. That person was allowed to live their life and Candice, at nineteen, was done with hers. It didn't seem fair, and I took a serious emotional hit at another loss. It didn't make sense to keep making friends if they were just going to be stolen from me. Snapping turtles, car accidents, heart attacks, cancer, and now murder, it was all too much.

I called Chad to make sure he was okay. It concerned me to have him so far away, able to be murdered, and since I was so wrapped up in my life I didn't reach out enough. Chad understood my sadness even though he and Candice were only acquaintances because of me. I decided that I didn't want to go to college and sleep over on a campus anymore (not that I was accepted anyhow). It was unsafe, and I wanted to live my life as long as I could, with little chance of sudden death. Everyone told me I was being ridiculous and that what happened to Candice was just a fluke. But I no longer believed in flukes, and it seemed the more you loved someone the higher the risk that they may die. I finished out the rest of my last high school summer and went to community college for English in September.

Mom was pushing for me to go to beauty school and become a hair dresser. I enjoyed doing my friends' hair and I mastered the art of braiding; however, I didn't want to be a hair dresser. I truly didn't know what I wanted to be. I was hoping community college would help me figure it out.

My first semester in college didn't go well. My grades dropped lower than my high school grades. At least in high school the teachers pretended to care about my grades, even if my parents didn't. Counselors and teachers alike always told me, "You could do so well if applied yourself" or "You know you are really smart, Danielle." But in college no one encouraged me— I was just another number.

No one knew my name, no one cared if I showed up for class, and no one asked me why my homework was late.

I sat in my classrooms with eighty other students and even though I sat in the front, I still found myself drifting into daydreams. The teachers weren't boring. I just couldn't sit hour after hour in one place. It wasn't their fault that I needed more stimulation and support than they were able to give. My brain became bored easily, and I daydreamed even when I was paying complete attention. This resulted in Ds as final college grades. Thinking school wasn't my thing, I needed to create plan B and fast.

I realized, even as a child, that anything was better than sitting in class after class. Sometimes I just didn't want to stay still in my seat. I wanted to interrupt because I had something important to say, and I'm not sure why I ignored my homework. I also learned that I liked any class that didn't require constant organization and didn't have multiple-choice tests. Writing and essays were my favorite types of tests to take: Hand me an essay exam, and I will give you A material. But put a multiple-choice exam in front of me and I will freeze. Every answer looked possible, and I couldn't decide. Normally time would run out before I finished, thus resulting in a low grade. That's why English and historical studies turned out to be my favorite subjects. They were the classes that required essays.

I even took a class in college for organization. It was an elective and recommended by my high school counselor, Mr. West. Years later, I would declare that this class saved my life— however, while I took the course, I was failing. My first semester at community college I received a D in an organizational class that was an elective. Honestly, I thought this class was going to be a piece of cake. My inability to stay organized has carried straight through my entire life and still exists today. I work on it daily. I create charts, write lists, buy calendars, use colorful sticky notes, and try my hardest to keep it all together.

During my second semester, freshman year of college, I decided to try to live on my own. Mom had had enough of me and, was telling me, that, "two women can't live under the same roof" on a daily basis. I had heard this infamous phrase from the age of fourteen on, and now was ready to make Mom happy. I moved in with my new college friend, Lilah, and her boyfriend, and the owner of a giant house in

Mount Holly, twenty minutes from my home. I rented one room in the house and was able to share the rest of the house.

My new room had a bed, a dresser, and ten black light posters I had placed, all over the ceiling. When the black light was turned on, the entire room lit up like tie-dye. I never brought anyone over to my new house. It was more my escape from pissing Mom off daily then a place to entertain guests. I struggled desperately trying to make her happy with our relationship and the fact that she didn't want me to return home was maddening.

Lilah was older than me, and she was trying to get her life back in order. We met at the community college and she wanted a female roommate. This seemed perfect. It wasn't until I moved in and was living with her for a few weeks that I realized her job was dancing at night to pay her college and debts. I really didn't know much about Lilah, and as time went on I was shocked to learn the details of her life. For instance, she had a child somewhere. Not understanding the impact this must have had on her at the time, I easily dismissed it. I had never met anyone like her before and I wasn't judging. She kept trying to talk me into being a dancer, but that was not happening. I was bad enough at dancing fully clothed and the idea of doing it barely clothed was laughable.

I didn't spend much time in my rented room. Instead I spent a ton of time hanging out with a new crowd of friends and one guy in particular, named Greg. Actually his name was Sebastian Gregory, but we called him Greg. We stayed up late playing video games, including killing aliens. I had been a gamer my entire life thanks to Dad, so the boys always let me play. I happily explained to a room full of boys that my totally cool Dad always bought himself the latest and greatest video games, including Atari, Sega, Nintendo, and Genesis each replacing the system that came before, and that he had taught me to play.

I used that knowledge Dad taught me to show off in front of boys who thought girls couldn't play. It was like a parlor trick that Dad has handed me without even knowing it! My girlfriends told me I was a nerd and to stop playing when they were around, because I made them look like nerds too. The truth was in the gamers' eyes— they were already nerds because they couldn't play!

It didn't take long before I was over failing school, video gaming, and living in Mount Holly with roommates. I decided I needed a serious change. My first thought was to apply for jobs. Maybe college just wasn't my thing. I was searching newspaper ads for jobs such as babysitters, envelope stuffers, McDonald's fry cook, secretaries, and then I saw it: an ad for a company in search of au pairs. I had no idea what an au pair was, so I researched it. I couldn't believe it was a thing. I had an opportunity to sign up at an agency called "Au pair Abroad" and become a babysitter in a foreign country. Seriously? *This* was a job. I rushed home to talk to my parents.

The conversation didn't go as badly as I thought it would. They agreed that I sucked at school. They agreed I was a great babysitter and that I had loads of experience and references, and that I really liked kids. This was the job for me! There was one major glitch. The application alone would cost me $350.00, and I might pay it and not be selected for the program. Even before the company would send me the paperwork to fill out, I had to pay the processing and handling fees.

I told my parents I had to do it, that I would make it happen and pay for it. But if I did get selected for the program, they would have to buy me a plane ticket. Dad laughed and gave me a "Yeah, right" nod and walked away. He didn't think I could pull this off. *Oh really?* Now it was a challenge. I would become an au pair. I would leave New Jersey and travel the world. I had never gone far from New Jersey. The farthest I had ever traveled was to Pennsylvania and Maryland to see Aunt Debbie with Aunt Barb, and Missouri with Jenny. The thrill of leaving the country was motivation enough.

First, I needed to make some money as fast as I could. So I moved out of my room in Mount Holly and back to Mom and Dad's house in Tabernacle. Mom was annoyed; however, it was the only way for me to save the money so I begged and pleaded for her to let me come home. I had to threaten her with becoming a stripper if she didn't let me move back. She didn't seem to care about that, oddly enough. However, once Dad realized that my roommate was dancing, he yelled "Mona, let her move back in." I smiled at Mom and said, "So, Mom, stripper daughter or au pair daughter?" She didn't find me funny, but let me move back home.

I settled back into my untouched bedroom, and it was as if I never left. I let all of my friends know that I couldn't go out at all if it was going to cost me any money. I began to take on any and all babysitting jobs offered to me, and I even applied to work at a local daycare center.

This was the first time I had ever saved for something I wanted. Two months later, after babysitting every day for the daycare center, picking up any weekend jobs, and not spending any (unnecessary) money, I finally sent my first check to the au pair agency. I then began to practice patience. In other words, I waited. I waited and waited, checking the mailbox every day. I felt disappointed every day as I walked away empty-handed from the mailbox.

After five weeks, the excitement of walking to the mailbox waned along with the expectation I had of ever finding a letter from the au pair agency. I kept checking regardless. But the disappointment was overwhelming and I began to believe that the paperwork would never show. I was just walking to the mailbox purely for exercise purposes. Every night Dad asked, "Anything come today?" Daily I would bow my head and say, "Nothing yet, Dad…" And then I would do it again the next day: open the mailbox, pull out all of the mail, and suffer more disappointment. Mom even showed some empathy and hugged me. "I know you really wanted this, Danielle."

Just when I was about to stop checking the mail, I walked out, opened the mailbox, and there, inside, was a gigantic manila envelope marked Danielle Mason. I shoved the rest of the household mail back into the mailbox and ran inside. "Mom, Mom, it's here! The package is here!" Mom wandered out of the bedroom and sat at the table with me as I opened the enormous package. She was more ready for me to go to Europe than I was!

It was the welcoming package from the agency and two hundred pages of follow-up paperwork. I couldn't believe it. It was really happening. I was going to travel on a plane for the first time ever to another country. My excitement dimmed a bit when I realized would have to fill out every page. These pages would include pictures, references, letters of recommendations, a two-page letter as to why I should be selected, a two-page letter to a prospective host family, drug testing, picking the country I would work in, language skills, background checks, and many other miscellaneous documents. I also needed to order a driver's license for Europe, a GO card, and my passport. I was overwhelmed and worried that this would be the point at which I failed.

It was the largest homework assignment I had ever taken on—not that I took on many. But at least I knew I had a full month to come up with all of the documents prior to receiving the passport, taking the drug test, and handing in the completed paperwork.

I worked on it for over three months. It took that long to get all of the documentation together, even with Dad's help. The references and recommendations were the most difficult part. I had no idea it would take so long for people to fill out a sheet of paper and get it back to me. I learned that people don't move as fast as you do when they're not the ones trying to leave the country!

Finally, after I collected all the proper documentation and received my first passport, I was able to submit my completed application to the organization. I put the finished application back into the mailbox and sent it to the au pair agency to be certified. As I sat and waited again, the agency searched for a host family in either the Netherlands or Greenland (my two countries of choice). Once again, waiting patiently proved very difficult for me, and I thanked work for keeping me busy.

Five long weeks went by, and I was very nervous that I wasn't going to be accepted. I often wondered what I could have done wrong. I worried that they found out that my driver's license was suspended at sixteen and maybe that would keep me from traveling the world. My father said, "You need to practice patience. It will all work out." His words would calm me for a moment and then a new anxiety would kick in. I started to worry that maybe they know about the time I had alcohol poisoning. Maybe that would stop them from hiring me.

When I signed the paperwork, I marked the box that said I didn't drink, which is completely true. However, the alcohol poisoning may be on some record somewhere. I had trouble sleeping as I waited for the agency to call or reply.

I realized that my teenage mistakes might cost me my dream.

Finally we received the phone call I had been waiting for. The au pair agency found a possible match and was ready for us to speak to each other. Nothing could stop me now. I was selected and I couldn't wait. I'd passed all the background checks, did everything I was told to do, paid all the fees, and now I had a meeting.

I called all of my friends to let them know I was leaving. Everyone was excited that it was working out. My friends and family knew I had been waiting for what seemed like forever. I compared my feeling to someone who just got into the college of their choice. I was living my dream.

My possible host parents, Cort and Adel from the Netherlands, were coming to Philadelphia to visit friends for two weeks. Dad and I went to meet them so they could have an in-person interview with me. My only job was to get them to want me as their au pair.

I have always been pretty good at interviewing, but the night before my meeting I stayed up much too late celebrating in New York with Greg and his friends. I rushed home, dressed, and drove with Dad to Philly to take my new family out to dinner on the ship Mushi Liu. Dad spent $200.00 on this meal to impress my new (potential) Dutch family. I believe he and his amazing personality sold my host family on me. I was so tired that I didn't have much energy and didn't talk too much. We all laughed with Dad and his hilarious jokes, and we discussed the job description. Everything seemed amazing to me. At the end they shook our hands and welcomed me as their new au pair. I would start on December 27, 1996.

I had two months to prepare for my trip abroad. I loved saying those words "I am going abroad." I was so glad my Dutch family accepted me and that they didn't ask to see my grades! I spent from October to December getting everything in order.

My family helped me plan my going away party, prepared me for my trip, and celebrated Christmas. All of my friends came to say goodbye, including the twins and I couldn't believe it but Stephanie was pregnant. I was leaving and one of the twins was pregnant. The last few days before I left flew by faster than ever. Christmas day, as promised, my plane ticket appeared as a Christmas present. Dad handed it to me and said "See you in three months!"

"Not funny, Dad," I said. "I have a one-year contract and I intend to fulfill it." We both laughed. This was my first big opportunity and I was not going to fail.

The day I left for the airport, I grabbed piggy and monkey and shoved them into my bag. I realize that I was a nineteen-year-old with a piggy and a monkey, but I didn't let that bother me. I just hoped no one would open my bags and see them. That would have been utterly embarrassing.

My former roommate, Lilah, and Dad drove me to the airport to say goodbye. Mom stayed home with our new puppy, Shadow. Chad headed back to the Marines in Virginia. And that was it. I was leaving my family for more than a week for the first time ever. Dad and Lilah waved goodbye to me from the window at the gate as I walked onto the plane. I was beyond excited, but worry and gloominess crept in. I worried about what I might miss while we were all apart. I tried to stop thinking about it and stepped on a plane for my first time ever, excited for this new adventure.

The plane ride to the Netherlands couldn't be any harder than it seemed. I had two layovers. One of the layovers was on the west coast and one was in the United Kingdom. I walked on and off the plane six times. I quickly learned the way of airports and navigated them with ease, as long as there was someone I could ask for help. I asked the security and bag checkers where I was supposed to be next. Everyone was kind and helpful. I was very grateful for that.

During one of my layovers, I had to run from my plane's terminal to the connecting terminal. I had twenty-two minutes to grab my overhead luggage, scurry off of the plane from Philadelphia, and grab the connecting flight to London's Heathrow airport. I was in the very back of the plane and fear of being late set in as people walked off at a snail's pace. This connection was the connection that I couldn't miss. This was the one that took me out of the United States and brought me to Europe. I ran as fast as I could, yelling to anyone who worked for the airport and showing them my paperwork to make sure I was heading in the right direction.

I ran to the terminal and it was completely empty. All of the other flyers had already boarded the plane. I ran up waving my tickets. "Am I too late? No, I'm not too late! I am on that plane." I kept yelling to make sure they couldn't say they didn't hear me. "Am I too late?" My facial expression must have said that any other answer than "No" may cause an explosion.

The flight attendant informed me that "they just closed the doors."

"Wait, what does that mean? Please let me on." My eyes welled up with tears at the thought of missing my plane.

She walked away. I stood in the terminal, feeling ignored. I was shaking when she came back and finally took my tickets. The plane was waiting for the pilot to return and I was lucky enough to have beat him—I headed down the plane terminal. Once I could see the plane my heart finally stopped thumping. I breathed a heavy sigh of relief and stepped on the plane with my bag following.

The bag-checking lady stopped me and said, "I'm sorry, sweetie, but you can't bring that bag on the plane. Your bag is too big." I tried to remain calm but went back into freak-out mode internally. Calmly I looked at the lady and said, "But, I was just on another plane with this same carry-on and they had no problem with it. Please don't take my bag." Apparently because I showed up last, there was no room for my luggage. My eyes welled up with tears. They were going to take my bag and put it below the plane. I was so afraid someone would lose the bag or steal from it. I began to take important items out of the bag, shoving them into my purse just in case, including strangely enough, Piggy. The pilot walked past me and I knew my time was running out. I handed them my bag and stepped onto the plane to Heathrow England, Europe. I had one more connection from Heathrow to Amsterdam. I waited patiently and then boarded my last plane for a year. That was it. I had moved to the Netherlands.

Chapter 11

American girls rock at adventures

People pushed off of the plane in a hurry. I stood waiting for my luggage to be returned. The flight attendant watched me for a moment then walked over to assist me. "What are you waiting for?" she said in England's, English.

"My bags," I said "The lady said they would be right here after the flight." The flight attendant called someone on the phone as I stared out at the luggage workers. "All bags have been sent to baggage claim." She pointed the way. *I now had to find my luggage in a Netherlands airport*—another challenge I needed to address.

I stopped worrying and followed the signs for luggage. It was easier to find than I expected.

I walked down the steps in the Schiphol Airport, listening to the foreign language coming through the loudspeakers then the English translation. Everything around me was surprisingly in English and the staff at the airport all spoke English. They pointed me in the direction of the exit, and I hurried toward Cort, my new host parent who was waiting for me. We said a quick hello due to short-term parking, and I followed him to the car, put my bags in the trunk, and we were on our way to the small town of Woerden. We chatted the entire drive. An hour later, I walked into their house, the place I would call home for the next year. I was completely jetlagged, burned out, and praying for a shower. I was ready to crash. Unfortunately for me, this was not going to happen. Cort opened the front door, we dropped my luggage in the hallway, and I was greeted by my new family's friends, a few neighbors, the nineteen-year-old au pair, Rendi, whose year was coming to an end and Rendi's two friends from South Africa. They were all celebrating Little Cort's fourth birthday.

I didn't realize it then, but entering my host family's world during their holiday break was helpful to my transition. The good news was that I wasn't beginning my au pair position until the old au pair left, so I had time to acclimate to the change in time zone. I tried to overcome the six-hour time difference by diligently fighting my sleepiness, forcing myself to stay awake until ten in the evening, only to wake up four hours later, at two in the morning. This continued for the first two weeks.

During the transition, Adel, my other host parent, had Rendi show me around town. We biked to the local stores, the train station, and the teenage hangouts. She showed me how to get to Little Cort's school, the neighborhood playground, and the nearby church. It didn't take long before I was navigating Woerden on my own.

My first travel adventure overseas began on New Year's Eve. Rendi and her friends planned a trip to Amsterdam for the holiday, and they invited me to join them. Since it was New Year's Eve, we waited until it was dark, and I biked with them to the Woerden train station, where I bought my first ticket to Amsterdam. We rode on the train for an hour before entering Amsterdam's Central Station. The overly crowded city embraced us, forcing us to walk with hundreds of people, the moment that we stepped out of the train station. I stood in wonderment of the lanes of bikes, people riding without helmets, and the beautiful buildings that surrounded us. This was my second experience in a major city other than New York, and I only visited New York once for a modeling opportunity. I wandered around Amsterdam following Rendi who thankfully had resided here for the past year.

None of my friends had ever been to Amsterdam, so they couldn't tell me what to expect. Whenever I told someone back home where I was moving they said, "Amsterdam is the most amazing city in the world. Marijuana is legal!" I assumed if it was legal, then people would be smoking in restaurants, at parks, and while biking through the city and to my disbelief, they actually were.

I followed my new friends into the coffee shop and was surprised when I realized that no coffee was served here—but marijuana was. I wondered why they called it a coffee shop. Upon entering the shop, the store owner greeted me with a menu of over twenty different marijuana choices. Feeling silly about not knowing different kinds of marijuana existed, I asked what the difference was. The store owner explained that each type of marijuana came from a different strain and had its own name. The menu included a description of how each one would make me feel. He held up each type for me to smell and explained that White Widow keeps you wide awake, Black Widow makes you sleepy, Jamaican and Juicy Fruit make you happy and motivated, and on and on. Everyone made a selection and purchased their product in a cute colorful bag. I stuck with the White Widow since I figured I'd remember that name the best when I wrote home.

Although I wished I could stay and smoke in the shop for the rest of the day, we grabbed our bags and headed back onto the streets of Amsterdam. I smoked the White Widow legally while wandering behind the old au pair and staring at the buildings and cobblestone streets. Along the streets, endless rows of bikes were chained to bike racks, light poles, or the railings of apartments. People rode them helmetless in the city and even commuted on the train with them. I wasn't as lucky back home, in my farm town of Tabernacle, to be able to commute by bicycle. Biking to the nearest grocery store would have taken forever. But it was different here.

I wandered the streets, staring at the different and remarkable sights as I drifted a few people back from Rendi and her friends. They had gone ahead while I took in the sights of the city. From time to time, I rushed to catch up but then I somehow fell behind again. At one point, I saw them cross the cobblestone street and disappear into the crowd on the other side. I picked up the pace, afraid I would lose them, hurrying across the street only to slam on the breaks a second later, when people screamed the moment my platform boots touched the cobblestone road. I couldn't understand what they said because they said it in Dutch. So I ran.

That's when I noticed that the street beneath me seemed to be ... on fire? Fireworks in the form of poppers covered the streets and started to pop all around me. The streets began to sparkle. In a state of utter confusion, I jumped back. People around me laughed hysterically. They may have been laughing directly at me, or they may have just been excited for the crazy street fireworks.

This, of course, is the very moment the White Widow kicked in. I couldn't help but laugh at the situation I found myself in. Smoking an entire joint was probably not the smartest choice I ever made. I was now in a foreign country, on New Year's Eve, as stoned as can be and separated from the handful of people I knew. My only saving grace was that we had planned to meet back at the train station if we ended up separated. But the trains didn't start back until six in the morning. I'd have to find a way to survive on my own until then.

I walked by myself, through the crowds, staring at the people on the streets. I wandered from bar to bar, staying away from the ones that charged a New Year's cover fee to foreigners. For the first time ever, I was a foreigner. Each bar I wandered into had a different Dutch band playing, and I smiled happily as locals bought me beer and passed joints freely. This was the first time that I was legally allowed to drink, and I had never seen drugs passed without the fear of being arrested. In New Jersey, the drinking age was twenty-one, and I was two years away from this milestone, so drinking legally at nineteen was hugely exciting. I felt like I was finally an adult. This country respected teenagers, and I was enjoying that teenage respect.

Around five in the morning, I walked back to the train station, asking for directions along the way, and located Rendi and her friends, who were waiting for the six o'clock train. They didn't seem bothered by our separation and honestly I wasn't either. Content that we were all safe and back together, I sat in the train station and reflected on my adventure, smiling at my New Year's Eve in Amsterdam.

We all waited for the train back to Woerden, falling asleep in the station and then sleeping the hour on the train till it was time to get off. We then had to ride our bikes back home. It was a short bike ride, but at seven in the morning after a night in Amsterdam, ten minutes felt like an eternity. When I arrived back at the house, I stumbled in the front door and climbed into bed with a pad and paper. Before passing out, I wrote my first of many letters to Mom about my travels. I explained the coffee shops in the letters, leaving out the part about my partaking in such activity. I was honest, but not dumb and I didn't want to say anything that could backfire on me later. I actually missed Mom a little. This surprised me. After all, *she* wanted me out. I let her know I missed her and that I hoped everything back home was boring without me.

This would be my last adventure with Rendi and her friends. A few days later, she would leave, and my host family, obviously very close to her, became surprisingly sad. My host mother even cried when she left. I found the whole thing pretty awkward. No pressure at all coming into a new home with a host family wishing they could keep their old au pair another year!

I let that feeling go and embraced my new job and my new family's schedule. I took care of the children from seven in the morning until five or six at night, Monday through Thursday. Once a month, I would babysit on a Friday. It wasn't very difficult to play with the kids, make sure Little Cort was at school on time, and hang out with Elsa, who was barely two, while maintaining the laundry and keeping the house clean. This last part was a challenge—and something my mother laughed about as soon as I'd been hired for the job.

I had a firm grip on most of my duties, but I found biking with the kids to be my biggest challenge. I had to put Cort on the back of the bike and buckle him in while keeping the bike standing and not letting Elsa run away. Once I got Cort situated, I instructed him "not to wiggle" as I held the bike up and put Elsa into the seat in the front. Mastering getting them both on safely was one skill, the harder part was to then ride with them both. I was honestly scared, as I recollected my Lauren story from childhood. It took me a few go 'rounds before I felt I had mastered this new skill. Once that happened the kids and I traveled all over Woerden. We went into the cheese shop and walked around the town with big chunks of cheese. Elsa loved the cheese shop and would laugh as I handed her a piece. We were blessed with so much to see in our little town. I loved the cobblestone streets, and the church at the end of the town was the oldest one I had ever seen. I enjoyed spending time with the children, but I missed having a friend my age to talk to.

Our street was full of stay-at-home moms, and I reached out to them often. In the houses to each side of our home lived families with young children. I grew the closest to Judy, who lived across the street with her husband and their three kids Esra, Zeb, and Izzy. I found Judy intriguing because she was an artist and had a very peaceful way of life. Her happiness spread to everyone and she possessed a calmness that spread to me. The street was full of kids for Cort and Elsa to play with, and they all loved Judy. The other neighbors kept to themselves for the most part, but when they did come out, I played with the kids and talked to their moms. Luckily, everyone knew *enough* English for me to get by.

Finally I made a teenage friend named Martyn. He and his younger brother, Frank, lived a few houses down from mine, and we shared the same walkway. Martyn was just as excited to have a new friend in his small town as I was to have him living so close. He introduced me to his friends and now I had friends too. Woerden was a small town, everyone knew each other, and the teenagers were friendly to strangers.

I learned through Martyn that the teenagers would host parties in Utrecht, go to raves in Amsterdam, and hang out at the local pub, a five-minute bike ride away. Martyn and his friends met up at the pub on the weekends before going out for the night.

He introduced me to Wendy, the daughter of the local pub owner. Wendy and I quickly became very close during my year abroad. She introduced me to her best friend, Lavinia, and the three of us were inseparable. I loved going to their homes and living like a nineteen-year-old Dutch girl—which by the way isn't much different from an American girl, except they can drink legally and no one cared.

It took a while but I eventually made friends with a few au pairs from the au pair agencies list. Jen, a girl from Canada, was placed with a host family two towns over. We had to ride our bike two miles and across a dirt bridge to get to Jen's house. Jen was shy but was willing to talk when she was with me. Agnes, an au pair from Poland who spoke little English, was only a ten-minute bike ride away. Agnes wanted to learn more English and I wanted to help her. We used terrible made-up sign language to communicate when she didn't understand something. She quickly picked up a more words, and it became easier to be friends. We all had different au pair schedules so we would hang out whenever we could. It was always nice having two au pairs hanging out with two small children instead of one.

I spent most of my time in the beginning getting to know the area, hanging out with Martyn and his friends, and traveling. I started to date one of Martyn's best friends, Edwin, after about four months. He lived four minutes away on bike, and we went to the bars, his house to watch movies, or just relaxed with other kids. His parents spoke no English and so hand movements and laughter became our means of communication. Edwin spoke fluent English and translated most of the time. He also was helping me learn Dutch.

I realized I needed better linguistic skills when I visited the post office and tried to ask for a box—and no one understood me. That was a turning point. I went home and asked Big Cort, "What is a little box in Dutch?" "Doosje" he answered. And thus my third Dutch word following hello *halo* and goodbye *tot siens* came into use.

By month three, I purchased a GO HOLLAND language book and began practicing my Dutch while Elsa took her naps. Little Cort spoke English with the last au pair, and he was learning more English through his conversations with me, while I learned Dutch from him. I studied the book and attempted Dutch with Little Cort. He would laugh when I said the Dutch words. My accent sounded silly to him, and he would correct my pronunciation. Throughout the year, I grew fond of this kid. He was smart, had a great personality, and played well with others. Elsa was so young and innocent. Having a little girl to take care of made me dream of the daughter I would have some day— no time soon.

Cort and Adel spoke only Dutch at dinner so that was helpful in moving my language skills forward. I tried to understand and speak only Dutch back to them. I learned how to have a tea party with my book and spent most of my time asking others if they would like tea and sugar! Everyone that came over to visit me was asked if they wanted tea. This lasted for a few months, until I could talk about other things. Edwin's mom was always so proud of me when I learned a new sentence or understood what she was saying.

By the time I left Holland I was able to understand conversations and to speak when I needed to, although I still messed up tenses and forgot the correct order of the words. The Dutch were forgiving and seemed happy that I was at least attempting to learn their language. I wondered if a foreigner in Holland not knowing Dutch is the same as a foreigner in America not knowing English. I wasn't going to be that foreigner.

Mom was shocked when I wrote that I was learning Dutch. She couldn't believe I was learning anything considering how "lazy" I was in school. She seemed proud of me in the letters. She wrote back every time I wrote and never skipped a letter. Her first letters talked about us getting closer, and I responded with wanting to be closer also. I wanted an end to the negative relationship we had. I didn't bring up anything about the past or how she treated me that may upset her. I wanted to move forward—she did too! Dad, on the other hand, wasn't much for keeping in touch. Out of sight, out of mind. This surprised me, but I wasn't upset. If I needed something, I knew he would respond with whatever it was.

I wondered after a few months if parents felt that having kids was a monotonous routine. My days with my host kids were always the same; however, my nights became more exciting as the winter ended and I began to explore my home. My new friends invited me to my first rave ever in the town, called Utrecht. The rave would begin at midnight and continue until six in the morning, when the trains started to run again. Edwin, Martyn, and I, and a few other of his friends, took the train to Utrecht and walked to the location of the rave. We stood outside for about an hour waiting to be let in. I was already exhausted by the time we arrived and knew that staying awake until six in the morning would be a challenge. We arrived an hour early in the hope that we could get in first. We stood along the tall metal fence waiting for the gates to open and to be let in. I was excited when I saw the roadies walk in with the DJ's equipment. I leaned against the fence, watching and waiting for something to happen.

As it neared midnight, the people around me became more excited and drunk. By this time, thousands of hyped-up teenagers crowded the area. At exactly midnight, the security guards opened the gigantic gates and everyone rushed the doors. This resulted in life-threatening pressure against the ten-foot-tall chain-link fence. Since my friends and I were closest to the fence we were pushed into it with no wiggle room to move out of harm's way. Thankfully, the fence, flexed under the pressure as my body pushed against it. If not, we probably would have died.

I yelled to Edwin, who grabbed my hand "Keep moving to the side," he shouted. "The gate is over there." He pointed and I followed.

The masses kept pressing forward, and even though I could see the gates, I wasn't able to move sideways toward them. Every step I tried to take was met with shoving and pushing. The rush of the crowd didn't let up. It was like a merging of traffic on a three-lane highway going to one lane except it was humans moving with a mindless urgency. I felt the once cold air warm up, and I was led full swing into my first-ever real panic attack.

I couldn't breathe. My heart was beating faster than I ever felt it beat. I thought I was going to pass out from the pressure of being pushed against the solid metal fence. The crowd forced forward harder, I lost Edwin's hand, and strangers waiting in line jumped to the front. I held tears back and kept trying to push forward. My breathing became fast and shallow, and I couldn't muster enough strength to yell to Martyn or Edwin. I wished I could find a way out of the situation; however, there was nothing I could do. I was sweating and freaking out in my head about the possibility of dying. The people continued pressing forward, and I was overwhelmed. I contemplated climbing the fence. I looked behind me to see if there was a different way to escape. A girl passed out and fell to the ground next to me. Her friends tried to get her out of harm's way before the crowd stepped on her. Everything was happening so fast, and I worried that I could become the girl who passed out. Martyn pushed me from the side and Edwin grabbed my hand and waved for me to keep following the fence line.

Finally I could see the gate opening; it was only a few feet in front of us. With Edwin pulling me and Martyn pushing me, we finally made it away from the fence, where I could breathe again.

The moment no one was touching me was a relief. I needed a second to compose myself and deal with the anxiety that I had just experienced. Once I was ready, we walked inside of the warehouse where no one came that close to me the rest of the night.

I don't know what I expected to find, but the inside of the warehouse wasn't very friendly. The dancers stayed on the dance floor, and the bleachers that lined the wall lacked comfortable seating for the wall flowers. So it was either concrete floor or metal bleachers. I opted for dancing with my friends (and theirs), but secretly I couldn't wait for my night to end.

DJ after DJ played their mixed style of dance music, sometimes in Dutch and sometimes in English and the crowd continued to go crazy. Apparently all of these DJs were famous in Europe, and it was an honor to be entertained by them. I had never heard of any of them. The DJ's light show reminded me of a Pink Floyd laser light show I saw in Philadelphia. I'd never forget watching what seemed to be a normal teenage crowd have dance-offs as they took ecstasy, smoked marijuana, and drank beer. It was unlike any party I had ever been to before.

By six in the morning, my rave night ended. I happily slept on the train, rode my bike back to my home, and lay down on my single bed in my cozy bedroom. I stared around at the walls I had decorated with photographs of my life in America. I doubted if I'd ever want to go on a rave night again—then my friend Wendy asked me to join her at one. She promised it wouldn't be the same.

I wrote home to Mom about the near-death chain-link experience, and she begged me to be careful. She didn't want her only daughter to die in Europe. I promised to be safer so I could return home to her.

My next rave experience was in Amsterdam. I took comfort in the fact that "this rave would be very different than the last one." I trusted Wendy and Lavinia, who also promised this rave would be better. The idea of going back to Amsterdam thrilled me. In Wendy's room, the three of us got ready for our night in the city. I styled my hair in a

Princess Leia double bun, put silver glittery eye liner on, and wore a pink hippie tight suit that my friend Samantha's mom gave me. I felt very Amsterdam even if I had no clue what that meant.

The night got even better when I realized Wendy would be driving. Not taking the train meant that we wouldn't be stuck until six in the morning waiting for the train. Now we could leave whenever we were ready. To someone who found it difficult to be awake till six in the morning, this was a real relief. We parked a few blocks from the club and walked right up to the front of the line and straight through the doors of the club as if we owned the place. I have no idea how it happened, I can only assume it was because we were cute.

Wendy was right; this time was better. We didn't have to suffer for hours with long lines, there were no panic fences, and no one pushing us out of the way. We checked our coats and walked around looking for a place to make our home base.

Feeling nervous, I found myself an out-of-the-way seat above the dance floor. I watched the hundreds of dancers underneath me. Once in a while someone would come over and try to talk to me; I tried to speak only Dutch so I wouldn't have to explain to anyone who heard my English why I was in Holland. I didn't want to get wrapped up in long conversations because the only way to talk was to scream and that makes me miserable so I refused to do it. I kept looking down and dangling my feet, just smiling if someone tried to strike up a conversation.

I had never been to a club like this one. It was musically the same as my first rave; however, the atmosphere was less dingy, with colorful couches, tables, food to order, and comfortable seats. The dance floor was wooden instead of a cold concrete floor.

After about an hour of feeling out the situation, I left my safe zone to dance on the dance floor with both Wendy and Lavinia. We spent hours laughing, holding hands, and dancing. They stayed with me the entire time so I wouldn't get lost in the club or swept into the mosh pit of crazy dancers. I watched as the mosh pit people danced their violent dance, pushing against each other and slamming their bodies. I wanted nothing to do with that.

As we walked around the club, I saw couches with teenagers making out, rooms closed off with black curtains, yet kids were freely walking through, and alcohol being consumed like I had never seen before. Wendy grabbed my hand to bring me closer to her and the other dancers. Overwhelmed by the energy of the people, I climbed back into my spot overseeing the dance club and dangled my legs from the ceiling. I stayed in that spot, dancing to the music until it was time to go home. Going from inside the loud, thumping, screaming teen world to the silent streets at three in the morning was shocking. It was as if I could hear for the first time. My hearing was picking up even the slightest sound. I climbed into the back seat of the car happy to have survived my second rave.

I wrote home to Mom to let her know everything that was happening. I told her about Edwin, the boy I was dating, and about my au pair family, friends, and the clubs we were going to.

Lately, most of Mom's letters revolved around her new love, Shadow. That puppy had taken over her time and she loved her. Dad came up in conversations too. She complained about his traveling and how lonely the house was without anyone—not that she was hinting she missed me at all.

Going back to work after a fun weekend off was easy. I missed the kids and they always seemed just as excited to see me. On the other hand, my host parents and I weren't spending time together at all anymore. We barely were speaking and we lacked a friendship. It was solely a working relationship—this saddened me. But I didn't know what to do about it.

At first, when I arrived in Holland, I would stay downstairs and spend time with everyone at night, but after the children went to bed I left Cort and Adel alone. A married couple didn't need their babysitter around 24/7. Mom never wanted me around at night and when I went on trips with my old babysitting family, Mike and Renee, they were the same way. So, if I wasn't working, I came back to the house less and less. I didn't spend much time with them at night, and I started to sleep out at friends' houses, and then Edwin's parents' house. I rode my bike back home before work in the morning and I went back to taking care of the kids.

My host parents often gave me Fridays off, and they had vacations planned throughout my year abroad— I wasn't invited to go with them. They encouraged me to travel alone on my vacation days or long weekends. So I made sure I did.

On my flight from London to Amsterdam I had made friends with a guy named Guy, so I decided England would be my next travel. Guy had been in the seat next to me, and we chatted the entire hour on the plane. He was from London, and he was visiting Amsterdam for work reasons. I told him all about my au pair job and moving to Holland. By the end of our flight, Guy gave me his address and said I should look him up if "I ever went to London." As soon as I had vacation dates I wrote him a letter to see if I could come visit for a weekend. He answered my letter, telling me he would love to have me come to visit and to call him on his telephone. I don't think he ever thought I would actually write and call. The next morning I called him to schedule my visit on my next weekend off. But it turned out he wasn't going to be around the weekend I had available. A moment later he said, "But you are more than welcome to use my flat." And I thought, *Is this guy for real?*

Without thinking that safety might be an issue, I traveled to London, England, on a ferry to a man's house, named Guy, who I barely knew to use his flat while he wasn't there. I trusted my own instincts and jumped on the ferry to England. I came off of the ferry and found my way to the train station and followed his directions. I spent an hour on the train until I came to his town. A man helped me hail a cab, which dropped me off at Guy's home. There was a moment that I worried that my instincts might have been wrong about him, and that the hidden key may not be there. And hailing a new cab was not going to be an option out here, where traffic wasn't exactly a thing. If I'd been wrong about him, I'd be lost and alone, and that scared the heck out of me. But the key lay under the vase on his doorstep like he said it would. And I was ecstatic.

I entered the stranger's flat and walked into a beautiful immaculate home. There was a note on the counter explaining all the places I needed to go while in England and how to get there, along with an invitation to eat whatever I wanted and make myself comfortable.

I looked at Guy's pictures and reacquainted myself with what he looked like, and I was happy that he didn't look like a sociopath murderer. That eased my mind. After all, our encounter was a brief one on the third plane of my travels. I wandered around his apartment and settled in on his couch. I sat there in the silence, embracing the moment. I was in England. Holy Cow! *I* was in England. I felt proud of myself as I sat there. I was alone and I was okay. I felt safe.

Moments later, I couldn't figure out how to work his English television so instead I fiddled through some old magazines on the table. It was late and tomorrow I had a big day planned for myself. I packed my bag for my day trip including water, my license (for proof of US citizenship), an umbrella, and food from Guy's refrigerator. I went into his bathroom to brush my teeth and get changed into nighttime clothing. For a moment I wondered if he had cameras in his room. I stared at his perfectly made bed, weirded out by the thought of sleeping in a stranger's bed.

Sitting on the edge of his bed my mind wandered to the worst-case best-case choices for the scenario I had placed myself in. The thoughts of, "What if he comes home? What if he has a roommate? What if this was a trap?" popped into my head. I stopped these disturbing thoughts and closed my eyes. I had a difficult time falling asleep that night, but I was comforted by the fact that I had told my host parents the address of where I was staying. I woke up in the morning and showered in Guy's shower.

I locked the bathroom door and looked around for cameras before stripping down. I decided I was safe after I was fully dressed and ready to travel the country of England.

I grabbed one of his bottled waters from the refrigerator, left his flat and traveled to London by train. Traveling alone wasn't as hard as I expected it to be. The trains were different in every country and figuring out the money was a bit of a challenge, but everyone became helpful when I put a confused look on my face. I walked off the train into Trafalgar Square and bought a map off of a local merchant. I was thrilled to be in a country that I had learned about in history classes my entire life. My first venture was to find Big Ben, and with my handy-dandy map it became easy. I walked through the city, looking like a tourist with my face in my map.

It didn't take long before I was staring at the world's largest clock tower. My heart stopped as I gazed at the legendary clock that survived World War II, feeling my own moment of accomplishment. I couldn't wait to tell Mom and Dad everything I was seeing. I continued to stare in awe; I would leave after hearing the clock bells ring.

I walked away reflecting on my happiness until I found myself standing in front of the House of Parliament. This building's striking beauty put me in a state of wonderment. Every step I took in London led to another building that I recognized from television or my school days. I followed the map until I ended up at the Palace of Westminster. I stood outside of the palace gates, hoping I would see someone of royalty, wondering if I would even recognize them if I did.

The palace guards greeted me with their stillness, devoutly doing their jobs and speaking to no one. I asked a stranger walking by to take my photo with them. I was impressed that the soldiers stayed completely still and weren't bothered by the American standing next to them. Other guards paraded through the gates upon horses, and everyone stepped out of the way. The guards and their horses marched away from the castle as gatherers stared in awe. Moments later the skies became darker shades of gray and within seconds, rain poured down. The crowds dispersed, and I took cover in the first local restaurant I could find.

I was excited to have my first opportunity to order the famous English fish and chips. I took the waitress's advice to put the vinegar on the side and dip the fish. I put the fish in my mouth and cringed, deciding I didn't like it. I did, however, enjoy the chips. I ate everything on my plate despite my dislike and didn't need to try fish and chips again.

Once the rain shower stopped, I headed over to Piccadilly Circus and shopped in the many stores that lined the streets. The shopping district looked like a combination of Amsterdam and New York City. Since these were the only major cities I had visited, I decided all cities must look the same. Once darkness set in, I returned on the train to Guy's apartment, where I passed out for the night.

My last day in England, I wrote a thank you letter to Guy. Next, I packed all of my items and straightened up his home. I ventured back out by taxicab and train to visit the British Museum and other attractions nearby. Later that afternoon, I had to catch another cab from London to the ferry back to Amsterdam, board a train to Woerden, and bike from the train station with my travel bag back to my home.

Every trip I took was more exciting than the one before. I went from living a boring life without travel to living in Europe and backpacking everywhere I could. I saved my money and bought myself the perfect travel backpack in Utrecht. I decided that I wanted to go somewhere warm next. I planned my next trip alone to Barcelona, Spain, after looking through a Dutch travel magazine. It was all-inclusive bus fare to Spain, six days in a hotel with a pool, and free breakfasts for the entire stay. I saved my money for a month and paid the travel agent I'd found in the ad in the magazine.

The bus travel to Spain from Holland took twenty-two hours. We stopped often for bathrooms, food, sightseeing, and anything else the tour guide thought noteworthy for the tour. I was enjoying the tour until the man next to me started to eat a sandwich that I believe was mayo and onions. It smelled so horrible; it was an effort to refrain from vomiting. I was elated when the bus arrived at the hotel and I could get off. I waited in line for the key to check into my room. Looking around and hearing the hotel guests speak, I surmised that most of them were from England. This was fine with me since the last place I visited was England, and speaking Dutch was difficult. The only Spanish-speaking people at the hotel were the wait-staff and the housekeepers. During the trip, I often wished I'd learned more in my Spanish classes.

The first thing I did after settling in my room was to lock my passport in my safe. I was told numerous times to be careful not to get my passport stolen. "This is the most important thing you have to protect on your travels, Danny," Dad had said as he saw me off at the airport. I remembered telling him, "I know, I know, got it."

I changed into my bathing suit, excited to find the beach. The moment I stepped on the beach, however, disappointment set in. The beach wasn't covered in soft sand like it is in New Jersey. Instead it was a broken shell beach, which made it difficult to enjoy the walk. Looking around, kids were running in the water and other people sat on the shell beach and they looked comfortable enough. I laughed and told myself to suck it up. I laid my towel down, climbed on it, shifted around the shells (which stabbed me) and basked happily in the sun for a few hours.

When the sun started to go down, I packed up my towel and headed back to the hotel. I had missed suppertime and hunger began to settle in. I jumped in the shower. As soon as the water hit my skin, I screamed. The hot water hit my sunburn, and my chest began to bubble. The sun was so strong that it burned my chest like no sunburn I ever had before. The skin just peeled off. The skin on my stomach did the same thing.

I stepped out of the shower, my skin on fire, thankful that I had covered my face on the beach. The freckles on my chest had literally been burnt off and my wounds oozed. I dressed carefully and headed downstairs to find medicine. The concierge directed me to the local shop; however, another lady standing at the counter offered to help me. She handed me Tylenol and aloe from her personal supply. I ran to the bathroom, took the Tylenol for the pain and put the aloe on, wincing at every touch. The Spanish sun was not my friend. I would need to cover up next time or risk scarring for life.

I returned to thank the lady that saved me with her aloe and Tylenol. She was staying in the hotel with her boyfriend and his parents. His parents, a nice older couple invited me to have dinner with them at the karaoke place in town. I spent the rest of my trip following this family on their crazy adventures. One of them was a trip to visit the Black Madonna in a monastery in Montserrat "serrated mountains" Spain. I found the holy sites in Spain breathtaking. The mountains surrounded us as our vehicle climbed the roads toward our destination. On the way, the tour guide explained that, according to legend, they found the Black Madonna in a cave in 880 A.D., after apparitions appeared in the sky that led them to her. The story fascinated me.

We traveled through a small village to a cable car that took us up the mountain to the holy place. What seemed like a thousand people wandered on the mountain visiting the Black Madonna. She sat high above the central altar of the basilica. My new friends and I climbed up a staircase through shrines of saints. When we reached the Black Madonna, I was taken aback by her size: She was only a few feet tall and sat upon a beautiful throne. I was told ahead of time to make a wish when I touched her. When it was my turn to have a moment alone with her, I thought long and hard before making my wish and then made it. I traveled all the way to Spain to the Black Madonna and wished that she could "make Mom well again."

I spent the rest of my trip to Spain traveling via subway to different must-see areas, purposely avoiding the horrible sun. The subways in Spain were significantly dirtier than the other trains I had traveled. There were homeless and beggars in the subway stations, and the smell of urine overwhelmed me. I couldn't figure out these subways. Everything was obviously in Spanish and the map I had didn't help at all. I was thankful that whenever I looked lost, a travel angel would stand beside me, speaking English, and get me back on track. The worry that I might be mugged was never far from my thoughts because the hotel concierge let me know that some tourists had been attacked a few weeks earlier. I kept just enough money and one ID on me. I wasn't mugged after all, nor did I encounter anyone who appeared to contemplate mugging me.

My last day in Spain was spent alone. The nice family I met had left the night before and we said our goodbyes. I spent my morning sitting at the pool, hidden in the shade and mentally preparing for the eighteen hour drive I'd face in a few hours. The bus trip home to the Netherlands from Spain was spent reflecting, writing in my journal or writing new letters home to Mom. I couldn't wait to see if I had missed any letters from her. I looked forward to reading about what was happening in her world with Dad and Shadow. Every letter she sent made me feel connected to her. I liked that she missed me when I was away. Honestly I never thought she would be the one to miss me the most. Dad sent one email so far, and it was to tell me he had mailed my rollerblades as I had asked.

Surprisingly I vented to Mom. Without being so close she didn't annoy me with her advice. She wasn't upset that I cleaned wrong or that I was doing something I shouldn't be. For the first time since turning ten, Mom didn't make me feel inadequate.

I felt such a huge sense of accomplishment every time I survived another trip and added another country to my list of places visited. During each journey I was finding more and more of my own strength. I was learning that I am brave enough to attempt anything I dream of.

My next trip would prove to be the shortest and strangest trip I had taken yet. I spent one day traveling by train to Brussels, the capital of Belgium, with my au pair friend Agnes and two of her Polish friends. Agnes barely spoke English and her two friends spoke none at all. They talked to each other the entire trip. I did not understand Polish so I just wrote in my journal while they chatted. After getting off the train, we walked to a youth hostel. This was my first youth hostel experience. We arrived and were greeted by an English-speaking Belgian girl. She checked us into our room, gave us each the key to the main door, and wished us a safe stay. As I looked around the room, safety was not what came to mind. The four of us shared a room of eight beds and a bathroom with four strangers. I decided I would travel Brussels keeping all my belongings on my back in my new travel bag. I truly became a nomad tourist.

As we toured the city, I found myself wandering in the main square, Le Grand Place, where Town Hall was located. I was overwhelmingly impressed at its design: It took the shape of a fortress ring. I had never seen any city this cool. I felt like I had walked into a story of kings and queens, and that I was merely a peasant among the beauty. People crowded the streets and Le Grand Place became as crowded as New York City. I spent an entire day visiting the local stores in the center of town. Even the streets of this glorious city seemed too clean and perfectly beautiful to walk on.
Wandering back to the youth hostel to sleep for the night, I worried about the stories I'd heard of people stealing bags while others slept. Determined that this was not going to happen to me, I placed my bag on my bed between myself and the wall. I snuggled my bag all night, making sure to keep one hand on it at all times. I felt safer than I

imagined—considering everyone was always warning me to not get robbed. No one wanted anything to do with my stuff or even me. The next morning the four of us headed back to the Netherlands.

Each time I returned home from a trip, there was another letter from Mom. I couldn't believe that she was the one who stayed in contact with me the most. At this point my letters to her were about my not-so-new boyfriend, each of my awesome trip experiences, my strangely weird relationship with my host family, and all the promises of how she and I were going to be so much "better" when I returned home.

It seemed to me that Mom and I just needed some distance between us to start to become friends. Six months into the year, I was sending and then receiving at least two letters a week, with photos of our dog, Shadow, our home in the snow, or whatever else she wanted me to remember. I became excited to return home to Mom—and wholeheartedly admitted that I never saw that coming!

A few weeks after my Belgium trip, my boyfriend, Edwin, and I took a long weekend together in Paris. The first thing I wanted to do when we reached France was to eat French bread. For this reason, after settling into our hotel, we went to the first bakery we found and purchased a baguette with cheese and a glass of wine to go with it. It was the most enjoyable sandwich I had ever tasted. I packed the remaining part of my baguette into my travel bag, and we set out for our first adventure Pere Lachaise Cemetery.

Edwin looked at me strangely when I informed him that I had to see the cemetery first. I had promised my childhood friend, Tina, who was in love with Jim Morrison, that if I went to France I would visit his gravesite and take a photo. I wanted to make sure I made good on this promise. Unfortunately, the promise ended up burning an entire day of our vacation. On the map, the cemetery seemed to be close to our hotel, but I realized quickly that just because something is located in Paris doesn't mean it is anywhere close to our hotel.

We traveled by foot for an hour, arriving at the graveyard, which covered over a hundred acres. And I had no idea how we were going to find Jim Morrison's grave in the middle of thousands of graves. We wandered around for another hour, admiring the romantic sculptures that included angels, couples in love, and doves, all set upon the concrete tombs.

I don't know why exactly, but as we walked further into the cemetery the sight of the many statues became disturbing. Hands reached out of the tombs as if they were real, dead bodies lay upon tops of their tombs, and half bodies looked as though they were trying to escape death.

With great disappointment, we stumbled across Jim Morrison's cemetery plot. Unlike the other, more artistic sites, Jim's looks like a square with a box in it. I laughed at the irony. I thankfully took my photo, walked around the other grave sites a bit more, and settled on being glad I had successfully kept my word to Tina.

After that, we decided to visit the Palace of Versailles–the most magnificent grounds I had ever seen, Versailles made me feel like a child walking into the Queen of Heart's garden from *Alice's Adventures in Wonderland.* Gigantic fish swam in the ponds, fountains rose higher than I had ever seen, and stairs climbed up to the heavens. I kept thinking, this *is the most beautiful place I have ever seen*, yet each new sight was more beautiful than the one before. The staircases of the castle reminded me of the scene in *Cinderella,* when she runs from the Prince before midnight. Versailles is the castle in every child's story. I reluctantly left this fairy-tale place at closing time, but I promised myself that someday I would return.

The next morning we went to visit the famous Notre Dame cathedral. So many people waited in a line to see the inside that we decided being outside was enough. We took a taxi to the Eiffel Tower and then back to the Trocadero, across from the tower, as suggested by the taxi driver, to take a photograph from the rooftop and eat lunch. Staring at the tower with the entire city behind it at night took my breath away. It was identical to every post card we walked past on the streets, lights shining everywhere behind a lit up tower with the moon shining bright. We rushed to see one more thing before our night (and trip) was over. The taxi driver dropped us off at the Arc de Triumphe for another photo opportunity. I swear driving in Paris with the taxi driver proved to be the best history lesson I had ever had. After coming back from Paris I waited anxiously for my final trip before I would head back to America.

One day I was reading a magazine at the aerobics class in Woerden, and I found a trip brochure for bike tours in Italy. A tour guide arranged the bikes, tents for camping, and the locations of several small towns we would camp at. Perfect! It seemed not too expensive, and it ran in the summer, when I had my longest vacation time of all. I reviewed the brochure with my host parents, and then I signed myself up.

I had no idea what to expect on this trip other than what the brochure stated. I stepped on the tour bus with my bags in Utrecht, Holland, with all of the other strangers who had signed up for the Italy tour. When we arrived in Italy, we were assigned a tour guide and a group. Our tour guide was a Dutch boy named Arjen. I had no idea at the time that Arjen was going to become my best friend on this trip. On day one, we were given our tents and explained that we will bike to our destination, set up our tents, eat at the local restaurant, and sleep till the next day. To me it seemed easy enough. We were given maps and, tons of water, and we set out on our first biking day as a group. Soon the groups began to break apart and the slow people stayed behind while the faster bikers sped ahead. I stayed behind.

I honestly believed that I was going to be perfectly fine on this trip after biking in Holland all year long. But Italy has enormous mountains and Holland, on the other hand, is flat. The difference was soon noticeable. I thought I was going to die the first day!

The first bike route was thirty-four miles, followed by a day of rest. As we rode through the hills, I fought the pain in my legs, the soreness of my butt from the seat, the hunger pangs and dehydration. I suffered through the sun pounding down on me. But I would not be defeated. I made friends with a group of teenagers, and we teamed up and rode together. I survived day one of biking and arrived at the campground, set my tent up, ate, and passed out.

The next day we relaxed by the pool, and I decided I needed a new strategy if I was to survive the whole trip.

First problem I had was my seat was too hard and my inner thighs were bruised. I took my towel and wrapped it around my seat in hopes of a softer surface. I bought a large bottle of sunblock, four one-gallon waters, and a chord to attach them to my bike. I also packed snacks from the store. Day two I was better prepared and able to enjoy the beauty of Italy as I pedaled up the mountains and experienced breathtaking moment after breathtaking moment.

The sun shined down on the mountainside for miles and miles. The ground was a perfect rug of yellows and greens. I walked down the hill and touched the eight-foot-tall sunflowers, my childlike amazement of them forever etched into my brain. A puffy mess of clouds scattered across the blue horizon. The earth and the sky became one as I watched the sun drop behind the hills. Moments later, pinks and purples reflected all around me. I stood in the midst of the magnificent landscape. When I made it to the other side of the mountain, darkness set in and the rest of the world became black with flecks of light. All of the beauty that surrounded us was lost.

To this day I can close my eyes and see the field as if I am standing there. The town that we were biking toward lay just beyond the field, and it seemed so far away but the beauty powered me to continue. I felt an inner peace at this moment. I never imagined I'd be alone in Italy overlooking a field of sunflowers like I had never seen before. I couldn't have imagined such beauty even in my wildest dreams. I felt an inner strength of accomplishment as I biked the last few miles.

I had managed to bike a few more days before I decided that I just didn't want to bike anymore. Not that I couldn't do it—I was just sick of it. During the days off from biking, the group traveled to other areas of Italy, visiting the ruins, small towns, restaurants, museums, and other area of interest. The guide, Arjen, explored Italy in his van on those days—and when I learned about this, I became his best friend.

We put my bike in the back of his van and set off to see other areas not on the tour.

We traveled through Florence, San Gimignano, and Siena, walking in the streets and shopping in the local stores. I begged Arjen to take me to the Ponte Vecchio, the golden bridge in Florence. I honestly believed it was a golden bridge similar to the golden doors at the Florence Baptistery; however the bridge wasn't made of gold. The stores on the bridge *sold* only gold. Here I purchased a gold miniature Ponte Vecchio for my charm bracelet as a reminder of Italy.

At the end of the tour, I was supposed to get back on the tour bus for twenty hours and head back to Holland. But our tour marked Arjen's last one for the summer and he had to drive his van back to Holland. We decided to stick together, the both of us taking turns driving his van. I was glad for the chance to drive through Germany, though I'm still disappointed that we didn't have time to stop and do some memorable sightseeing or exploring. Arjen dropped me off at my doorstep in Holland, and we promised to keep in touch. We met up in Utrecht a few times for lunch and laughed at our adventures in Italy. I promised to write when I returned home.

I spent the fall preparing for my December 23rd flight home. I purchased clogs for everyone for the holidays and tried to figure out how to pack everything. My friends and host family threw me a going away party and, even though I couldn't wait to see my real family, I was going to miss the new life I had created. Leaving Europe after a year living abroad was heart-wrenching. I adored my new friends, and they had allowed me to be a part of their world. Edwin said he would come visit me in America, and I hoped that he would. My only concern was that Mom wouldn't want *some guy* coming home, no matter how nice he was. I understood her concerns and promised to come home alone. I hoped *everyone* would come and visit me, but I knew there was little chance of it.

I walked away from my European experience knowing I could do anything I set my mind to. I felt pride in having seen seven countries. I knew my new language skills wouldn't come in handy back home, but at least I now knew that I could study and learn. I was sure this would help my college career in some way. I said goodbye to the Netherlands, but I would never forget any part of this amazing experience and what it taught me.

I promised I would come back to visit and I kept my promise— three years later I returned.

Chapter 12

There is no place like home

I walked back into the Schipol airport and onto the plane heading back to America stronger and more mature than ever before. I was ready for the next stage of my life and prepared to go back to school and work toward straight A's. I was now a traveled teenager, and I felt the difference in my soul. The entire plane ride home I imagined what changes New Jersey may have undergone. I assumed everyone must have had as many fantastic experiences as I had during the year.

I was very excited when I saw my father waiting for me at baggage claim. He'd parked illegally so he rushed me and my two-hundred-pound bags off the carousel and into the car. When he asked me why the bags were so heavy I said, "Everyone I know will be getting a pair of clogs from the Netherlands!" He laughed.

I wrapped my arms around Dad's waist and hugged him. It felt as if it had been ten years, not just one. I'd missed our talks and laughter. I talked his ear off the entire ride home, and we compared the places each of us had been. Dad, also well traveled, loved telling me funny stories of his work trips, especially the one about a "Spotted Dick" dessert from England, which is some sort of pudding treat. Unfortunately, I didn't see anything like that when I traveled or I would have brought it home. We laughed and laughed as I shared my adventures and he shared some of his.

The drive home seemed longer than the hour it lasted. I was beyond excited to see everyone. I ran into the house, leaving the two bags of luggage in the car, screaming, "Mom, I'm home!" just like Desi does on *I Love Lucy*. I was first greeted by Mom's puppy, Shadow, who was as big as Mom had described in all of her letters to me. Shadow barked incessantly as if I were a stranger. She'd forgotten me. I pushed passed the crazy barking dog and hugged Mom. "How much did you miss me?" I asked.

Mom hugged me tightly and then responded with "Go clear out the car and take your bags to your bedroom. We can talk after you settle in." Ending the unusually okay hug I walked outside to grab my bags from the car. "Some things never change!" I announced. I walked back in, down the steps, missing my old room and looking forward to having space again. But as soon as I opened my door, a strange and unpleasant smell emerged and the faint feeling of wanting to throw up followed.

Apparently the entire time I was away in Europe no one had thought to even clean my room. It was one hundred percent the way that I'd left it a year ago. Plates of left over pasta lied rotten on my dresser, next to tea cups green with mold, and beer bottles left over from my going away party gave the room the smell of a frat house. I had written letters asking Mom to "Please straighten up my room so I don't have to do it when I come home." I also, in our letters, admitted to her that "yes, I know you didn't make the mess!"

I closed the door to my foul-smelling room and brought my stuff to the room that used to be Uncle Hanky's. I forced myself to stay cheerful despite my inability to move into my bedroom. I was home for eight minutes, so asking Mom, "Why wouldn't you clean my room at least once in a year?" would definitely start a war. I took the lesson she was trying to teach me and decided I wasn't going to give her the satisfaction of a reaction. Day one was not going to be spent fighting. Things were changed. We agreed to a better relationship in all of our letters, and I was committed to that now that I was back home. I longed for a relationship that was as good as the one we shared in our letters back and forth. Our communications were so positive while I was over there, and we had missed each other. *She said she missed me!* I wanted to prove to her that not only had she changed but I had also. I knew once I took school seriously and got a new job, Mom would be proud, and we could finally have a normal relationship.

Ignoring the smelly bedroom fiasco, I embarked on a two-hour discussion convincing Mom and Dad that I should move into Chad's old room. I didn't think this would bother Chad since he was in the Marines. Mom and Dad quickly filled me in on Chad's world, which Mom had *never* mentioned in her letters. Apparently Chad married Shelby, a friend from high school that he had been dating when I left. During the year I was away, they had a baby daughter and for their own reasons stopped talking to Mom and subsequently Dad too.

I had been home twenty minutes and I started to wish I wasn't. I understood why my parents wouldn't tell me this was happening and it didn't involve me so it was better left unsaid. It did strike a nerve, however, and I questioned if this explained all of the kind letters Mom had sent me. Was she nervous I would follow Chad's lead and write her off too? I truly didn't have time for, nor did I want to get involved in, a family feud that had nothing to do with me, and luckily Mom wasn't the type to get me involved. I decided not to call my brother yet. I was home for one day, and I didn't want to make Mom sad by choosing to reach out to my brother or to piss my brother off by assuring him that "Mom had changed since I was gone" and that she'd "written me letters every day." It just didn't seem like a strong enough argument. Instead I spent my time bonding with Shadow.

I took her outside, into the backyard, and smiled as I looked at the pool. I couldn't help thinking; *Mom must have loved using the pool this summer without us kids anywhere near her.* I stood outside with Shadow, reminiscing about how Uncle Hanky and Dad built the deck attached to the pool and all the years I spent swimming with my friends. It felt good to be back in familiar territory.

Back inside, I got on the phone and started making calls, inviting all of my old friends over to visit with me. I wanted to find out what I had missed over the past year. My friends, over the phone, filled me in, and what I learned during these moments was profound: In the year that I was away so much had changed for so many people, but none of it had affected me. I was too far away to be involved or helpful. One year can change so much, yet change nothing at all at the same time. I had truly missed everyone the first three months of my year away, but once I settled into my new home, I moved on from mostly everyone—except for those who wrote me regularly. Out of sight, out of mind is a truth I finally understood.

The most exciting news I received was that my childhood friend, Stephanie, had her baby girl, Savannah. Going to visit the new baby was my top priority. I do wish I could have been there for her, but at least I was home now.

I was home for two weeks before I enrolled at Burlington County College for the second time. If I could last a full year abroad, then I certainly could finish college with A's and B's. The first thing I had to do was talk to my academic advisor. I worried about my grades from the year before. My advisor had suggested that I retake any classes that had a D as a final grade. If I retook the class, I could then combine the GPA. I dreaded the thought of retaking a science class—and, even worse, that stupid organizational class.

The fact that I had to get an A or B in this class in order to fix my GPA infuriated me. Not to mention, I had to pay the college for three more credits for the same class. The professor smiled knowingly when I walked through his door for the second time. Apparently I was dreading retaking his class as much as he dreaded me taking it again. But, serious about acing the class this time, I followed the organizational rules from day one. The professor taught me how to create flow charts, write better class notes, and keep my folder one hundred percent in the order he asked for. In the end, I was happy I managed a B! I also ended the semester with A's in my other classes. Plus, I became friends with the organizational professor this time around.

I knew I needed to find a job again and friends told me waitressing was a way to make fast money. Fast money worked for me, so I tried it. I went to all the local restaurants and handed them my new resume with a year working abroad as an au pair in Amsterdam as my latest job. I was impressed with my own achievement and knew employers would be too. After a month home, I took a job as a server at

Prospectors Bar and Grille. I was working full-time and going to college full-time.

The first two weeks of server training were intense. We had to learn the new computer systems, the restaurant manager's expectations, what all the food looked like, and an alcoholic drink menu. Serving came easily to me, and I no problem talking to the clients, dealing with the other workers, and handling upper management and their constant schedule changes. I was also lucky enough to meet Alex, my soon-to-be boyfriend.

Alex came to work after I had been there two weeks. He had been on a vacation with his family or he would have been the one to train me. One night, two months into my job, he invited me to a party where the Prospector crowd hung out. We were inseparable following the party.

By month three of being a waitress/server, I wasn't sure it was the job for me. I learned pretty fast that people are hellishly rude. Yes, a ton of people are kind and sweet, but each night of work I faced at least one client who purposely tormented me. I couldn't believe that people could complain as much as some clients complained—or tipped as low as some people tipped. Worst were the ones who ate ninety-five percent of their food, then claimed that it was somehow unsatisfactory and asked to be reimbursed. This job made me realize not everyone is kind and that people can be horrible.

One night a large group came in and sat in my section. This group had me running back and forth more than any other had in the past four months. I delivered all of their orders dead-on correct, their drinks came out on time, and everything was perfect. At the end of the meal, they paid their bill and left it on the table. I grabbed the bill and knew with a glance that they left *no tip*. They'd wasted two hours of my life, taking up my entire section, and left no tip. At that moment I did something the wait staff is warned strictly *not* to do.

I marched straight up to the first man I could reach from that table and said, "There must be some mistake." The man looked at me confused and said, "Excuse me?" I repeated myself, saying, "There must be some kind of mistake because you forgot to leave a tip." He then said, "No. We don't tip."

And I lost it.

I explained to the client that I have to tip the bus-boys on the money I made (this was mandatory since the bus-boys did half of my job) and now I was losing money because his group didn't tip. He said, "That isn't my issue."

My manager walked over "What seems to be the problem here?" he asked.

I knew that I was in trouble. I heard my father's voice in my head, "Sometimes you need to just walk away, Danielle." I thought for a second, considering an answer of "nothing, sir" and walking away, keeping my job. But it was too late: I had broken a major rule and I broke it standing in the front of the restaurant next to the hostess and in front of other customers. Mortified and afraid I may get fired right then and there, I quit. I explained how this isn't the job for me and that kindness from strangers obviously doesn't apply to a waitress working her butt off. "I am not cut out for this kind of work." I stated holding back angry tears.

My manager didn't make me tip out on that bill at the end of the night. He tried to talk me into staying as long as I promised never to make a scene again. I honestly couldn't make that promise so, I left the restaurant business and decided waitressing was not for me—and never returned to the restaurant industry again. Instead, I became a very large tipper.

Luckily, it didn't take me long to start a new job at a day-care facility. I liked running an infant care daily, and my au pair experience helped me make more money than babysitting had. I found the coworkers and their constant complaints about the kids or the kids' parents to be the most difficult part of the job, but it was easy to ignore those issues for a paycheck, so I did.

The only thing I stayed connected to from my waitressing experience was Alex, my new boyfriend. He was a student at Stockton College and worked as a waiter to pay for school. He was also one of the top waiters. We started to hang out whenever we had free time between both of our jobs, college, and his college baseball schedule. We managed two nights a week in the beginning, which evolved into hanging out any chance we got soon enough.

Mom and I barely saw each other when I was home. Luckily, she was feeling better those days and Dad encouraged her to do something for herself. Her seizures seemed to be maintained and her depression wasn't noticeable to me. I bet it was my wish on the Black Madonna in Spain that healed her! *Or maybe having no kids in the home.*

I was surprised to learn that while I was in Europe she had taken up line dancing. She practiced the dances on VHS, then went to Prospectors, my former place of work, and danced all night. She was glad when I quit that job. She didn't want the two worlds colliding. However, when I turned twenty-one I went to Prospectors the dance club side and ran right into her. I was excited to see her, so I hugged her, yelling, "Hi Mom!" over the band. She pulled me outside and told me not to call her "Mom" in the bar. Apparently no one knew she had a child my age. She looked really young and having a twenty-one-year-old daughter cramped her style. The rest of the night she stayed with her friends and I stayed with mine. I found the entire situation seriously strange.

Mom wasn't drinking because drinking wasn't her thing, but she was definitely dancing straight through to the last song of the night. When I got home I told Dad how she reacted, and he just laughed. He then informed me that maybe I shouldn't go there, that maybe I should just let that be her place. Dad was just happy Mom spent less time complaining and more time making new friends. For years she was closed up in the house and now, without her children around, she was creating her new world. I promised I would leave that bar to her. Besides, line dancing was her strong suit and I just looked like a mess trying.

Between Mom going dancing, and my busy schedule—going to school, working, and trying to see Alex—we became two passing ships. My trip to Europe seemed to have fixed my relationship with her. We went from fighting all the time to getting closer and promising a happier future via letters to having no time to for each other now that I was back. Not fighting was better than fighting, so I accepted our new relationship and considered it a positive.

School, work, and Alex became my life for the next year and a half. I graduated from community college with straight A's and B's, and I would transfer into Stockton College to major in advertising in the fall of 1999. Everything was coming together, and I was living my dreams!

Chapter 13
Life is about change

The summer of 1999, my relationship with Alex started to get rocky. He had graduated from Stockton and landed a job working with his sister, at an importing and exporting firm. Suddenly there was less time to see each other, and our relationship went from solid to unsteady.

After his graduation, he had complete freedom, but I was still tied to college. And that caused many arguments. Graduating from community college was just a first step for me. Starting Stockton College was the next step and it would be two more years before I'd be able to show off my bachelor's degree next to my associate's. My life was school, and Alex's life was about going out after work and meeting strangers who became his new friends. Our relationship had changed, and one day we mutually decided to take a break and go our own separate ways. A few weeks after our breakup, we reconciled.

We were having a rough patch in our relationship and I started to feel nauseous and tired all the time. The doctors suggested I rule out pregnancy—I did not think I could be pregnant, but I bought a pregnancy test anyway. With my girlfriend Cindy at my side, I waited for the results for three anxious minutes. I mentally prepared for either situation. I was going to be okay no matter what.

I was pregnant.

I was sick to my stomach when I realized what this meant. I always planned to be a mom one day, but the timing and situation were slightly off of my original plan. I drove home from Cindy's contemplating how to tell my Dad, my unstable relationship, and dreading telling Mom.

I told Dad first, pulling him outside. "We need to talk," I said. Dad came outside willingly and stared at me. "Well?"

I swallowed hard and announced, "I'm pregnant."

I expected my father to freak out, yell at me, lecture me— or something. Instead he looked at me and said, "You'll need to get medical insurance." *What?*

Just like that he walked inside the house. I sat outside alone for a moment thinking, *that was way too bizarre.* Mom would be a ton worse. I walked up the stairs to her bedroom, sat next to her on the bed, and said, "Can we talk?" I didn't want to beat around the bush even though I was prepared for the worst, so before I could even say the words Mom said, "What? Are you pregnant?" I hated her uncanny ability to do that, "Yes Mom, I'm pregnant."

She stared at me for a moment, smirked, and then said, "I'm surprised it didn't happen sooner!" My first instinct was to react to her comment... *didn't happen sooner?* I held my tongue on this one, finally heading Dad's constant statement "Just learn to shut your mouth, Danielle."

I planned to take the weekend to wrap my brain around what was happening before I contacted Alex. He might not agree with my decision to have the baby, and he might try to persuade me his way, so I wanted to be clear that I made my choice with the understanding of how a baby would affect *my* future first. I figured if Alex wanted out I'd be fine alone. Dad said he would help me until I finished college and Mom, rolling her eyes, agreed.

Unfortunately for me, Cindy, the girlfriend who stood by me when I took the pregnancy test, had taken the liberty of calling Alex and letting him know before I was ready to tell him. I was infuriated. Instead of me calling him after I'd had time to think, he called me to "discuss my situation." The conversation didn't go well. Alex and I weren't staying together, he had a new girlfriend already, I had just finished two years of college out of four, and I was pregnant.

A few days passed during which Alex expressed his opinions, his family expressed theirs, and I felt completely alone. Alex's parents were openly livid. Alex had just gotten his life on track by finishing college and landing a good job, and I now was going to impede that forward-moving process. From their perspective, I had "trapped" their son, even though to me it seemed like he wasn't the only one in this situation, so it was a joint trap. The whole "trapped" thing annoyed me. *Did they not realize that he must have been there too? Why wasn't anyone holding him accountable? We both weren't ready for a baby but, the baby was obviously ready for us.*

Annoyed, I wrote everybody off and told them all I could do it alone—meaning with my family's help. I moved forward, feeling a sense of calm and peace with my situation— and yet somehow feeling completely lost. Mom was oddly quiet and left me to deal with my situation.

In need of guidance, I sought solace in the local church called Saint Mary's of the Lakes. I opened the church's heavy outside doors, walked through the second set of doors, and entered a deadening silence. The church was completely empty. Only one light, the main one that hung from the center of the building over the top of the altar was lit. At first I worried that I may be trespassing. I was a stranger in this church. I hoped someone would come out and greet me, but no one came. I walked up the aisle, toward the altar, and sat in a pew closer to the light. I began trying to picture the life I wanted, asking the universe for a positive start for my pregnancy. I sat still, praying that everything would turn out perfect, and then I started sobbing.

The sobbing filled the silence of the church, which only made me sob louder. Then someone's hand touched my shoulder, and I startled. A priest stared down at me. I jumped up, grabbed my backpack and apologized for trespassing. He smiled at me and asked if he could sit. I spent the next thirty minutes talking to a man I didn't know; never saw before in my life. He listened to me and then explained, "This is your journey."

147

I nodded in agreement, thinking of the baby who was now going to depend on me. He then said with certainty, "You're going to achieve your dreams; it just may take a bit longer."

I held onto those words. In one moment, he helped me believe I would be fine raising my child as a young single mother. He gave me advice on how to continue to pursue my goals of college and still be a good mom. He didn't preach about God or the Bible. He helped me stop the fear of failure from ruining my goals.

This priest, a stranger, helped me in a way that no friend could have. I felt better, like my life was starting again. I left the church, drove home, and walked back in the house. I thought about waking my atheist Dad to tell him "everything is going to be okay, Dad. Don't worry. The *priest* at the church spoke with me and now I feel better." I could just imagine how that conversation would go. Yesterday I told him I was pregnant and today I would tell him I was religious. I decided to avoid this scenario and chuckled as I walked down the steps to my bedroom, feeling some relief.

I was able to deal with my circumstances after that day.

I went through my first semester of Stockton not noticeably pregnant. But from September to December I started to get bigger and bigger. Every time I looked in the mirror, I noticed the change in my stomach. I squeezed myself into my normal jeans and sweaters for as long as I could. I tried to keep my pregnancy hidden until I finished the semester. Not many people in school knew I was pregnant.

By December, though, I was showing enough for friends or people who pay attention to notice the baby bump. Whenever I ran into friends, they would rub my baby belly, tell me how cute I looked, or once in a while I'd get a surprised, "Are you pregnant?" Despite being pregnant, I was determined to be a real college student. I spent time in front of the mirror, telling myself, "I am young and pregnant; however, I am the same as everyone else." But I didn't really believe it. I felt uncomfortable being pregnant in college. I knew that I was probably the only girl in my classes who was.

One night my new college friend Beth invited me to go to a local restaurant bar in Pomona. I stayed after school and hung out in the library until she finished her classes, and then I met her at the bar. She invited a few friends and she knew many of the students who were hanging out. I didn't know anyone. The fact that I transferred as a junior left me at a disadvantage when it came to college friends.

Beth and I ordered food and began to talk. She was a sweet girl who didn't care that I was pregnant, though I asked her to keep it between us. I was worried that I would be alienated if anyone knew. The later it became that night, the more of Beth's friends showed up. I stayed in the booth, smiled, and said hello to the strangers.

At one point, a brown-haired, blue-eyed guy named Rich joined our table. Everyone ordered drinks and I ordered a virgin pina colada, explaining that I had an hour drive home and would be leaving soon. Immediately after drinking the pina colada, I felt ill. I excused myself from the table and headed into the bathroom. I went into the stall and sat down on the closed toilet seat. Everything around me became fuzzy and a moment later I blacked out. The next thing I knew, Beth was knocking on the door to see if everything was okay. I was so embarrassed that this had happened and so confused as to what was going on. The only thing both Beth and I could think of was that the virgin drink actually contained alcohol. After I was feeling better, we asked the bartender, and he assured us it was a virgin drink.

I was so humiliated when we walked out of the bathroom. Rich was still there and he asked, "What happened? Are you okay? What's wrong?" I didn't want to explain that I was pregnant, so I said, "I'm not sure. I'm just not feeling very well."

The embarrassment was overwhelming so I left shortly after. The entire drive home I considered what could have happened. I was nervous that whatever it was could affect my baby.

I called my obstetrician the next morning. He believed that my body couldn't handle the large amount of sugar from the pina colada, and he wanted me tested for gestational diabetes. I went to the lab the following week after fasting for twenty-four hours and had my glucose levels tested. Five minutes after I took the test, I fainted again and the lab techs stared at me in confusion. Apparently too much sugar all at once caused me to faint. For the rest of the pregnancy, I stayed away from juices, candy, and cakes. It was torture, but I was determined to never faint. Twice was humiliating enough and next time I may not be so lucky. I mean what if I had hit my head on the toilet and passed out on a dirty bathroom floor?

A few days after my fainting incident, Beth's friend Rich called me to see how I was. To my surprise, he also wanted to know if I wanted to hang out again sometime. He spoke freely about college, his parents, and his punk rock music. I listened to him, all the while dreading when he finished because then I would have to explain to him that I was pregnant. One thing I learned during this time was that it was easiest just to blurt these things out and see who runs from you the quickest. The moment came: He stopped telling me about his awesome life and asked, "What about you? What's your deal?"

I said, "I'm pregnant and the baby is due in February." I expected him to either hang up or say something in shock. Strangely enough he said, "I don't care about that."

He didn't care? Shouldn't he care? He proved he was serious, and he kept asking if I would just say yes to going out with him. I said, louder this time, "I am six months pregnant. Do you really want to date a pregnant college student?"

Again he said he didn't care. I couldn't have predicted any of this if I tried.

So after some more persuading on his part, I said yes. He was very sweet and sympathetic about my pregnancy. We started dating regularly, and after a couple of weeks he wanted to introduce me to his entire family.

Before this time, I had never had an issue meeting new people. I am not shy, but meeting his parents at seven months pregnant traumatized me. I couldn't help but consider the fact that I don't think I would want my son dating a pregnant girl at twenty-two years old. He was about to graduate college and get his life together, and I was pregnant. It wasn't his kid, and yet he wanted to date me. Everyone in his family oddly enough accepted the situation and that was it. Rich and I were officially together.

Mom was excited that Rich came into the picture. Her hope was that I would marry him and he would take care of the baby and me. She was not crazy about the idea of me and my infant permanently residing in her home.

Tensions between Mom and I rose once again, especially when Mom started to suffer pains in her neck. I was trying to survive college as a pregnant junior, and she was trying not to have surgery. And neither of us was holding back. I felt that my dream of a happy family was diminishing, and Mom's frustration was running amuck. She missed dancing at Prospectors and having Dad to herself, and when I had my baby; it was just going to get worse.

With one and a half years left of school, I had no intention of moving out. I wanted to get established first, and Dad kept telling me "Mom will be fine once the baby comes." He didn't want us to leave as soon as the baby came. This became their fight. I stayed busy and tried to not say anything that would set Mom off.

I focused on my new life and making a new start. Alex and I were avoiding each other at all costs, which lowered the tension between us. I was about to finish my first semester at Stockton and everything was coming together perfect enough.

One night in December, I was driving Mom's old truck home from the Red Lion Diner. I had just had dinner with an old friend and was on my way home. Driving down Route 206, a huge buck ran in front of my truck. I swerved in an effort not to hit him, but I wasn't lucky enough and hit the buck on his back end with the front end of my truck.

Smoke filled the air the moment the air bag busted open and smacked into my seven months pregnant body. I parked the truck, dazed and confused, and opened the door. I walked around the truck to assess the deer and the damage. There was no blood, no fur, nothing. The buck was gone. He must have run back into the woods, uninjured. A moment later, the police from the station across the way showed up. I felt dumb explaining that I'd hit a buck.

"I know the buck isn't here," I said, "but look at the damage. I hit a buck."

The police officer asked me if I needed an ambulance. I was sure I didn't; however, it dawned on me that I should go to the hospital to make sure my baby was okay. On the drive home, I worried about telling Dad that I had crashed another one of his vehicles. I calmed down and did my best to explain what happened. Dad agreed that I should visit the hospital, and by the time we arrived there, severe pains rattled my chest. I felt like someone was stabbing me. Being pregnant made it difficult for doctors to assess the damage. They couldn't X-ray the area because it could hurt the baby. Meanwhile, the pain grew worse.

Rich showed up hours later after they did an ultrasound. The doctors concluded that I must have broken a rib. I didn't remember hitting the steering wheel, but apparently the pain I was having indicated this type of injury. Then they said that my *son* was in perfect health. Son? Dad and Rich joined me in my excitement, and I couldn't wait to call Mom to tell her the news. She was praying for a boy and now her wish had come true.

The doctor wrapped my ribs tightly and the pain stopped. The doctor wished me luck being pregnant with a broken rib, and I went home. The truck had taken a serious hit and the next day it was in the shop for repairs.

I learned to deal with the rib pain, but it was at its worst when I sat for classes. I was relieved when I finally finished the college semester in late December with a 3.5 grade point average. I then suspended my schooling because my baby was due in February. I figured if I took one semester off and went back in the fall everything would work out fine.

In January 2000, my girlfriend who had told Alex I was pregnant, Cindy, threw my baby shower at my home. Mom wasn't up for organizing a shower so Cindy and my aunts ran the show. Dad's sisters Aunt Barb and Aunt Terry helped make the shower perfect. It was a beautiful day and they did a great job getting it all together. My friendship with Cindy had floundered since she told Alex I was pregnant, but I forgave her, knowing she honestly had thought it was the right thing to do. She agreed to not meddle in that business again. She invited all of my friends and family to the shower. The support was uplifting. I mingled with my guests, taking pictures with everyone. My child hood friends, the twins, Lauren, Samantha, and Tina all were there.

I loved feeling supported and excited about my new baby boy. Throughout the shower, I fought back the tears, and hid my concern as to whether or not I could be a good mom from everyone. But I'd held it together, and now everything was going to be okay.

At the end of the gift opening, Cindy handed me a pile of presents from Alex's family. The room went silent, and everyone stared at me. I wasn't sure what to do. My first thought was, *"No, I am not opening these gifts. What the hell?"*

I couldn't understand, given the circumstances, why Cindy thought this was a good idea at this exact moment. Alex and I were not speaking, and she snuck these gifts in—*to my shower.* The feelings of fear, that now his family wanted to be involved, flooded me. I glared at her, wondering why she would do it. But in the end, I sucked up the pain and betrayal I felt, opened the gifts, and placed them to the side. No one said anything to me about those gifts because the look on my face must have said it all.

I fought through the melancholy I was feeling and found a way to enjoy the rest of the shower. I said goodbye to the last guest at around six o'clock after thanking everyone for coming and thanking Cindy for making it happen. Mom and Dad retreated to their room for the night, and I went into the living room to organize my son's gifts.

At one point, as I sat in the middle of these gifts, my heart began to ache because I had to do it alone, without the father of my child. I looked at the gifts from his family and felt outrage. I couldn't understand why Cindy thought it was a good idea to bring them to the party. Whose side was she really on? I wanted her to take a side, and it wasn't supposed to be Alex's. I didn't want anyone around who was on both sides. Alex and I weren't friends, so I just ignored the situation.

I sat for over an hour, folding the cute clothes, organizing the diapers, putting together the bouncy chair—and then I made a decision. I thought, "Maybe I'll stop feeling so sad if we just could have peace." I decided to call Alex, to offer an olive branch.

I let him know that I had the shower and maybe he should come over to see what everyone gave the baby. I also let him know that I wanted the war to end. I wasn't prepared for his response, which went something like, "I'm sorry I can't talk to you. I'm with my girlfriend." At that, my brain almost exploded in pure never felt before anger. I wanted to lash out, to throw every gift across the room. I restrained myself from driving over to Alex's and beating him and his girlfriend up. I saw rage. Then quickly I felt sadness.

I hung up the phone, sorry that I'd been stupid enough to put myself out there. I had shown a moment of vulnerability, and he squashed me. I stared at all of the gifts and took the ones that Cindy brought from his family and boxed them all up. I didn't want anything from his family, or from him, and I became even more annoyed that she brought those gifts to my house. I decided at that moment that Alex and I would never be friends.

Two weeks before our son, Ryan (named after my childhood friend who passed away), was due to be born, Alex e-mailed me. He asked to be called when the baby was born so he could be there. I had decided that I didn't under any condition want him and his girlfriend waiting at the hospital as I gave birth. I'd spent the entire pregnancy dealing with this situation without him—and now I was bitter. He was welcome the next day. Could I have a *moment* of peace, please?

Rich remained supportive of my schooling as I finished my semester at Stockton. I often wondered, *what is wrong with this guy?* The further along I got in my pregnancy, the more I wondered. We hung out all the time. He either came to my house to hang out, or I ventured into his crazy life of punk rock shows, karate tournaments, and his friends' parties. Everyone became used to the fact that I was pregnant, and even his friends were excited for the baby to arrive. Rich was extremely supportive and I tried to just be a normal college student, minus the drinking or drugs.

Rich was so entangled in my world that I recruited him as my Lamaze coach. He went to the Lamaze classes with me without reluctance. I was shocked that he didn't complain. We were the couple in the corner laughing hysterically at the breathing exercises. We didn't explain to strangers that the baby wasn't his child. We just let that go. It was too much to try to explain anyway.

As my due date neared, I was physically uncomfortable. It was the first time the pregnancy disrupted my life. I couldn't sleep anymore. Lying on my stomach wasn't possible because I was built like a huge basketball. I weighed one hundred and fifty pounds up from my normal one hundred and twelve. The weight was all stomach, and my broken rib was killing me. The doctor said, "Until the baby is born, your rib doesn't have a chance to heal. Once he is born, you will feel much better." I couldn't wait for this to be true.

February 24, 2000, I went into labor. Thank goodness Rich was around to drive me to the hospital. Mom had just had a fusion surgery on her neck, and Dad had to be home to take care of her. I called my friends, including Cindy, excited to let them know I was going to the hospital. I wasn't even halfway there when I got a phone call I didn't expect. It was Alex. He "heard" I may be in labor and wanted to make sure I let him know what was happening. I knew right away who had called him and, as I headed to what should have been the best moment of my life, I was ready to murder her. Cindy was supposed to be a part of the delivery, but the first choice she made before I even got to the hospital was to call Alex to let him know. The betrayal I felt was unbearable.

So there I was, driving to the hospital to give birth to my son while, arguing with a woman who thought she could hijack my moment. I couldn't understand why she couldn't wait for me to call Alex after the baby was born. He wasn't going to be in the delivery room anyway— that had already been agreed upon. I was livid that Cindy thought he deserved to know. I couldn't imagine why she thought she had a right to meddle in my decisions.

Shortly after twelve in the afternoon on February 24th, I was in the hospital bed waiting for the doctor to see how dilated I was. My contractions, in full swing, made it difficult to talk to anyone. My friend Stephanie showed up around two, after finding someone to watch her daughter, Savannah. She was in charge of relieving Rich, so he could leave the room, eat, and rest. I lay in the bed with contractions hour after hour, wishing I could take something for the pain, but the doctors were waiting for me to dilate and for my water to break before anything else could happen. The doctors wouldn't send me home because I was past my due date; however, they weren't helping me understand what was happening. Stephanie kept asking the nurses to do something and poor Rich was just stuck in the middle of all of the excitement. My obstetrician was on vacation, so the doctors working with me were strangers. Nothing was going the way it was supposed to go.

Seven in the morning on February 25th a new doctor came in and checked my vitals and the baby's. My baby was distressed, and I still wasn't dilating. He wanted to come out, and my body wasn't responding the way it needed to. Immediately she ordered Pitocin. I did not know what Pitocin was and I was worried. Without explanation the nurse injected the medicine while I kept asking, "What's happening? Is something wrong? Why isn't the baby coming? Why is he distressed?"

No one offered reassurance. Stephanie marched out to the nurse's station and demanded answers. By the time she got any, thirty minutes later, I was in the worst pain I had ever felt. The doctors informed me that until I became seven centimeters dilated, they couldn't give me the epidural because it would stop the labor and I needed to get him out. They also explained that if the Pitocin didn't work, I would be having an emergency C-section. I was not prepared for any of this. I lay in the hospital bed from seven thirty in the morning until twelve in the afternoon waiting for them to stop the pain. No one had informed me that any of this was a possibility.

For the first time during the delivery, I wished Mom was with me. She had a C-section and could help me through this. She knew what to do. I couldn't talk Mom into being in the delivery room even though I had tried. First, she hated blood and gore (except on horror flicks), and second she had her neck fusion and couldn't sit or stand for long periods of time. I cried for Mom even though I knew she couldn't come to my rescue. I was on my own with my friends.

Steph explained that I wasn't dilating on my own and my water wasn't breaking even though I was in labor. This is what caused the baby distress. The doctor broke my water with a tool, and then we waited until I dilated to seven centimeters. Luckily for me, the anesthesiologist was ready the second I reached seven. As soon as they gave me the epidural I could talk again and laugh with Steph, Rich, and Tina (my childhood friend), who showed up to relieve poor Rich and Steph. It was miraculous how effective the epidural was. One minute I was rolling around in agony and the next I was fine again, wishing I could eat something other than ice chips.

Tina was having a difficult time with my delivery. She was six months pregnant with her baby girl and the experience was making her sick. So Steph and Rich stayed in the room for the actual delivery, and they were the first to meet my baby boy.

At 2:07 p.m., I celebrated the first most amazing thing that would ever happen to me. After they cleaned him off, the nurse handed me my beautiful baby. He opened his already sky blue eyes and I said, "Hi, buddy!"

Once we were settled in the hospital room, I invited everyone to see the baby. Friend after friend visited, though I was exhausted from the delivery. Even Uncle George came and brought me bagels. Excitement filled me knowing that Ryan was going to be loved by everyone that ever loved me. I was relieved when it was just me and him alone. I loved this baby the second I met him. I wasn't scared to be a mother anymore.

Another nurse came in carrying the birth certificate that I had to sign. It was important that I sign it before Alex came up, so we could hand it into the registrar. I wrote *Ryan Joseph* proudly on the paper and then waited for the nurse to pick up the paper. She walked in and said, "This is the fifth Ryan this week, must be a popular name."

"Wait," I told her. "Can I have that back, please?" I then stared at the piece of paper and then at my son. I didn't want my son to be the fifth Ryan that week. I wanted him to have an original name. My biggest thought was, *Ryan wasn't popular and now out of nowhere it is. What is happening?*

Rich came back to the hospital to visit the baby, and I explained my naming dilemma. We tossed around names, going back and forth. Finally Rich said, "What about Nolan Ryan?" I knew even Alex, who once aspired to be a professional baseball player, couldn't argue with a great name like that. I took the birth certificate and rewrote his name. Nolan Joseph-Ryan.

All along I thought he would be Ryan, so when people came to visit, they were confused. Even Alex looked dismayed when he showed up at the hospital to see his son. I hadn't informed him beforehand that I had selected a different name. Honestly, it all happened so fast there was no time. And secretly I wished that I was a fly on the wall, the moment he signed the birth certificate and saw Ryan's new name, Nolan.

The first few months became yet another war with Alex, this time over the custody of our son. He wanted to know when he could take him, and I never wanted him to take him. I was still angry at how everything went down, and at twenty-two years old, I didn't handle it well. By the time Nolan was three weeks old, we were in court battling custody issues. I didn't have a lawyer, but Alex did. I didn't think I needed one, but once I saw his, fear set in. My father came with me to all of my court dates. I have to admit this was not my finest moment and I was completely selfish; however, I did what I had to do to keep what I wanted. I truly didn't think that overnight visitation when Nolan was an infant was a good idea. Nor did I think I should be forced to part from my newborn after the past nine months of carrying him.

On this particular day my sister, Jenny, sat in the car with my baby, because I was nursing and all I wanted to do was keep my son close to me. I sat in the courtroom with my dad as my support, staring at Alex and his lawyer across the room. I was scared to death that they were going to take Nolan. The moment the judge asked me if I had anything to say, I stood up and told the entire courtroom something quite shocking: "I don't believe that Alex is the father, and I would like a paternity test." I announced.

My dad didn't see this coming and gave me a "We will talk in the car!" look.

I knew this approach would at least buy me more time. Alex and his lawyer looked beyond shocked. I looked over at Alex and saw sheer, one hundred percent anger. I was holding my breath to see what could possibly happen next. The judge ordered the paternity test, charging me half the fee, and gave Alex visitation at my home with the baby. I was glad that this would stop his stupid girlfriend from seeing my baby for the time being.

The first visitation was, in a word, *awkward*. Alex and I both acted as though we weren't enemies, and he was great with Nolan. I wanted to stop hating him, but I just couldn't. I was holding onto everything that had happened and was still deeply angry.

All of the visitations went fine short of Alex feeling uncomfortable about having to be in my home with his baby while waiting for a paternity test to come back. I remained uneasy wondering what visitation the court would give him once the test came back positive. I was lucky this strategy had bought me extra time with my son. The unbearable thought of every other weekend away from Nolan ripped my heart out. During the visitations, I could see that Alex truly wanted to be Nolan's dad. I started to feel bad that I was torturing him and wished everything didn't happen the way it had happened—but I was ruled by anger and still going to fight for what I wanted.

Rich was great about the visitations, and he didn't have any issues with Nolan's dad coming to see him. Our relationship was great; I would see him two or three times a week, depending on his work and his intense second-degree black belt karate schedule. Outside of the court stuff, things were coming together. I even brought Nolan to Alex's sister's house on Easter when he was two months old so Alex's family could spend time with him. I left Nolan with Alex for three hours.

When the three hours were up, I went back to get Nolan and Alex came outside with our boy. The next moment, Alex's girlfriend of almost a year came out to introduce herself. I have no idea why, but I became infuriated with the thought that she assumed I wanted to say hello to her. I blame what happened next on hormones, because I have never been so rude in my life. I couldn't help but judge her, and I was still upset about Alex not taking a few moments to talk to me after the baby shower. The words, "I'm with my girlfriend right now and can't talk," flooded me—I was livid.

His girlfriend was heavier than me, even though I just had a baby, and she had bleach blonde hair, so I turned to Alex and declared, "You picked Miss Piggy over me that day?" At this moment I realized I was jealous that they were going to try to pretend to be my son's family and play house.

Then I marched away with my son, buckled him into his car seat, and drove away. I was actually proud of myself for being so witty and smiled at the fact that they were probably having a fight because he didn't stick up for her.

Anger isn't an emotion I am good at maintaining, so once the court stuff ended, Alex and I got along fine. The paternity test proved he was the dad, of course. The court established the rules of Alex's child support and visitation—three days a week, for three hours each day. We worked together to care for Nolan and when the baby was two years old, Alex's custody broadened to every other weekend and Wednesdays. By the time Nolan was eight, we shared custody fifty-fifty. The fighting had ended by the time our son was eight months old. All was well and got even better when Alex broke up with his girlfriend and started dating his present wife, Lila.

Rich and I dated for the first two years of Nolan's life. His mom became the saving grace I desperately needed. You see, my mom was not going to watch Nolan unless I was showering or doing something else in the home. She felt that she and my father had done enough just by allowing me to live in their house. Dad sometimes watched Nolan, but he was at work during the day so I had to figure out another game plan in order to finish college.

I'm so lucky Rich's mom, Mrs. H, watched Nolan during the day while I attended school. She wanted to make sure I had the chance to graduate from college. I drove to her house, dropped the baby off, and then drove twenty minutes to school. She loved Nolan as much as a blood-related grandmother would. On the days she couldn't watch him, my girlfriend Jackie, who had two children of her own, helped me out. Nolan cried more often than not when we weren't together. I felt bad for everyone who babysat him. The only time he wasn't crying was when Alex, Dad, or I was nearby.

Having a six-month-old and commuting to college was the biggest challenge I ever faced. I stopped pursuing advertising, because my preceptor advised me to. "Advertising is too time-consuming when you have a baby," he said. "Maybe you should go into education." I agreed, so I switched over to historical studies and education, and began my new college career in these areas. It was going to add one extra year, but I would graduate with two bachelor degrees in two different areas. The professors understood my situation and offered support when I needed it. I often lay in bed at night studying with Nolan sleeping next to me. As he got older I would put him on the floor of his bedroom and let him play while I wrote notes from my schoolbooks. Sleeping was not an option the first two years of baby and college, and I accepted that.

I remained in my parents' home, despite Mom's snide comments of how this wasn't how it was supposed to go down, and I remained grateful that I had shelter and could finish college. Mom liked to say, "You'd be making money if you would have listened and became a hairdresser." There were moments I had to agree, but nonetheless I pursued my degree. Dad loved having Nolan around and secretly, despite her complaints, I knew Mom had a soft spot for her grandson too.

One day, I was forced to bring my son to school. I kept him in his stroller next to me because Rich's mom had an emergency and couldn't watch him. In this way, I finally showed the people in my college world that I was a mom. Another girl in the class, Robin, also was a young mom and we instantly connected. I feel so lucky to have found her, and we have been friends ever since. After that day, we planned play dates for her daughter, Taylor, and Nolan, and we discussed the difficulty of surviving college, maintaining our grades, and being young moms. She was married, but that didn't seem to make her situation any easier. I was just glad to have a new friend who understood my life.

Everything was going well. I was doing great in college. I saw the twins all the time and Steph's daughter, Savannah, loved Nolan. My relationship with Alex and his family had evolved into something manageable, and my boyfriend was great. I was on target to become a teacher and take care of my amazing son.

I floated on this cloud of happiness until one day Rich came over to talk about going to Florida for six months to train in Karate. He wanted me to come, but I couldn't. I wanted him to stay, but he wouldn't. We hit a wall—and I was devastated. The feeling of abandonment was overwhelming.

I had yet to recover from my relationship issues with Alex, and now I was losing another guy I had spent over two years with. I had thought that since he was there with me and Nolan through so much, that we were going to be together forever. We never discussed the next step. I guess that was my own dream and not his. Looking back, I should have been happy with his decision to go to Florida and to grow as a person; however, I was twenty-four and I felt like Nolan and I were being abandoned again. I wouldn't wait for him to come back in six months, so Rich and I broke up cordially and I focused on my baby while finishing school.

Since Rich and I remained friends through the breakup, his mom continued to watch Nolan for me, and I was grateful. She truly helped me raise Nolan the first two years. She guided me as a parent and sympathized with me for being so young. She always listened to my troubles and tried to help. If it weren't for her those first two years, I wouldn't have been able to finish college.

The days that I left my home in Tabernacle to drive the hour to drop Nolan off were taxing. I would beg Mom to help once in a while, but this just angered her. When I would ask for help she would say "I didn't have a baby, Danielle, you did." I understood that Nolan was my son. What I couldn't understand is why she was so against helping—almost always. Nolan would have it easier if he didn't have to endure the commutes, but we did what we had to. I kept swearing to the universe that I would be a totally different mom to my child than my own mother was to me.

My close friend Jackie also assisted in saving my life. She would take Nolan so that I could study, take my one-hour classes and on the days Mrs.H was busy she kept Nolan for me. Poor Jackie dealt with crying the entire time I was away and still she never abandoned helping me to finish college.

I was exhausted from driving to drop Nolan off, then driving to the college, then attending my classes, and then driving back to get Nolan and returning home by eight at night. Each night when we got home, I grabbed Nolan's food from the kitchen, brought him into my bedroom, and sat him in his seat to eat as I started my homework. I broke down some times from the exhaustion, and once in a while begged Mom, "Can't you please just help me a little?" She was teaching me a "lesson of responsibility" she would say. I felt she was teaching me what "no support" looks like, and that pissed me off. The more tired I became, the more I worked to get straight A's with a baby, the more she annoyed me. Dad just answered my complaints of Mom with, "You know your mother."

Shortly after Rich left for Florida, Dad came home one day and needed to talk to all of us. Chad and Mom made up finally after three years of ignoring each other, and Dad had Chad come over. He sat all three of us down. I hated sit-down conversations with the family because it meant someone either died, was dying, or something was about to get taken away. I hoped this time wasn't any of that. "I'm having a minor surgery tomorrow," Dad started.

"What? What kind of surgery?" I said, wondering why we were only finding out now.

"They are going to put a simple stent in to help me breathe," he said.

"Where is the stent going?"

"My heart," he answered.

Mom knew what was happening so she wasn't shocked like Chad and I were. Chad asked several questions, and Dad answered them calmly and assured us that he was going to be fine, and that it was "all routine."

Dad was having surgery on his heart the next day. The next day! What the heck? I felt my chest closing up and couldn't breathe. Dad was the one in perfect health. He never had any issues. *Mom* was our sick family member.

The next day, Dad went to the hospital as planned, and Chad and I stayed with Mom. With twenty-four hours notice, my sister Joanne flew in and met us at the hospital. Aunt Barb was on her way from the Poconos. Nolan stayed overnight at Alex's. The surgery was supposed to take an hour. Two hours later the doctor walked out. He apologized for not talking to us sooner; however, they were still in surgery and there had been some complications. The moment I heard *complications* I could feel my heart thumping in my chest and a knot formed in my throat. I listened, taking cues from Mom and Chad. We all sat back down in the hospital chairs in silence, waiting for Dad's return.

Hours later the doctor came out again. He explained that when they went into Dad's vein to put in a stent they found many more clogged arteries. They began open-heart surgery. He had a triple bypass. I couldn't believe what I was hearing. A routine procedure had just become heart surgery.

"Don't be shocked by how he looks," the doctor said.

I had no idea what that might mean. My heart was breaking as the doctor continued to speak. I vaguely remember what he was saying. After he finally walked away, Mom turned to me and my sister, and with complete authority, told us that "when Dad comes out, we would not be allowed to see him."

Aunt Barb agreed and then the two of them sat there as if the matter where closed. I freaked out first. "Who do you think you are? You can't keep me from my father. I am the next of kin!" I started to shout and then my sister, Joanne, who flew all the way from Missouri, chimed in too.

To this day I have no clue what those two were thinking, but my sister Joanne almost lost it on them both. "I will see my dad," she declared. The nurse came out, and Mom and Aunt Barb went to see Dad first. We waited for them to return. When time seemed to be enough, Joanne asked the nurse at the nursing station when we could go in. But Mom had told the nurse's "not to let us in." I laughed at the nurse and said, "What? What did you just say?"

"I'm sorry, wife's orders," she told me.

I wanted to scream. Right there in the middle of the hospital. I wanted to scream so loud that my father would wake up and hear me. Mom has lost her mind, and Aunt Barb followed her crazy. I hated both of those woman and their selfish nature toward *my* father. I am his daughter and like it or not, so were Jenny and Joanne. My face turned red as I held in my anger.

I looked at Joanne, and she looked at me, both of us rattled in disbelief. Dad needed his daughters and we were being closed out. I refused to accept the nurse's "wife's orders."

Irate, I marched with Joanne in tow, straight into the room. We moved both my mom and aunt out of the way, and I hugged my father's head while Joanne held his hand. He was still groggy from the pain medicine when I whispered in his ear "Can you believe those crazies weren't going to let me in? They'll never understand our bond!" I hugged him, crying.

"I just ate a bad clam," he said.

We both laughed and then he cried in pain from where they'd cracked his chest open.

For the next four months, I told Nolan he couldn't climb on his grandfather because he had surgery for "eating a bad clam."

I was relieved when things were back to normal and Dad pretty much went back to being himself again. I started to distance myself again from Mom as Dad recovered. Her extreme outlook on how Dad was supposed to be taken care of and that "I am the wife and will do it" attitude started to irk me. Dad always told me to walk away, that she was smaller than me and not worth the fight, and that I was stronger. I followed his lead, but felt deeply that she was wrong. How she acted was wrong; the things she said were wrong; and the separation she attempted to cause between my father and his daughters was wrong.

I fought hard to continue to love Mom. That is what we are supposed to do—love our mothers. Respect was falling to the wayside yet, this was *her* home, despite the fact that I grew up here. I had to let it go. We never spoke about that day at the hospital or why Mom and my aunt went wacky. I did, however, tell Dad that if it ever happened again, I wouldn't be so kind. He said, "That will never happen again, Danny."

Chapter 14
Regret sometimes happens

Making strange decisions must be in my genes. It just comes naturally to me. When I was younger, my parents would stand on the sidelines, shrugging their shoulders, as if to say, "Oh boy, here she goes again."

Coming home from Vegas at twenty-four years old and announcing that I was married to a man I dated successfully for three months after dating him unsuccessfully for three months did, however, came as a shock to them. This was without question the most spontaneous thing I had ever done. I thought my behavior was justified because my new husband and I had known each other since grade school.

When I was twenty-one and didn't yet know I was pregnant with Nolan, this guy named Seth ended up on my back porch with a mutual high school friend named Mikey. At the time I had just broken up with my boyfriend Alex, Nolan's dad. Turns out, we went to grade school together and knew tons of the same people. Seth and Mikey stayed for an hour, chatting and laughing, and then left.

Mikey called about two weeks later to say, "My friend really likes you." I thought Seth was really cute in his own way. I said, "That's cool. He's cute!"

Then, oddly enough, Mikey said, "No way. Don't do it. He is really a jerk." I was confused. Why was he telling me that his friend liked

166

me, if he didn't want me to be with him? So I moved on, convinced that if Mikey thought Seth was a jerk, I better believe he is a jerk.

Once I met Rich and became engulfed in that world, I never thought about Seth again. A few months, after Rich went to Florida for karate and I was single again, I ran into Mikey's friend, Seth, at Nicklebees, the local pub. I rarely went out to bars after having my son, but my girlfriend from high school, Jane, had called, upset with her husband and asked if I would hang out with her. We sat at the bar talking until she saw someone she knew across the room and left me alone. That's when I noticed Seth at the other end of the bar. I called his name "Seth!" smiled and waved. He left the girl he was sitting next to at the bar and came over to talk with me. We spent the rest of the night talking until the bar closed and everyone left. Seth hugged me and that was it. He left. I walked over to Jane ready to get home myself.

Jane was excited because we were invited to an after-party and according to her "we needed to go." I argued for a few minutes before following her to the party, but I honestly would have preferred to go home to sleep. I wasn't looking forward to going to a stranger's house at midnight but, I also wasn't going to leave Jane alone.

I was very surprised when I walked in and Seth was there. We gravitated toward each other and spent the next two hours talking outside, in the rain, under a table umbrella. I learned that he was in the Navy for four years, just got out, and was now a loan officer. He also had a son a year younger than Nolan. It seemed too good to be true. He was cute, successful, had a son, and was interested in me.

We traded numbers this time, and so our relationship began.

I was really excited every time I had a chance to spend time with him. We spent the next three months going places with the kids, camping at Camp Jam in the Pines Music Festival, hanging out at Seth's house, playing with our boys, and beginning a great relationship. I was sure that everything was happening as it was meant to and that this was the next step in my journey.

Then, two days before Thanksgiving, he told me that if we continued to date, his son's mother wouldn't let him see his son.

I didn't understand how she had that right to do that—or why he accepted her ultimatum. I also knew that I had no place in a situation like this. With nothing to say, I left his home crying. A day later, he sent me an e-mail confessing everything he felt about me, how he truly loved me. He ended the e-mail with, "I will love you until snow covers the earth."

I was confused and pissed. I decided I would never talk to him again. He was a jerk and Mikey had warned me. I took the blame because I should have listened. I went to Mikey crying and all he could offer was, "I know, I told you Dan." Ugh, he was so right!

So, I moved on … or so I thought. A few months later I met a nice guy, and I was happily dating him. I'd determined that I wasn't getting attached to anyone after the crazy quick breakup that had just occurred. I came to realize that in the three months Seth and I had shared, I'd learned nothing about him except that he had a son one year younger than mine and he was so in love with me—until one day he wasn't. I accepted that he was a mystery.

A speeding ticket ended our three-month separation from each other. I didn't want the points on my license so I took my chances fighting a ticket in court. Having no sitter, I was forced to bring Nolan with me. I sat on the floor in the courtroom, hidden in a corner, while keeping Nolan entertained by coloring and playing with his toys. Out of the corner of my eye I saw Seth's son, "Little." My heart began to race, and I hoped that neither of the kids would see each other. But Little did see Nolan and he walked over. I sat back as far as I could behind the water fountain hoping Seth would not be able to see me. Unfortunately, this wasn't the case. He looked over and we made direct eye contact.

"Looking beautiful as ever, Danny," he said.

"Hi," I responded sharply.

We exchanged a few useless words, dealt with our court issues, and left.

Two days later, he called to ask if I would at least have a conversation with him. I hesitated and then eventually agreed. He picked me up in the truck he'd purchased after we broke up, and we went for a ride in the woods. I don't know why I agreed to talk to him, even if it was to hear his apology. The fact that I wasn't responding to his advances frustrated him. "You know I miss you, right?"

I shrugged and looked out the window.

He began to drive faster through the woods. Driving fast in the woods makes me nervous and I didn't like that he was doing it on purpose, probably to scare me.

"I'm dating someone new now," I said and he slammed on the brakes. When he shouted, "Look at me!" I did. I stared into his face, feeling extremely angry at the way we had broken up. I knew in my heart that I hadn't moved on; however, I *was* dating someone new. "You still miss me," he said as he started to drive again. "I will win you back." I felt sick to my stomach that he thought I was a prize to be won.

Days later, with a thousand apologies, he asked me to give him another chance. While I wasn't ready to fully forgive him, I *was* willing to go on another date with him, with his understanding that I would continue to date other people.

I was not about to put all of my eggs back into a broken basket, but I also knew that something about this guy kept me drawn to him and I wanted to explore that more. I would soon realize that he was reckless— and I was used to guys who were extremely safe. Something about his spontaneous, wild, do-whatever-he-wanted persona attracted me. It was different; it kept me on my toes.

He agreed to date other people and understood my obvious concern. Suddenly his baby's mother didn't care if he was dating again or maybe he had been lying about that. I blew it off. Our arrangement of dating others lasted for three weeks, and then one day he erupted. It was Valentine's Day, and I wasn't spending it with him. He was hysterical crying. "Come here and see me," he kept texting. I found it very difficult to be on a date while getting texts. I cut my date short, claiming I had an emergency and drove to his home all the while discussing what was happening with Jane as I drove to him. He was sobbing when I came to his door. "I don't want you to date other people. Marry me," he said.

My first instinct was, *This isn't normal.* He gave me an ultimatum: I was either going to get on the plane with him to Vegas or I would not be dating him anymore. He handed me an emerald ring, no real proposal, and said, "Are you going to come to Vegas?"

I said, "Yes." At that moment I truly believed that he had found "the one" and I was it. Looking back, I hadn't really considered if I had found "the one." After Alex's and Rich's rejections, both of whom moved on with their lives quite fast, I believed that this was true love. They ran away, and here was Seth, wanting me desperately. I couldn't see beyond *this person loves me and wants to spend the rest of his life with me.* He was so certain, and his certainty overtook my common sense.

I accepted his offer to "go to Vegas" with the belief that love was stronger than anything else in the world, and we could make a marriage work. I also thought of our two sons and how they would make a cute family. I was finally about to graduate college, and we were going to move forward together. I wouldn't have to deal with Mom's annoyance when I graduated and still lived at home with Nolan while trying to find a teaching job. It would all work out perfectly; I was sure, despite not knowing this person very well and knowing that we were on shaky ground already.

I told only two friends about the Vegas trip, and they promised to keep it a secret, knowing that everyone who cared about me was against my getting back together with him—a factor I also conveniently ignored.

This time around, his intensity and affection for me was like nothing I had ever experienced. He made the world about me and lived in a place of kindness. He kept apologizing for the so-called "stupid choices" he'd made months prior, and he wished he knew then that this was where we were supposed to be. Our relationship was meant to be—just look at the number of times fate had pushed us together.

We eloped and were married in the Little Chapel of the West. We returned home four days later and told our families what we had done.

Despite our newfound happiness, his mother freaked out when he told her (expected). My dad was like, "Whatever. Good luck. You know where your home is." My mother was glad it wasn't costly for her and that I'd be moving out. His father called him an "idiot."

So that was my start as a wife.

170

My aunts (Mom's sisters) were livid when they found out how I got married. They spouted rhetoric about how I cut Mom out of her mother/daughter moment, a moment that she and I could never get back. I should have let Mom throw me a bridal shower, we should have done the wedding planning as a family, and I should have went shopping for my wedding gown with her. Not being able to tell if this was just my aunt's opinions or if Mom was really upset, I determined it all to be ridiculous.

Let's be realistic, the last time I went shopping with Mom, she bought me clothes from a fancy consignment store. I was nine. The clothes were cheap (but still adorable). I didn't mind shopping there. After Mom started showing signs of becoming depressed when I was ten, Dad realized that she wasn't willing to leave the house to do these mom-like things anymore. So he sent me shopping with the wife of his friend Jim. He gave me my school clothes money, and Jim's wife helped me buy my new clothes.

The truth is I didn't believe that shopping for a wedding gown would be the time Mom finally came shopping with me, or even that it would bother her to miss it. At the time, I also didn't think my eloping would be an issue for her. To this day I will never know if my marriage, and the wedding we had, upset her or if she didn't care either way. Her sisters say that she did. However, I'm still not sure they truly knew Mom.

We threw a second wedding two months later to make Seth's mom happy. Then, almost three months later, I moved out of my parents' home, he moved out of his rented house and we moved into a new home of our own. I didn't own much furniture since I lived with my parents, so moving Nolan and me was easy. I spent the first week decorating our new home and running back and forth to my old home. I cherished our home and everything was glorious and even our kids seemed happy to have each other. Seth brought everything from his house, including furniture, dishes, and let's not forget guns. I wasn't comfortable with guns, but I knew he had them. Plus, his father had warned me, "If you married a hunter you need to accept the guns." We bought a gun safe and when we redid our closet, we hid them in the back.

Our house was set up and it was all ours. I adored it. The new neighbors seemed awesome and everyone welcomed us to the neighborhood as we moved in. Life was as perfect as it could get. We were moving forward. Even Mom was happy because I was finally settled and out of her hair. She changed the locks on the doors and from this point on I had to knock to go home. I let all of her craziness go and embraced what happiness should look like, swearing that "I would never be that kind of mom."

Despite the quick wedding, the first twelve months of our marriage were solid. We were in love and happy. Everything was easy. We were a cute, young, hippy couple. We went to parties together, passed joints among friends, laughed often and I never wanted to leave him or our house because there was so much to do. I loved painting the new bedrooms for our boys, opening all of our packed boxes, taking photos of everything we did, developing our first family portraits, and most of all living as a family. Seth would go to work and when he came home, an entire room had changed colors or its furniture had been rearranged—again. This home became our world.

I loved dinners together, snuggling on the couch, and shutting off the lights at the end of the night. We relished in the positivity and newness of our world. I was even more excited when I found out I was pregnant with my second child. I always wanted another child, and I secretly hoped, after having the two boys, that this was my girl. Unfortunately this baby didn't want to show us what he/she was. The ultrasound proved unreadable in that regard, and we left the ultrasound appointment not knowing its sex. I couldn't wait to design the spare room so I painted it green on the bottom and blue on top, and waited to see what I would do next.

I couldn't wait to meet the baby. I finished my final step of college, student teaching, while I was pregnant. As soon as I finished, I graduated and now was officially a certified teacher. My dreams were all coming true. Nothing could have made my life happier.

My marriage took a strange turn when I was six months pregnant, Seth and I had our first major fight. Up to this point our minor arguments were normal newlywed arguments and easy to navigate. I wasn't the same fun girl I was when he married me. I was pregnant so partaking in fun wasn't the same. One day, I was heading out on a Saturday to visit my best friends from childhood, the twins. I was so excited to see them and their families. We had planned this date for a month. My boys were with their other parents, and I was heading to the twins' house to show them my baby belly!

But before I left, Seth stopped me.

He had decided that he was going to strip the ugly wallpaper off the dining room walls. It was very rare at this point that I did anything without him. I was so caught up in our "new" marriage and setting up our home, dealing with the life we created, figuring out kid schedules, and inviting people to our house that I rarely left his side. I hung out with him all the time unless he was at work or I was at classes or work. This was the first time that I was breaking away for the afternoon—and he was pissed.

I was so confused. I wasn't sure what I had done wrong.

He started off by screaming, "I need help."

And I agreed. "I am absolutely fine with helping any other day." But he wanted to do it at that exact moment, and he was angry that I had made plans without him. No one had ever been so angry with me. I couldn't understand what was happening. I was going to visit friends and yet I felt as though I had done something horribly wrong.

This evolved into a yelling fight in the foyer of our home. No boyfriend of mine had ever told me I couldn't do something. I was getting so angry and I worried that my anger wasn't good for the baby. But I stood my ground about leaving—and his anger raged.

He started yelling about how ignorant I was for leaving him there, how I was always selfish, and that I didn't care about him. I ignored what he said because I wasn't backing down. I wouldn't even back down against Mom if she *ever* treated me like this, why did he think I would for him? I was going out. A moment later he screamed, "Just leave!" and threw the kitchen chair in my direction. The thought that I had just become a terrible person for *leaving the house* made no sense to me. "Just go!" he shouted. "Go, be with your friends and leave me here alone."

The chair hit the hardwood floor, and I inspected the nick it made on my way out. I was shocked and infuriated. I walked out to the Jeep and climbed in. He chased after me but stopped when he saw the neighbor standing outside. I cried all the way to my friends' house, ignoring his calls to my cell phone. I wasted my entire visit with the twins on crying to them about what just happened. Stephanie despised Seth that day, and she knew I was in trouble.

I learned something important: It didn't matter how kind I was or how sweet, loving, affectionate, or how much I cleaned and took care of the kids, when Seth wanted something his way, it better go his way. I didn't know at the time that this wasn't just a bad moment for him, but the beginning of a very hard marriage for me.

"Someone has to be the bigger person and usually it's the woman," Mom told me when I told her about it. In the future, she would listen every time I called to rant about another fight we had just had. For 99.7 percent of my marriage, she was very kind to Seth. It seemed to me that she went out of her way to be extra kind. On more than one occasion Seth made comments like, "Your mom likes me better than she likes you."

I believed he was right and blamed it on the fact that he's a guy. Mom liked guys. She loved her father, loved Dad, loved Chad, adored Nolan, and was kind to Seth. She was ever so difficult with me, and she struggled with female friendships and family members—even the granddaughters had to fight their way into her good graces. The few friends she truly let in were very lucky. She chose selectively.

Dad continued to be of the opinion that I never should have married Seth in the first place. But I just thought that was Dad's way of being overprotective.

Still he made an effort to hang out with Seth because I begged him to. "Can't you at least make an effort?" I asked. He did. One night, he took Seth with him to spend a night out with his work buddies. Everyone was drinking as they always did on late "work" nights. I was asleep when Seth came home. Dad had dropped him off.

The next morning, hung-over, Seth explained that he might have thrown up in my father's car. If he was right and it was true, I knew that would probably ruin any chance of friendship they would ever have. I dreaded talking to my dad about it. I had forced him to befriend my husband and now this happened. *Why couldn't anything go right?*

174

My father didn't mention the throw up the next time I saw him, so I didn't bring it up.

Months after the incident, however, I was at my parents' house dealing with yet another one of our many fights, and my father brought it up. I laughed so hard when Dad told his story—and Mom defended Seth.

"Sometimes you throw up," I remember her saying.

I appreciated her attempt to empathize with him, but it annoyed me at the same time. I rolled my eyes and returned to Dad's complaining about needing to have the car professionally cleaned. Needless to say, my father stopped attempting to hang out with Seth after that ordeal.

I felt great during the last three months of my pregnancy, but the doctor saw a speck on the baby's brain on the final ultrasound. He wasn't sure what it could be, but a tumor was a possibility, so suddenly I was in the middle of a high-risk pregnancy. The benefit of more ultrasounds was that I could finally find out the sex of my baby. The moment we found that it was a girl, I was ecstatic. I painted flowers and fairies on her bedroom walls and started the girly planning.

The daily arguments continued between Seth and me. While we dealt with the high-risk pregnancy, Seth entered into a custody battle between him and his baby's mother. The hardships of a blended family started to surface. The fact that Little and Nolan had other parents, with other personalities and other rules, caused struggles in our home too. Seth yelled at me when he didn't like the way I was raising his son, and I never wanted him to yell at Nolan.

Seth and I began spending less time together, which was a blessing. During the summer of my pregnancy I went back to work at a camp I'd been working at on and off for years and luckily both the boys came with me. We left at seven in the morning and returned at six at night. By the time we got back home, I rushed through dinner, tossed the boys into bath time, and then passed out from exhaustion. I worked up to the day that my daughter was born.

In August of 2004, I gave birth to the second love of my life, Rory Francis. The instant Rory opened her eyes, I felt in my soul that this child was going to change the world—or at least change mine. Her small fingers curled around my thumb and I couldn't miss noticing her vibrant eyes, a dark blue that never changed. Loving this child came naturally.

Secretly, I had hoped that the birth of our daughter would bind the family and calm the fighting. The first year of Rory's life consisted of me spending time with the boys and her, photographing all of them whenever I could, and trying to keep the home in order. (This was the hardest job I had ever had!) But I happily became a full-time stay-at-home mom with a hobby of photography.

The issues in the marriage didn't go away with the birth of Rory. Instead we added some new issues. The kids were getting older, which meant I wasn't spending enough time alone with Seth. Every weekend had a child in them, whereas before the boys went home to their other parents every other weekend. The house started to fall to the way side, becoming messier with a newborn, a three year old, and a four year old. Three kids proved harder to care for than two.

Everything was changing, and we had to adapt. When Rory was six months old, we entered into a full-fledged custody battle with Seth's ex over his son, Little. This fight drained Seth's energy and our bank account.

Between the money troubles and trying to survive weekends filled with kids, the stress became too much. Everything was a battle. Every day Seth told me I was doing things wrong, when I was trying my best to do everything *right*.

With each new fight Dad happened to catch wind of, he would ask me, "Do you want me to be involved Danny? Do you want me to say something?" I always said, "No, Dad. I'll be okay!"

Looking back, I wish I would have let him protect me. I wish I would have put some fear of Dad in Seth. Maybe that's where I went wrong. I kept Dad out of my marriage even when he should have stepped in. It's hard to figure out where your daddy fits in when you are trying to be an adult and deal with your own life. But I feared something bad happening to my dad if he got involved. There was no way to tell if the wrath Seth directed at me could turn onto Dad, and I refused to risk it. This could result in many bad outcomes, and I wouldn't put it past Seth to want to put Dad in his place. After all, many times he blamed Dad for how bad I turned out. And if it wasn't Dad, it was the *"happy bubble"* I lived in.

Mom believed I could deal with it all, and she encouraged Dad not to get involved. She knew that the more involved he became, the greater the chance I may come back home. I went to Mom often with my stories of the marriage. She suggested that we keep it between us because it could hurt Dad's heart, and he didn't need the stress. She never told Dad any of the bad stuff that was happening because she knew he would want me out of the marriage. Mom made sure he was isolated from the pain I was going through.

The stress of our marriage hit an all-time high when the mortgage industry collapsed. We were the first wave of people to feel its impact, because Seth was a loan officer. He was very successful for a long time during the housing bubble and then suddenly one day we were broke. His unemployment lasted two years and was very difficult for both of us. I panicked daily as the bills piled up. I took a night job, through my sister-in-law, Shelby, working as a registrar at a hospital. The job was offering medical benefits to full time employees and it was the night shift. It fit our needs so I could still be with my kids all day long.

Work started at seven at night, and it took thirty minutes to get there. So, at six thirty I kissed all of my children, told them to be good, and left. Although, it broke my heart to leave the kids, not tucking them in and kissing them goodnight hurt the worst. Briefly, I considered going back to teaching and using my degree, but it was the middle of the school year and I was hoping Seth's unemployment would be temporary.

Things had gone from an already kind-of-bad relationship, to glimpses of goodness to hold onto, to a horrible relationship and no glimpses at all. All we seemed to do was fight, and I questioned the benefits of being married anymore. We repeated a circle of the same fights for almost two solid years. I wanted to quit my job at the hospital and told him he *needed* to get a job because I couldn't work the night shift anymore.

He blamed me and said things like, "The gravy train ended so now Danny isn't happy." This infuriated me. It wasn't the gravy train that was my issue. Honestly, aside from the fighting, I didn't want to be the people who were happy living on unemployment at thirty years old, and I couldn't for the life of me understand why he wasn't *trying* to get another job in another bank, or looking for new opportunities in other fields.

Other people managed to keep themselves in the mortgage industry through the financial crisis. I couldn't understand why he wasn't even trying. To add to my frustration, every time President Obama extended the unemployment another six months, I wanted to throw up. *Who was that favor for?* The free money from the state kept my husband, a perfectly capable man, from trying to find a job. If it weren't for needing medical benefits, I might have been unemployed as well.

So, I continued to work.

Morning drives became more dangerous than ever before. Every morning I left the ER at seven in the morning so sleepy I was barely able to stay on the road, and thankful the towns put yellow stripes down for my safety. Home at last, I'd park my car and walk into the house ready to start my role of wife and mother of three. Exhausted, I'd suck up my lack of sleep and play with the kids. On the days that went smoothly, life was fine enough; however the days I entered into another meaningless argument with Seth were enough to break me.

Five minutes after arriving home I learned that the days-old laundry, which didn't seem to matter to me so much anymore or a lack of socks was *indeed* a big deal. Shockingly these two topics caused a new level of chaos in the house. *The laundry? What? Why?*

Tired and shaking my head in annoyance, I'd decide this discussion wasn't happening, or at least I wasn't joining. Snide comments such as, "Don't worry, I got the kids the rest of the day" passed through my lips in a tone of "I am *so* done with *all* of your crazy shit." *Snide*, I had become snide. And he didn't appreciate snide. But I didn't care anymore. I never felt so *over* the same conversation in my entire life—not even with Mom—who would smack me in the head if I was snide to her (or at least she would threaten to do so).

Thanking God for my three beautiful children who ran in yelling "Mommy, Mom, Danny." I'd grab my littles and lie down in my queen-size bed with all three curled up around me. I'd sleep-watch whatever cable show their little hearts desired. Hearing the downstairs door slam, I exhaled relief that the fight was over. I assumed he had left out of anger and that he'd be back later, as usual.

One evening, I had volunteered to photograph a fundraising event. For some time, I had been thinking about making photography my profession instead of working at the hospital (teaching wasn't an option because Seth needed me home daily in order to keep fifty percent custody of Little.) And I was determined to get this new career off the ground for my sanity first and for money second.

I worked late at the hospital, entered into a fight at home, fell asleep, and Seth left. Hours passed, the kids and I slept, and when I woke, I phoned Seth. And phoned him and phoned him, to no avail. Finally, at 5 p.m., he sent me a text saying "Down the shore." I had spent many nights not knowing (or caring) where he was, what he was doing, waiting for him to come home late, so this was nothing new. But not knowing where he was this time was unacceptable because he knew I needed him to watch the kids so I could work my first photography job— or "joke of a hobby," as Seth called it. This was the job that would hopefully launch my new company.

No one else could watch the kids for me at this point, so I was stuck. Seth knew I would be stuck, so he went to the shore. The children couldn't come with me to the benefit. It was a Relay for Life benefit at a bar, and I'd be doing group portraits. A cancellation on a two-hundred-person event could ruin my fledgling reputation.

Seth had waited for the perfect time to ditch me. I called Dad and Mom begging for help, and Dad said, "Don't worry, we will take the kids." They saved me.

I left my parents' house and rushed to the benefit. I was already late, which added to the feeling of nausea in my stomach. The fight I found myself in was draining my soul. I fought the urge to cancel the shoot, even though everything in my world suggested I should.

I was flustered when I walked into the benefit. I wanted to be set up and ready to shoot as the guests came in the door. Instead I was chasing the guests down in the dining hall asking them if they would like their picture taken. Though my frustration was at an all-time high, I had to be a businesswoman and control my emotion. I couldn't stop thinking about my failing relationship as I photographed all the "happy couples" attending the benefit. My best friend from high school Sam was there with her parents and I couldn't help but wonder if they were miserable in their home lives too. Mom always told me that "no relationship is easy and everyone fights," and that, "it's not supposed to be perfect, and it is all normal." I remembered these words throughout my marriage, but even more so on this particular night. I tried to hold onto the great moments we shared the first year of our marriage. That's what helped me keep it together all these years.

Whenever I thought we'd hit rock bottom, I relived Vegas and our first year together. I wanted to reconnect with Seth. I wanted that time back. I needed us to work. I dreamed of the fun moments we'd shared, like the first festivals we went to together, the parties we threw at our home, the move into our new home, and other amicable moments. I held onto these memories for the sake of my own sanity.

During the benefit's dinner break, I called Seth to let him know what time I'd be home so we could talk. But he wouldn't answer his phone. I left the photo shoot and headed home, expecting to find him there. Instead I walked in to a quiet house with only the animals scurrying around. Seth had not come home. He wasn't waiting for me to talk. He was gone, purposely not answering my calls, and I felt terrible. I had no children, no husband. I experienced an emptiness I had never felt before. Even when I traveled to Europe all alone I never felt this alone.

I called Seth again to let him know I was home. He finally answered. I remember how glad I was to reach him, to just hear his voice and to know he was safe. For the first time that evening I could breathe. I mistook his annoyance with me as reassurance because he was actually talking to me. I was frustrated that I felt relief, because I knew I didn't deserve the silent treatment and the worry over not knowing where he went or his uncanny ability to ignore me when he wanted to. I knew that this was his way to torture me and make me uneasy inside of our relationship. I followed his lead and fought harder for us to be better. I was begging for him to come home and talk to me.

During the phone call, I heard people in the background talking and music playing. I asked him again, "Where are you?"

"Down the shore. Get a grip, I am with my Mom and Aunt in Cape May," he snapped.

An hour and a half away from our home. "Seth, are you coming home?"

"Nope, not coming home," he said matter-of-factly. *I didn't see that coming.* Then he mocked me while I was on speaker-phone to an audience outside the bar. "My wife is on the phone. She wants me to come home right now. She's *so* hilarious." He laughed and strangers laughed, and he continued to mock me. "Anything else you want to know or can I go back to *my* fun now?"

I became enraged. He was making fun of me in front of strangers. He was degrading me. And he thought it was funny. I asked him again, "When are you coming home?"

"Are you dumb? Can't you hear? I am *not* coming home." He then said something that changed our life for the next six months and probably the rest of our marriage. "I am not coming home until *you are gone.*" He then hung up the phone. Unbelievably, I tried to call him back to find out if he meant it. No answer.

After that I became so angry that I stopped searching for the truth behind his words and I stopped calling him. I stood in my kitchen, staring at the world that we created. I was all alone. I began to cry. I fell to the floor of my kitchen and sobbed. I felt my heart breaking. His words, "I am not coming home until *you are gone,*" replayed in my mind over and over again. I felt a level of anger that I had never felt before.

No one had ever told me they didn't want me around, that they wanted me gone and hoped I left and didn't come back. In the past, I'd excused his cruel behavior by convincing myself that it was just his knee-jerk reaction to a fight or that his past relationships caused him to act this way. For some reason, though, this was different.

I had reached my limit.

As I came upon this truth, I stood up, stopped crying, and composed myself. I straightened up the kitchen out of sheer routine and stumbled up the stairs. I stared at my walls of photographs on the second floor of my house. I envied the girl in the photographs from five years ago. I was jealous of the innocence I once had. I remembered falling in love with Seth after I married him. I longed for us to work. I stood at the bottom of the second floor stairs, questioning everything, while I stared at our family photographs. I journeyed up the stairs to our third floor, walked into our bedroom and lay alone in our empty bed.

I stared at my bedroom, thinking of all the fights we had. I knew at that moment that I was holding on to a relationship that had endless flaws. Something had gone horribly wrong along the way and now I was just trying to survive. In that moment I understood what extreme loneliness felt like. To me, it was the feeling that even though I had a house, a car, children, a husband, a job, and one million material possessions to account for, I still felt powerless and alone.

As I lay in my bed, knowing he wasn't coming home, I called my brother and said, "I have to get out of this marriage."

Chad knew that I was trying my best and the wars were continuing behind the closed doors. I reached out for advice from my big brother whenever I could get it. I knew he would be there if I needed him and today I needed him. This fight, which had lasted three months already, needed to end. Our relationship was at rock bottom. I knew that now, and I was ready to get out.

Dad (who still had my children) and my brother went back and forth on the phone from ten o'clock at night on, with a family friend named Tom. Tom was a landlord, and after hearing my story, he said he could help me quickly find a new place to live.

I told my family what was going on, how much we had been fighting, the way he had been talking to me, and that I was very unhappy. I believed that I had made a mistake marrying him and I couldn't get out of my situation. The marriage was not going the way I wanted it to go. I honestly believed that we would be kind to each other, love each other, and be there for each other. This was not the case anymore. Six years in, this marriage had become a survival of the fittest. He was winning.

The next morning, my friends and I moved me, my daughter (who was three years old), and my son (who was seven) into a town house. My brother called his friend Dave, who I had grown up with. He owned a landscaping company with two giant trucks. Dave jumped at the opportunity to help me. He liked Seth, but his loyalty lay with my brother and I.

Dave and my brother showed up in the morning with three landscaping trucks and a few workers. Nolan's dad, Alex, came as well. It was eight o'clock in the morning, and no one knew what time Seth would be coming home. It was pouring rain outside. This was not the optimal situation for a move; however, the time was now.

Dad showed up with the children after everything was in the trucks and we were ready to move into the new place. The kids seemed unaffected. Moments like this were normal, and we all had learned to adapt to arguments leading to yelling fits by someone in the family—and sometimes someone left. During these fights, Rory grabbed my hand and said, "Come on, Mommy. Let's go play." I learned to follow her; after all, maybe she was the one that would learn to stop the fighting.

I promised my children a new beginning with no fighting. I talked about the new house and how they each could have their own bedroom. Rory was young enough that she was excited to stay with Nolan and me. Nolan witnessed some of our fights, so he was happy to see me leave.

My heart dropped when my cell phone rang. It was Seth. He was freaking out because a mutual friend had driven past the house and called to tell him there were people "emptying out his house." He screamed at me while I had him on speakerphone. I became terrified at the idea of facing him. I had no idea how far he was from home, but I knew he was furious and driving very fast. I was afraid of what might happen next.

I rushed everyone out of my house, and we all packed into the cars. My heart was beating uncontrollably as I drove closely behind my father's car with my two children inside of it. I couldn't stop crying. I was crying out of fear for what may happen mixed with the thought that *maybe I was overreacting by moving out. Maybe he didn't mean to be so mean. Maybe we can fix this.* It was too late and I couldn't turn back. There was part of me that wanted to stop what *I* had started. I wanted to make the twenty-four hours that had made this fight one hundred times worse go away. I wished that he had never told me to

"Get out." But he couldn't take it back and now neither could I. I was broken inside, and I had no idea what was going to happen next. I knew I had set a new world into motion and it happened so easily. I didn't need this horrible life, yet something kept me drawn to it.

We arrived safely at the condo, three towns over, twenty-five minutes later. I was beyond frazzled. The entire car ride was met with disturbing text messages, and if I answered the phone he would tell me how big of a "piece of shit" I was and how *I* was destroying our family. Reminding him that he told me to be gone was falling on deaf ears, but I refused to take the blame for this.

He returned to our house an hour later. He called me again after walking through our home of rain, mud, and half furniture. "Where are you?" he demanded to know. Ironic, that now *he* wanted to know where *I* was. He kept asking louder and louder. I didn't answer any of his questions because I would be alone in this house—alone with my children, and very scared.

I kept him on speakerphone so I could protect myself and make sure that I could justify to myself and everyone else that I wasn't crazy for leaving. Everyone stood outside of the condo staring at me as he spouted off angry threats directed at all of us. My father took my phone from me and hung up. Seth was very lucky that my father and brother ignored his ramblings and considered him an angry person. I found myself explaining that "he was extremely angry and didn't mean any of it." I made excuses for him to everyone, just as I had made excuses to myself. It is what you do when you are trying to protect the person you're married to.

Every person present, including Nolan's dad, Alex, hugged me and said they were sorry.

I set up the new apartment with the kids. I gave Nolan his own room and Rory her own room. I slept on the couch and decided I didn't need a room. In the days and weeks to come, the children and I found solace in the new home. It was quieter than what they were used to, without any yelling or fighting.

After three weeks, Seth calmed down enough to talk, and we started to work on our issues while living apart. After six months, we agreed that I was going to come home with the kids and he was going to get a job. We were going to go to counseling and start over again and the fighting had to end.

I broke my lease, apologized to everyone who helped save me, and went home.

Somehow, months later, Dad and Mom allowed Seth into their home once again. My family wasn't happy about our getting back together, but looking back now, I was in my own world and I didn't let how they felt have an effect on me. No one agreed with my choice to give Seth another chance. I felt my family's disappointment with me, and I know they wanted to protect me from my own choices.

I believed people could change, and I gave in when I detected the slightest hint of remorse from Seth. He even apologized to my family—I couldn't have stayed with him otherwise. I took him back this time even though every fiber in my being told me to run. I convinced myself it would all be okay, and I acted like it was all okay. It did become momentarily better. But then it became worse.

Chapter 15
Look before you leap

I knew that I had returned home for all of the wrong reasons. I feared leaving my house on the lake and abandoning the few neighbors that I actually liked. I hated the idea of us not sleeping in the bedrooms I'd made for us. I didn't want to be the cause of my children losing their stable lives, struggling financially, or being forced to start over. The past six months made me realize I wasn't ready to financially support us on my own yet, and the torture I would be inflicting on Mom if I moved in with my parents was not something I could consider. She didn't want company at *her* house. "You know Danielle, two woman can't live under the same roof, and besides, Dad and I are finally enjoying ourselves now that we have the house alone." Mom declared. *She* was extremely satisfied with the child-free life she was living, and I wanted no part in ruining that for her.

Moving back home with Seth, however, only put me back in the same position I'd been in a six months prior. He had the same control over me that he'd had before, and I beat myself up mentally for making such a big scene and moving out. I had not been strong enough to stay away and pursue the separation. I could never ask my family and friends for help like that again. On top of it all, I had proven to Seth that I needed him, and that I was never going to leave him.

Seth kept his promise to go back to work, and eventually he started doing energy audits. He was lucky to have his longtime friend,

Antonio, invest in his new company. I was thankful that we were given this chance. Antonio had saved our family financially. We finally had solid paychecks instead of unemployment checks. Seth stepped into this new field at just the right moment; within a year he became one of a few companies doing audits for state programs. This took some of the pressure off of our marriage and allowed me to quit my hospital position and concentrate on my two stable loves: the children and my photography.

Seth worked long hours to get this career off the ground, and the kids and I had peace and quiet at home. The more space Seth and I had between us, the better everyone's life became. I stopped resenting him for his inability to work for the past two years, and we stopped struggling to make ends meet.

Just as we adjusted to our new living situation, and I was convinced we had weathered the worst of our marriage, the fighting resumed at an all-time high. Seth reacted bitterly about working full-time and this led to fights about dirty dishes, overly busy kid schedules, sports for the kids getting in the way of *his* free time, laundry that had been washed but not yet dried, and how nightly homemade dinners just weren't always possible. I tried to work with him at his company but just like the home life, us working together was a new war that no one needed to witness.

I rolled my eyes and kept my real feelings to myself. Each fight about *whatever* would always end the same way, with Seth saying, "Just leave if you don't like what I am saying to you. You left before. I don't need you here. There's the door."

I wasn't going to tear the kids out of the house again unless I was one hundred percent sure I was done, and done wasn't an option because I wanted to keep my family together.

I was at my happiest when I was with my children, working, or when friends were visiting and we could all pretend to be the "Cleaver Family." Behind closed doors, my lifelong dream of being a happy wife became a distant memory of what could have been.

My work in photography was moving along. I had merged with a partner, Julie, and we opened a beautiful full service studio on Main Street in town. I was lucky to have the chance to be with my kids all of the time unless I had a shoot or they were at school. Everything was as good as it was going to get. I settled for happiness in two of my three worlds.

I became a zombie in the marriage, attempting to have dinner on the table nightly and the household chores completed to the best of my ability. I knew that I was trying my best and that pushed me through the days when Seth explained my failures of house hold chores "The toys are everywhere, can't you get a grip on that?" Or, cooking: "Whatever, you made chicken, big deal!" Or happy children: "Why are they fighting when I get home?" Or, god forbid, I forgot to do something he had asked of me: "Do you even think about my needs?"

Sometimes I flared back with a snarky comment but that always proved fruitless. The list of my abundant flaws grew more apparent as the years passed. My self-worth took a hit (as my seventh marriage therapist pointed out) with these remarks, but luckily no one else spoke to me this way—not even my Mom. So I maintained my positive bubble as much as I could.

One night, our new neighbor Jill dropped off her daughter, Faith, to play with Rory. I wanted Rory to be friends with her daughter, no matter what. Rory struggled with friendships at this point. She could be a bit bossy. It seems obvious now, but I didn't realize at the time her friendship issues were related to our situation at home. As much as I tried to pretend she didn't see us and hear us fight, and wasn't absorbing the crazy energy or learning passive-aggressive tendencies, she was. I was sweet and loving to Rory, but that wasn't all she needed in order to be sweet and loving back. The negativity was hers to absorb, and she did so without anyone noticing. Pushing a friendship with the newest neighbor felt important to me and it was. They are still best friends.

On this particular play-date, when Faith was ready to go home, her stepfather came to pick her up. Rory was having an off day and being a bit ornery toward Faith. Faith didn't seem to mind, nor notice, and I was on top of the situation every time I noticed a negative behavior. I kept pulling Rory aside to discuss kindness, love, and respect of friends. I'm not sure why she should have listened to me. I mean, looking back it seems so hypocritical. It was the best I could do. I didn't want my daughter to be all the bad behaviors and actions she witnessed. The girls said goodbye to each other and then Faith's stepdad began walking Faith out through the back door. As they were leaving, I heard Seth say to Faith, "I would understand if you didn't want to play with her. I wouldn't either."

I marched out of the kitchen and said, "That isn't okay to say."

The neighbor smiled and left quickly. Seth turned around, infuriated. I was infuriated, too. He hated being disrespected, and I refused to let anyone disrespect my child. I imagined that I'd just entered into a fight that would probably last weeks.

In anger he grabbed my shoulders and pushed me up against the countertop by the dishwasher. He looked me straight in the eyes and yelled in my face, "You will never disrespect me in front of another man again. Do you hear me?"

I was so livid that I couldn't even respond. Then it happened: Out of the corner of my eye, I saw something that broke my heart. My eleven-year-old son, Nolan, was peeking over the balcony and could see everything happening in the kitchen. Before I could even speak up, with his arms pinning me down, Seth yelled again, "Do you hear me?" I wanted to say yes so that he would release me, but I must have hesitated.

It was the worst mistake I could make. Without warning, Seth looked down at me with an anger I had never seen before. Before I could say another word, he sucked in air and spit right in my face. Then he forcefully pushed me away. In complete shock, I stood straight up, wiping my face. Every horrible moment, every fight, every emotional, mental, physical situation did not matter the way this moment did. I felt my heart crack. I could feel in my soul that everything was wrong. I wanted to hug my son. I hated my husband, and for the first time ever, I said nothing. I didn't react. I couldn't react. There was nothing left to be said.

My son had disappeared up the stairs, and I didn't approach him because I didn't want him involved when Seth was this angry. I walked up my stairs in disbelief, locked myself into the spare bedroom, climbed into the bed and spent hours crying before I passed out from exhaustion. Seth banged on the door a few times, asking to talk, and eventually he broke the lock and opened the door.

"I'm sorry" was not going to work this time. I had heard enough. After a few attempts to repair the damage done, he retreated to our bedroom. I rolled over and sobbed into the pillow hoping he couldn't hear the pain he had caused.

I called Mom the next day. As I told her what had happened, I broke into hysterics. On the other end of the phone, Mom began to cry. Crying was not what I was used to when it came to Mom and news of my marriage. For the first time ever, she had no advice to offer and instead she apologized that this had happened to me. "No one should ever be treated like this, Baby. You need to try another counselor. Your marriage is getting worse," she said.

Mom was finally feeling the anger I'd been harboring. The years of her making up excuses, saying this was normal in marriage, and it's-just-supposed-to-be-hard lectures were ending today. Mom wasn't standing up for Seth anymore. And her fire was exactly what I *needed* behind me to get out.

My plan was to keep what had happened a secret from everyone else. My heart wanted to scream from the rooftops, "I have a terrible, horrible, frightful marriage and I hate *every* second of it." I had to leave. I knew this, and knowing was debilitating. Our relationship was irreparably damaged.

Anger, pure anger, was the only emotion between us— and yet I stayed. I planned my long term way out in secret and endured more of the same.

Luckily, Seth's energy company maintained a solid financial stream of business, and Seth worked from eight to five daily creating much-needed space between us. He had moved from a small office to a 5,000-square-foot building he leased from his uncle. He had a few trucks, several employees, sale guys, and an office manager. He hired friends and they all wanted to see the company succeed—and it did.

At home, he gave me my space too. Seth found solace in new hobbies he pursued in the garage. They ranged from whittling sticks, new equipment like lathes, building a gigantic rock tumbler, and when the reality TV show *Moonshiners* started, an interest in stills. Between his job and his hobbies, we were separated—and this resulted in less fights between us.

At dinner one night, Seth said he'd like to sell his company. I didn't care what he decided. After all, it was *his* company. A few weeks later he actually had a buyer. He was going to get out from underneath the energy industry and start over again. And so, he sold the company.

We finally had real money. And it quickly disappeared with the purchase of a new kitchen, a camper, a buggy, a vacation. Soon we were back to zero again.

During the sale of the company, Seth signed a rental lease with the new owners, which made him the middle man between the leasers and his uncle. A few months later, the leasers bailed out of the lease, found a smaller location, and left the space vacant. From what I gathered, they were unhappy with the sale. The new owners complained that the company was not as lucrative as Seth made it out to be, and they felt cheated. Seth was lucky his contract was solid or we could have been sued.

Luck ran out when Seth's uncle refused to let *us* off the lease. Suddenly we needed $70,000 to pay it off or we needed to rent the building to pay off this debt. *Somehow* this became my problem too. We were financially obligated to his uncle for the rent of the building.

Within two weeks we created a thrift store. It started with just the items from our garage that we could afford to get rid of. I worked hard on getting the new store organized while running back and forth from my photography studio.

Oddly enough, Seth and I came together during this emergency situation. I couldn't understand how Seth's uncle would hold him to such an arrangement and that anger fueled me to make the thrift store a success and pay him off as quickly as possible. My husband, in my eyes, was a victim and I still wanted to protect him— even though I was angry he had put us in this situation. Refusing confrontation I went to work, put a smile on my face for the customers however, I despised his cruel uncle and later Seth. As customers started to stop by the pretty much empty store, they asked if I would sell their items as well. I was so happy to have more items. Within two weeks, the store started fill up with merchandise. Once it was up and running, the plan was for me to step away and let Seth run everything.

Unfortunately for me, Seth was offered a new job. He had to take it so we could pay our household expenses. The thrift store was suddenly mine to run, and I had no other choice. I was stuck and I was angry.

My business partner, Julie, rolled with the fact that she was now going to be alone at our store front while I dealt with another bad blow. My dreams of being a photographer were put on part time again, and I resented this new situation from the moment it began.

Regardless of my feelings, I designed the new thrift store with the help of a few amazing friends, who were fully aware of how horribly I felt about this situation. I ran the thrift store for two years, took on over a hundred consignors, hired people to be there when I didn't want to be, and tried my best to make another negative into a positive. Only a few friends knew the predicament we were in as a family, and the reasons behind this new business. Otherwise, we successfully faked the appearance of a happy couple pursuing an adventure.

On January 23, 2013, I went to work at the thrift store like any other day. I turned all the lights on, switched the sign to open, and began looking at the numbers from the day before. I was five minutes into my routine when Seth came in the door. "There's an emergency," he said, "and you need to come home."

I locked up the store and we went home. On the way he explained, that the police were at our house and he wasn't sure why. "Did you not pay your child support?" I asked. "Why would the police be at our house? Are the children okay?"

Apparently one of the neighbors had seen the police walking around our yard and called Seth. He had no other information to give me.

We rushed home, but we weren't allowed to go in. The police were in the process of getting a warrant to search the inside and outside of the property because they saw a still on the back porch— a *nonfunctioning disassembled* still. I had no idea that a still and an anonymous call could cause something like this to happen. The police allowed me to leave, but Seth couldn't.

I sat in my parents' house with Rory as Seth sent me text after text, explaining each item that the police were confiscating and labeling. The first text stated that they took the outside still apart, and found no evidence of moonshine. They began to search our garage and inside our home. The second text stated that they found marijuana hidden- my heart sank. The last text was about Seth's guns.

Seth was arrested when the search was completed. No more texts were sent. They took his phone.

We lost all communication and I was left in the dark. Rory and I stayed at my parents' house until my neighbor texted that the police had left. I took Rory over to Jill's house to have a sleepover with Faith, and I went home. The house looked as clean as it had when I left it with the exception of all the drawers being messed up and the garage torn apart.

I couldn't breathe. I couldn't understand what was happening or why. Seth sat at the police station, and I ran home to my parents. On my way I called his family begging for help. They all informed me that "their son was on his own. He was a big boy now." I couldn't even believe this situation.

Mom stayed calm, as if she had been through this before.

"You need money?" she said.

"And a bail bondsman, apparently" I added.

Luckily, a few days before, Seth had sold his truck, and I'd given the money to Mom to hold for me, because whenever there was money in the home, it was as good as spent. Mom held us accountable so we wouldn't just grab the cash for any reason. We needed an emergency fund. I took the seven thousand dollars she was holding onto, having no clue if that was enough, and researched bail bondsmen, as suggested from a mutual friend.

I rushed to the police station to meet the bondsman, discussed the case with him and handed him the money. Apparently, this was now a federal case. The bondsman told me to take a seat and wait. I did. I was shaking uncontrollably at this point. *Federal case.*

Just then two women walked out the door to another office in the station. Panic set in when they headed in my direction and then asked if we could talk. I knew they were from the Department of Youth and Family Services, more commonly known as DYFS.

Before that moment, it had not dawned on me that this could become a DYFS case. My heart stopped. The mean looking lady looked at me and demanded, "Where are your children?" *No Introduction. Nothing.*

I couldn't breathe. I began to panic and let out a blood-curdling scream, "No, not the kids." Tears fled from my eyes. My worst nightmare was happening and I was alone to deal with it. "The kids don't have anything to do with this." I pleaded. "Please leave them alone." I refused to tell them where my children were.

The heavy set lady repeated the question, this time as a demand, "Tell us where the children are."

"No, they have no idea any of this is happening. Please leave them alone." I repeated.

The police officer pulled me to the side and spoke sternly. "You need to make this easier on everyone. You have to let us know where your kids are."

In a state of panic I wasn't ready to give in. I begged the police officer, "Please, you need to guarantee that they will take them to my mom's house. I refuse to allow them to go anywhere else."

He walked back to the two DYFS women, and I heard him ask if that would be okay.

"No, we don't do that" snapped the heavy set lady.

"We have an approved home that is ready to take these children now," the mean looking lady said as if she was in a hurry.

These women had no empathy. Sobbing, I turned around and barged into the conversation, "What is wrong with you? Why would you refuse that?" I cried.

I was going to do whatever it took to prevent the children from getting sucked into foster care. I was willing to go to jail to make sure the kids stayed with my parents. Thankfully, no one wanted to arrest me.

Moments later the bondsman had pulled through, and Seth walked out of the police station door to the lobby. For a moment I felt it wasn't me against the world. He begged the ladies from DYFS not to take the kids from me. He told them that none of this was my fault. But the ladies wouldn't budge. They didn't care and there was nothing he or I could do.

They had deemed our house unsafe, and it was my fault as much as Seth's because "I allowed it." I was losing my babies. I wasn't allowed to leave the police station until I told the authorities where the children were; however, I wasn't under arrest so I could use my cell phone.

I walked outside the door of the police station where they could see me on the security camera. It took me a moment to catch my breath and calm down. Once I could speak without crying I called Alex, Nolan's Dad, to let him know what was going on. This was the worst phone call I ever had to make. I forced calmness in a moment of terror. What made everything worse, I knew I lost Alex's trust, and I was convinced it would be forever. He was sick of the issues I had with my marriage and even more sick that his son had become involved in whatever this was.

I called my step-son's mom and she offered me advice on how to handle the situation. Her advice saved me, mentally at least. Apparently, the DYFS workers could indeed take my children to their grandparents' house and get it approved as a foster home. I am not sure why they didn't want to do this for us but I didn't care.

I marched back in, less frazzled, and ready to fight for what I wanted. With my back to the DYFS workers, I looked at the police officer as I spoke, "My parents' home can be deemed a foster home for the duration of this situation. They are willing and able and I want that choice." "No" said the mean case worker.

What is your problem? I wanted to scream. The heavy set DYFS lady finally agreed to let Rory go with my parents, to my relief. We were able to use Mom and Dad's house "as long as it passed inspection." *I would make sure it would.*

Little's mom agreed to keep her son, on Seth's visitation days while we dealt with everything. DYFS showed up at both of our ex's homes at two in the morning. They had to verify that the kids were safe. Little's mom understood what was happening, so she didn't freak out, but when the door-bell rang at Alex's, and woke his newborn baby, a brand new rift between us formed.

While this was happening, I called Jill to let her know that I was going to have to pick up Rory. I drove with Seth to Jill's house with a police car and DYFS following. The cop followed me into the house. I picked my daughter up off the couch where she slept and calmly explained that we would be going to Nanny's house again. I fought back tears attempting strength for my daughter.

I walked outside with my sleeping daughter in my arms and went to put her in my car. The mean DYFS worker woke Rory up when she shouted "Put that child in this car!" I begged her to allow me to go with Rory. At first they said no, but the police officer promised to follow us and that it would be okay. I climbed in their car with my eight-year-old and sat next to her, petting her head. "Everything is going to be okay," was all I could say. I knew it had to be.

By the time we reached my parents' house, it was three in the morning. My mom was up, and I took Rory downstairs and put her back in bed. Luckily she fell fast asleep. I walked back up the stairs to where the cop stood and the two DYFS workers. One of the DYFS workers said, "We may not be able to keep her here."

They then walked around, pointing out the construction that would have to be completed in order to abide by foster house standards. The police officer rolled his eyes, and it was obvious he didn't agree with what they were saying. My poor mom was exhausted, and these ladies were tormenting her. Dad was asleep and didn't know any of what was happening. Mom didn't want to wake him and insisted she could take care of this herself. I couldn't believe that Mom was saving me, us, my daughter. I was overwhelmed with the entire situation and scared for the future of my family.

I asked if we were done, and once we were, I started to walk downstairs, eager to crawl in bed with my daughter.

That's when the heavier set DYFS lady said, "What do you think you're doin'?"

"I am going to sleep," I said.

"No you aren't. Not here. You need to go home. This is now a safe house and the only visitation you have is six in the morning to nine at night."

I couldn't be strong any longer. I started to sob. *Visitation? They just placed a visitation schedule on me with my own daughter.*

"Why am I getting visitation? I haven't nor am I being convicted of anything," I stated.

"You have a court date on the twenty-fifth of the month for the custody of all three children. You both need to get separate attorneys" she answered.

"I don't understand what is happening. I deserve to understand," I said.

"You are an unfit mother. Your children were in an unsafe house and you will be held accountable," she said contently.

I felt sick. "unfit mother" Never in my life did I ever feel like an unfit mother! I'd do anything for my babies. She was wrong, and I was going to prove that—and fast.

I wiped the tears from my eyes and went downstairs, kissed my sleeping eight-year-olds head and walked out of my parents' home, angry and ashamed. Shame was not something I had felt before.

The drive home with Seth felt surreal. He explained why he was arrested. The gun safe was unlocked and there was a pistol that wasn't registered inside. The antique *Moonshiners* still, although empty and no signs of moonshine were found, was confiscated. Marijuana found in the home mixed with the guns labeled Seth dangerous and with the intent to distribute. Add in the Chinese throwing stars from China town, fireworks from Pennsylvania, and we were certainly unsafe.

My head spun with anguish the entire night. I never felt nor were my children ever *unsafe* in my home. I didn't sleep a moment and I kept replaying all that had happened over and over again. Seth kept trying to console me, but there would be no chance of that until this was resolved. I was so angry, and even though I knew I had to take responsibility too, I couldn't help but loathe the situation at that moment. I lay in bed all night, formulating a plan to get everything back to the "normal" it once was.

Even a horrible marriage was a much better option than this scenario.

The next morning, I visited both of my children's school principals to explain the situation. I then met privately with Nolan. The fear of

197

losing my son was destroying me. I drove crying from Nolan's school all the way home to Mom's. When I arrived I crawled into bed with Rory and just lay there, staring at her beautiful face. When she finally woke up, she said "Hi, Mommy!" The sound of her voice gave me strength. I brought her upstairs, made her breakfast, and put on her favorite cartoon. She sat with Mom and watched Dora as I called around for an attorney. Seth was at work, and I refused to go back to the thrift store until I was ready. We had a court date in two days, and I was determined to get these kids back. Mom was extremely patient with our situation however hoping that it solved itself quickly. I feared it may not.

Financially we were about to take the biggest hit of our lives. We both needed attorneys, and we both needed money fast. We both went into our own form of survival mode with the DYFS cases. I went in one direction, fighting to get the kids either back home or fighting so they could stay with my parents, and I could have my visitation rights. He was fighting criminal charges to clear his name.

The two DYFS workers clearly didn't want us to have the children back, and in their reports they claimed that we were unfit. In person they said, "we wouldn't have them back for a year." I refused to accept this.

I woke up on January 25th ready to face our situation. I suffered the first smack in the face when I went on Facebook and saw the horrific news article that had been posted, reporting everything that had happened minus the DYFS details. Our phones began to ring off the hook, as friends inquired whether it was real or not. I told them yes and hurried off the phone as quickly as possible. My sisters called me from out of state because Seth's picture was on the news in the Midwest. Our home was also in the news. My biggest fears were coming true: Everyone knew it had happened. They knew about the arrest, the guns, the still, the marijuana, and now we were the biggest headline in town.

Through all of it, Mom tried to keep me calm. "Don't care what others think, Danielle. It's the only way you will survive this."

Easy for you to say *Mom… Your life is simple.*

I left for court, crying and feeling very unstable. When I arrived at court, the DYFS lawyer was speaking with my attorney. My lawyer wanted to resolve this situation as fast as possible and to get my children home; however, the DYFS worker disagreed. I wanted to throw up. The fate of my children lay in the hands two women who I had screamed at two days prior and a lawyer I had hired via the telephone. My lawyer waved me over to the table they spoke at. I felt sick when the DYFS worker spoke about how unsafe our home was. When they kept bringing up how the police had found guns in an unlocked safe during their police search, with bullets kept close enough for a child to harm themselves. I tried to argue that not only has the safe been in our home from the beginning of the marriage and our children were trained not to go near it but, I have never even touched one of those guns and neither have the children. My argument didn't work. I "allowed" the guns.

Since our home was deemed unsafe, we would have to pass an evaluation on the safety of our home. Once that was completed, the kids could come home— as long as Mom and Dad were there to supervise the visitation. I also needed to do everything DYFS said, and I was allowed unlimited visitation with the exception of sleeping over. Nolan was to keep his normal fifty-fifty schedule with Alex and now fifty-fifty with Mom or Dad. Seth and I weren't *allowed* to drive anyone anywhere. This was the best situation I could have. I accepted it as a blessing.

I left court feeling better knowing that my parents were in control and not DYFS.

The first chance we got, we spoke to all three of the kids and explained everything we needed to do to get us all back together in one home. Explaining that there was a huge chance that their father could go to federal prison because of the house search was the most painful conversation I ever had to have. I seemed to be having a lot of painful conversations lately. The kids beautiful faces all looked so sad. I kept reassuring them, "This is the worst-case scenario." We all prayed it didn't happen this way.

Rory and Nolan went back to their normal school schedule. Each day I picked up Mom, Rory, and Nolan. I drove Nolan to school, dropped off Rory at her school, dropped Mom off at home, and headed to the thrift store. Little stayed with his mom, and she brought him over when things settled a bit. Everyone was involved in the DYFS case whether they liked it or not. All parents of all the children involved where checked out by DYFS. This was my life and I became used to it.

My friends would stop by the thrift store to check in on me and to see what was happening with all the court stuff. I worked the store like a zombie, paying back our unforgiving debt, and trying not to lose my mind. I hated the courts, Seth, his uncle, and anyone standing in my way of getting my kids home—and the farther into the DYFS situation we moved, the worse my marriage became. I was fighting for the chance to get the kids back to their home, without visitation, and without Mom and Dad.

My case manager from DYFS insisted that I wasn't going to be able to get my kids back if I continued to live with Seth. "He has to go so they can come home," she said. "You need to prove you'd choose them."

I explained to Seth what I was told and that he needed to stay at his father's in order for the children to come home. We would get him home after that. I was not about to wait until his September court date to get the kids home. I couldn't.

After Seth reluctantly agreed to leave the house, I was on my own because Seth and I fought daily and eventually he stopped talking to me. "You shouldn't have listened to the DYFS workers," was his defense.

I was in a fight I couldn't win. I had two choices: I could listen to DYFS and get our children home or listen to Seth and hold the marriage together. I chose the children.

I tried to not hate Seth even more. I sat at our thrift store fuming while the kids were in school. I resented every choice that he ever made that was impacting our life now, including the store.

News started to spread and some people were saying that it was a kid that previously worked with Seth who called the police. Then it was a neighbor that hated him. Then a Girl Scout mom that saw the moon-shine still at my home— who's brother was a police officer in Medford.

No one could be trusted. Acquaintances were calling daily, gossipy people where spreading more news, and school moms were very interested in what was going to happen next. It was all too much for me to handle.

My true friends would stop in on me at work, some friends stopped talking to me because they couldn't be affiliated with what had happened, and other friends made me feel even more horrible with "Maybe now is the time to leave Seth." This moment was the one I felt we had to unite the most. My children were in the middle of a war and I couldn't fight another battle.

Every time I called my attorney, it cost me more money. My children's schools started to become a hassle because DYFS kept showing up and pulling the kids out of classes. I was berated by the secretary when I went to pick Nolan up. The office insisted they needed to call Alex, though Mom was with me. Rory's school wouldn't let her take her bus home to Faith's house. No one was allowing us the things that would provide a sense of normalcy. I contacted the DYFS office and demanded a new case worker. It was obvious mine was not trying to get our family back together.

They gave me a new case worker—thank God. But on top of everything else, my own attorney infuriated me when she couldn't give me an idea of when the nightmare might be over.

Meanwhile, I was trying to make everything as normal as possible for the kids. I brought everything they loved to my Mom's house, including Rory's extremely loud gymnastics bars that Mom protested vehemently about having in her home.

Mom had a fit when we set them up. Every time Rory did a flip on the bar, the metal frame smacked the old wooden floor. "Bam, Bam, Bam." Dad said, "Ah, leave the kid alone, Mona." Mom then pulled poor Dad in the room for a lecture on "sticking together." My whole life Mom was trying to force Dad to stick with her. I believe he found it hard to do because she put the kabash on anything that would actually silence the kids and keep them occupied for an hour. But no one wanted Mom to worry, feel responsible, or freak out if one of the kids got hurt so Dad and I stayed on high alert. Once she was used to the new arrangement, Mom calmed down. We all knew we needed to coexist—and it wasn't easy. It took a full month to adjust to the new situation.

I tried to be at the house every second the kids were there. I wanted to make sure this situation was the least problematic possible for sixty-year-old parents. At nine o'clock every night, I drove home to an empty house and cried my eyes out. Our court date was still two months away.

I fired my attorney when she told me, "I don't think you will be getting your kids back in April." I couldn't even believe what she said. "There are more things DYFS wants you to do," she had explained. I went into a state of shock driving home, hyperventilating most of the way. I went inside Mom's house and lay next to her in her bed. She petted my head as I told her what happened.

After we spoke, I got fired up. My family had a trip booked to the Dominican Republic for Easter break, and I was determined to get my kids back and take them on the trip. I mustered the strength to call lawyer after lawyer and interview them. After I found the one I thought was the best because he said, "Yes, I will get your kids back," I introduced him to Dad and signed the papers. I had a new lawyer and a new caseworker—and they both wanted to help me get my life back. We all agreed on our strategy, and for the first time in months I felt confident.

After jumping through all of the mandatory hoops, I walked into my court date with new confidence that this was about to be over. I had a lawyer, Seth had a lawyer, DYFS had a lawyer. Alex was there, ready to take custody of Nolan, and Little's mom was there to take him. The world seemed like it was against us, but I was still confident that I was going to get it all back together. Seth and I formed a united front for the courts.

I couldn't breathe. I needed things to go my way. I kept praying "Please, let this all end today."

Both sides made their cases. Some were against us having our kids back and others were for us being reunited. The judge listened to both sides. I waited anxiously for him to make his final decision.

Here were his terms: Seth wouldn't be allowed to sleep at the home until DYFS gave the go-ahead, random drug screenings were to continue, another inspection would have to be done on my home (none was ever done), and visits from DFYS would continue. I was willing to do anything they needed in order to send my babies home.

I started to cry the moment I realized it was over. We walked out of court, done with visitations. The children were returning home that moment and the case worker was responsible for finally seeing the home for the final inspection.

I called Mom to tell her the happy news and to thank her for saving our lives the past few months. The kids were coming home. Everyone would sleep in their home except Seth. He was not dismissed from the DYFS case until three weeks later. Slowly, we all recovered from the four month trauma that this situation caused our family—or so I thought.

Weeks later, I was outside of our home cleaning out my Jeep. I turned to walk away from the trunk, and a police car slowly passed in front of my driveway. I started to have a panic attack and ran to the back porch, hysterically crying. Realizing that my house could be raided at any moment caused me a new fear— of police. I now felt the system was broken, and I suffered severe anxiety. I walked my hallways at night, checking on the kids to make sure they were still there. The fear of losing them again was the hardest part to deal with. I was in counseling for post-traumatic stress disorder. The agony of knowing that this could happen again plagued me.

Seth still had his court date coming up. Every day I worried I might be pulled into that situation next. They only charged him alone, but the fear that they may change their minds and charge me as well hovered over me. Seth let me know that they have two years, after his court case, to charge me too. I fell asleep in fear of this daily.

We finally made it to his court date, and we would now know what was next for our family. We sat in the courtroom, praying that everything would just be done. I was shocked when the judge dismissed everything. We had to pay a large sum in fines, but it was over. Everything was over for Seth.

I was never going to be the same; the marriage was never going to be the same. And unfortunately, the kids learned a horrible life lesson. I imagined everything was going to at least get better.

Part 4:
Awake & Determined

Chapter 16

Fate always steps in

October of 2013, the marital war continued and money became our main conflict again. One day the bank account had money in it, and the next it didn't. No deposits were being made. Without my knowledge, Seth had opened a bank account and took over the bills. This was particularly vexing because my mother had always told me "Never let a man control you with money." Now I understood firsthand and the lesson sunk in. When Seth took control of the money, we entered into the war that would never be resolved.

Seth claimed he was taking over the bills because I "couldn't do it" even though I handled them the past ten years. After the moonshine fiasco, we'd burned through more money than I care to remember. We had sold our camper, our Volkswagen Bug, and any other possessions worth any money to pay for Seth's attorney. The spending money was admittedly tight, but the bases were covered and we were doing fine. In other words, his reason for taking over as distributor of the family funds was unjustified.

We literally stopped talking and working together. One day, I grabbed the kids and we took a vacation with Mom and Dad at their house, just to "spend more time with them" I told the kids. After the DYFS situation, Mom had grown used to having my kids at the house.

She let us come without any fight and actually welcomed us more than ever before.

During this time I started to look for a new home again. On Thanksgiving night we went home despite the fact that I should have stayed away.

The marriage never improved. I was totally disconnected. Texting became a horrible means of communication, and we destroyed each other verbally in the texts. My resentment had skyrocketed, and everything he said put me in an angrier state. I finally thought about getting a divorce as a serious option. But all I really wanted to do was end the crazy war that we waged— I still wasn't able to commit to ending the marriage.

Eleven years. I had spent eleven years fighting to keep this family together. I kept wishing our marriage could get better, but I kept one foot out the door, never feeling safe there.

My marriage finally took a serious backseat in February of 2014, when I received a phone call from the emergency room. Dad was on the other end of the line. I thought, *What if it's his heart again? What if this time he may die?* He must have heard the stress in my voice, so he explained: "I am not at the hospital for me. It isn't my heart." Relief flooded over me, but then a moment later the relief disappeared. "We are here for your mom."

My heart sank again.

"Mom is still coughing," he said, "and the doctor said to take her to the hospital this time."

The idea that Mom might be dying was never one I entertained. We all joked that she would outlive everyone.

"Do I need to come to the hospital?" I asked.

He said, "I am sure she will be okay."

I hung up the phone with a very uneasy feeling.

A few hours passed, and Aunt Shelly, mom's sister, called to let me know that they were moving Mom to another hospital. The hospital tests revealed a mass in her lung, and she needed to go to a pulmonary specialist because she was unable to breathe.

"Her veins are showing through her skin," Dad said, "and are more prominent than usual. Uh, and Danielle don't be shocked—she is turning blue."

"Blue? What?" I cried out.

"We will talk when you get here." Dad hung up.

I called Seth and asked him to take care of the kids that evening so I could head to the hospital.

I hadn't seen Mom in a few weeks. She'd missed Christmas due to wanting to prevent her horrible cough from getting anyone sick. I knew she had been sick, so I tried not to let it bother me that she was missing Christmas for the first time ever. Years and years of having a "sick" mom had made me numb to the fact that her ailment might actually be serious. Over the years, I'd learned to accept that she skipped events, and I certainly never worried about her actually being sick.

This time, though, Dad seemed worried. Normally he ran the course of going to the doctors with her and getting her diagnosed with whatever ailment reared its annoying head. A few days later she would be fine again. A few days after that, another issue would come up, requiring more doctors and yet another diagnosis. This was the routine. But this time Dad seemed more concerned.

The next phone call put everything into perspective. As Dad's words came through the phone line I felt my world change. "They think a mass in her lung is causing these issues. There is a chance it may be cancer."

I was nauseous by the thought of losing my mother. Every other sickness that she had been plagued with—neck surgeries, car accidents, epilepsy, knee pain, back pain and so on wasn't going to hurt Mom, but I knew cancer might.

I went to the hospital to sit by Mom's side and find out what was happening. Mom looked horrible when I arrived in her room. All of her veins in her neck stood out, obvious and blue. Her face and body had swelled, and she didn't look like herself. Mom was suffocating—not much oxygen was getting to her lungs. The worst was the "elephant in the room" the mass needed to be removed and we all knew it.

I hated having no idea what was going to happen next. I dreaded the possibilities of the months of treatments we would have to endure in the future, and I kept reliving the worst-case scenario of Dad telling me, "Your mom has cancer." We were introduced to a foreign world at that moment. Doctors of all specialties came into the picture, trying to figure out what was happening and how fast they could solve the issues Mom was having. She didn't seem scared, but I was terrified. She kept saying, "It will all be all right, doodle bug," like she used to when I was a young girl. I prayed she was right.

The days that followed became a blur in my mind. I drove back and forth to the hospital daily to make sure she was okay. It was the most time I'd ever invested in her. I wanted to make sure she knew I was there for her, that I understood this was serious, and that I wasn't going to abandon her. It took two weeks of constant doctors, tests, and probing before they let Mom leave the hospital.

The look in my father's eyes spoke volumes. I saw him age before me. Things were about to get serious, and he was the leader in the pack. He refused to accept less than "she would get better," and I followed his lead.

The day we took Mom home, he said, "I am not going to leave her side." He kept his word and didn't leave her side. At first I was coming over four or five days a week, bringing food, cleaning, or just saying hello. I spent more time with Mom those days than I had in years. My life was torn in two horrible directions, with a dying mother and a failing marriage.

Mom's diagnosis of stage-four lung cancer woke me up. Realizing what was important in life verses what wasn't appeared to me clear as day. I put my shattered marriage on the back burner, and in the midst of another fight, I warned Seth, "If we continue to fight while I am dealing with Mom's sickness, we will not survive our marriage."

I knew I was at the end of my mental rope. Watching a loved one lie changes you. Life is too short became my motto. All the clichés of life *Don't take a single day for granted, Never look back,* became my gospel truths. I started to feel how short my life was while watching Mom fight for hers.

I researched the chances of survival, and the results were depressing. Still, I tried to stay optimistic and hope for the best. I wished I had someone beside me, to help me. I was again mentally all alone.

I put all of my energy into seeing Mom. I sat on the side of her bed daily as we wrote in a mother-daughter journal. I asked her questions about her childhood and young adulthood—I had no idea about half the stuff she told me. We talked about my birth and how *I almost killed her.* She laughed as she told me this. If anyone was going to kill Mom growing up, we both knew it would be me. She told me her earliest childhood memories of dressing up and traveling through the town with her older sister, Aunt Marlene. She smiled as she talked about being a city girl with horses because she begged her daddy and he gave in. Mom was wealthy and spoiled, and I believe that the day she told me all of this stuff, she finally realized it!

When we weren't writing notes about her life, I worked on getting her friends to come visit and planned parties for her. The first party we threw celebrated her sixty-first birthday. She never had parties, for some reason, and this year she was happy to have one. My brother worried about this idea. He was afraid the people coming to the party might unintentionally get her sick. But I was afraid she may never have another birthday, so I threw the party anyway. Mom was excited to see everyone. She was still in contact with three of her childhood friends, and they showed up to spend time with her. The room filled up with people who loved her, and she opened her presents with an ecstatic look on her face.

The second party we threw was a cancer benefit to help offset the incredibly high co-pays from the medical bills. Dad was dead set against the fundraiser. He didn't want anyone to assume they couldn't handle it or were poor—because they weren't. Mom, at first, was very excited to have the benefit, and she knew I would make it happen. She flip-flopped wanting it and then when the date came closer she was concerned that she looked terrible. She didn't want anyone seeing her looking so bad.

Looking back, she did look different but she was never, "not beautiful."

The night of the event she had to use a wheelchair. She wouldn't be able to walk up and down the steps after months of chemo and radiation. She was fine having Dad push her around. She looked like royalty. I was so happy that everyone showed up for her.

Mom was a member of the Flying W in Medford (an airport fly-in "resort") in the middle of the pines with a small motel, indoor and outdoor bars, and an amazing airplane-shaped swimming pool. We hosted the party at the indoor bar. They donated the use of the venue because they loved Mom. They even gave her a key to the pool! Mom sadly enough never made it back to the Flying W, but she loved that she didn't have to pay again.

Over two hundred friends, family members, people who worked with Dad, my friends, and (thank God) my brother showed up with his wife. Chad is much more private than I am, and I believe if Chad were dying he wouldn't want anyone to know. If I were dying, I would want to see everyone just to say one last goodbye. But Chad originally said that he wasn't going to make the event. When Mom heard that, she said she wanted to cancel the whole thing. She never wanted to do anything to put her son out. I had already made many arrangements: The hall was locked in, bands were scheduled, auctions were acquired, a team of medical professionals was built to assist … everyone was in full swing. I couldn't cancel at this point.

Mom kept asking Chad to come, and finally he agreed. He did it for her. And it made all the difference in the world to Mom.

While I was cleaning up after the benefit, I realized it took all of my energy to be actively involved in Mom's world and I had never taken that step before. I had to make an effort to make sure she felt loved. I knew I hadn't done that enough the past eleven years since I moved out. I wanted to show her she was more important than she ever felt. Mom often told me that she felt like "she didn't matter to anyone in the family." It was never that she didn't matter; it was more that her constant sicknesses were viewed poorly by most of the family, including me. Knowing that this was her one concern, I made it my goal to make sure she felt loved—I just hoped it wasn't too late.

Following the amazing benefit, my marriage finally broke. *I* finally broke. I endured from October to May, fighting with Seth about a home that wasn't getting any cleaner and dinner happening later and later. I couldn't keep up with both lives, keeping Mom's world clean and everyone fed, while keeping the same in my own home, while watching Mom wither. I did everything I could to stay busy and to avoid falling into a depressed state. I couldn't handle the marriage anymore. I relied on my friends to help me through the pain. Between my restless nights crying over my mother and enduring fight after fight with Seth, I grew more and more tired. I started signing the kids out early from school and taking them to spend time with their Nanny. Being a good daughter became my top priority, and I knew I was making the right choice.

By the beginning of May I was one hundred percent ready to get out of my marriage. We weren't sleeping in the same room anymore. I slept on a trundle bed in the spare bedroom with my daughter in the main bed. I knew what I had to do despite feeling scared. Seth was ready for it, too, or at least he said he was daily. He was going away for the weekend without me, and I was moving out. Mom had agreed that the kids and I should move in with them. She was over the marital issues too. I was over it all and moving in with my parents to help Dad with Mom while saving my soul made the most sense.

Seth left for his festival and I hired a friend to help me move. For the first two weeks, my children and I shared a king-size bed because I was in denial about the separation leading to divorce. I couldn't get myself to admit that this was my new home even though Seth declared his happiness without me. My parents' garage was packed and remained full of all of our stuff, requiring me to climb through and search for hours when we needed something. The idea that this was where I would be living for the foreseeable future had not yet become a reality for me. I had no road map of my life anymore.

Once I ended the pity party for my failed marriage and finally listened to Mom, "Move on. It's sucked too long, Danielle," I found the motivation to make a space for us. The downstairs of my parents' house that once made up my bedroom, my brother's room, and an old living room currently was an empty room and two storage rooms. We needed to put a new carpet in the living room and the old bedroom, to put up trim in all of the rooms, and to paint the walls. I had my work cut out for me, but I knew that I could make it happen.

Mom was excited to have my help around the house. We both found this to be humorous, considering my childhood. Numerous times she said, "If something happens to me, please make sure you take care of your father." I promised her I would always take care of Dad. She smiled back knowing that was a promise I'd keep.

Thankfully, Mom and the kids had learned how to live together during the DYFS situation. That time, Rory had been very angry that she had to live at Mom and Dad's house. She hated that Mom had a gazillion rules. The rules showed up every time Rory did something wrong.

"This is normal," I told her, laughing. Rory was lucky Mom wasn't as rule oriented this time. She was too sick to care and just wanted to love on all of us.

I was glad she got to live with her Nanny and that they really got to know each other. Prior to Mom getting sick, my children visited their Nanny and Pop-Pop at least once a month for a sleepover, if we were lucky two.

During the sleepovers, Mom watched movies with the kids—inappropriate movies that I would not have ever allowed my kids to watch. At home, my children kept asking to watch *The Walking Dead*, and I kept saying "No." It was way too gory, and I didn't want to expose them to that. The kids were eight and thirteen when they started asking.

When Mom became diagnosed with cancer, and we were at the house all the time, I caught them all sitting in the room with Mom watching *The Walking Dead*. They had been sneaking the show whenever she babysat them. Thus the reason they kept begging to watch it every Sunday. They settled for dates with Nanny to watch their show. After I moved in, I threw in the towel and began watching it with them. We all lay in Mom's bed and watched the creepiest show ever (in my mind) and the best thing that has ever been on TV to Mom and my children. *The Walking Dead* remains in our lives every Sunday, or Monday, if I fall asleep.

Everyone grew closer with Mom during the three months we moved in. Everyone's goal was to help her get better. Mom and I talked every day about life and what I was going to do now that the marriage was ending. It was the first time since I was a teenager that she wasn't explaining how "two women can't live under the same roof." She wanted me home, and she wanted me to leave Seth. She encouraged my moving forward, and she kept telling me, "You deserve a man who loves you. Please Danielle, find yourself a good man." I laughed, promising her I would.

Chapter 17
Two woman can live under the same roof

Despite Mom's sickness, living at my parents' house was quite peaceful. Daily routines no longer entailed the arguments, walking on eggshells, or passive-aggressive behaviors we were used to. Some of this was because I now looked at Mom differently. I started to see the person that my friends had seen my whole life. It seems odd that I could see an unsick Mom when she was indeed the sickest she would ever be. At this point, forgave the years of her not being able to be a "normal" Mom and I just enjoyed her personality.

Everything for the first time in years became easier.

My war continued with Seth, at a distance, but he wasn't my focus as I watched Mom fight her cancer battle. Numerous phone fights ended with, "I can't do this right now. The relationship isn't a concern." And though most of the phone calls ended, the evil texting lasted for months.

My heart ached every time I received one of his texts, but my friends were sick of listening to it and my Mom wanted me to "move the heck on."

Mom kept reassuring me I was making the right choice. "Life is too short and getting out is your only option," she said.

Mom wanted to see me happy. She knew I wasn't happy.

"I am so sorry I didn't tell you to leave sooner," she said. "I should have." She held my face and tears streamed down hers. Instantly I forgave her. I cried on Mom's shoulder for an hour that day. Not only for the death of my marriage, but for her honesty and sincerity. I knew she was right, and I was thankful to finally have her support.

Now Mom's main concern was to make sure that the man she loved didn't end up alone. She knew I would stand by Dad's side. My relationship with Dad, which she once considered an annoyance, now had become a blessing.

Within the first months of living in my childhood home, I decided that I was not going to sit home and watch sappy movies or, cry while the children went for their parent visitations. Mom and Dad hated seeing me sad, and they encouraged me to move on.

I embraced Mom's excitement when I mentioned that I may hang with this guy, Matt, I had recently met. I told her what I knew about him. He was a comedian, and we'd spoken after his comedy show. I wanted to know if his jokes were real. Or did he make it up for his comedy routine? I truly knew nothing about him except that he was a comedian who *did* have a dog named Jack, he liked the snow, and he was separated from his wife and surviving happily. I wanted to be living happily. Mom encouraged me to reach out to him and to leave her and my father alone by getting "the hell out of the house." *Some things never change.*

I did as she said and called Matt. I liked how he spoke about life, and I knew he completely understood where I was in mine. I liked the calming sound of his voice. I was excited to talk to someone separate from my old world, someone I could confide in, and someone fun. I had no intention of dating or moving forward. I was just trying to find my way and enjoy my freedom at the same time.

We spoke on the phone and planned on seeing each other a few days later. He would come over to my parents' house. I warned him that we would have to paint the trim (actual trim), in my new room, because that was what I was doing at this point in my life. He came over dressed in his normal clothes, and I think he may have been surprised when I set up the wooden trim outside and actually began painting. He told me later that he had a change of clothes in the car to

216

paint. Dad walked out with the dogs and just shook his head at me. I introduced Dad to the new "painter assistant" and explained to Matt that "he could meet mom when she gets a little better."

I felt embarrassed bringing a guy to my *parents'* house at my age, but it was my situation. While we painted, we laughed at the fact that I actually had him painting. I wasn't considering it a date, so painting seemed innocent enough. He had me laughing joke after joke about the girl who makes men paint. After the trim had its first coat of paint, we headed down to the local bar, *One More Bar,* and sat talking over a sampler appetizer. I dumped my entire situation into Matt's lap. Literally I told him everything about my marriage, Mom's sickness, and why he couldn't meet her. I must have sounded like a crazy person, and he still wanted to continue hanging out with me. He seemed understanding and fine with everything.

On our drive home from the bar, Matt reached over and held my hand. *Really!* I thought to myself. I literally was internally kicking myself for spilling my *whole* life story on this guy and he wants to hold my hand. I couldn't believe it. He knew everything, and it wasn't because I trusted him. I didn't have time to develop trust. I just didn't want to start anything without the truth being number one priority even if it made me look crazy.

I held his hand as we talked for the next ten minutes on the ride back to my home and, then we painted the second coat.

For the next few weeks, Mom became happily engaged with Matt conversations. Every time I would go out with him, Mom would ask for all of the details. She was excited that my life became less about Seth and our war and more about this new guy I was talking to. She kept saying, "I want to die knowing you are happy, Danielle. You deserve that."

"You're not going to die, Mom, but I promise to be happy anyway!" I said.

I didn't introduce Mom to Matt initially because she was getting sicker, and I waited to introduce her to him when she became better. The chemo and radiation were taking a toll on her body, but the mass was almost completely gone, and the chemo was supposed to stop any further growth. There would be time to introduce them in the near future, and I waited patiently.

Mom allowed fewer and fewer visitors as the time went on. She did, however, allow my childhood friends to visit with her since I was living with her. She was so excited when Lauren came to visit from Virginia. She hugged Lauren and said, "Look at your hair, look at my hair. Oh, Lauren, I wish I had your hair." She then made us both promise that we would never cut our hair again. Even Dad had to promise. Lauren and Mom sat on her bed laughing hysterically as they talked about their past together. Apparently, when I was away in Europe Mom spent her time saving Lauren from her crazy self. I had no idea that they had become so close. Lauren would call Mom if she found herself stuck at a bar unable to drive, stuck because someone left her somewhere or because she picked a bad dude and needed help. Mom rescued Lauren with no questions asked. Unbeknownst to me she even stayed at their house for a few days. I wasn't too surprised, though, because I knew Mom always had her sneaky mysterious side. Stephanie (of the twins) also came over to visit, and we laughed for hours remembering our childhood. Mom always said, "You should all write a book, and I better be in it!" We assured her she would be a star. It broke Steph's heart to see Mom like this.

Thankfully, the summer passed slowly. Decades later, at thirty-five years old, I found myself daydreaming about my childhood while sitting on my now twenty-two-year-old decrepit back deck. The barn too had seen better days. It once was bright red with red asbestos siding. There were no windows, just two large red barn doors and a loft. Over the years my father put up sturdier wood panels that covered the red siding, but the original parts still peeked out from behind the newer plywood. We couldn't hold more than two horses in the barn at a time. Any more than that and it would have been overcrowded in the winter time.

On this particular day, a loud crashing sound disrupted my peaceful silence. It sounded like the lid of a trashcan coming together again and again. A few moments later, I heard another BANG! I stood up from my resting position on the deck, wiping the wood particles from my pants, and looked around. I still had no idea what that sound could be. It did not return so I went back to recollecting my past. As soon as I settled in, another loud BANG made me stand up. I looked further into the yard. And then it caught my eye: The culprit of the loudest bang in Tabernacle was our barn door.

The wind grabbed our rusty, old red barn door and smashed it back against the old rotten fence. The fence took the beating and pushed the door back until the wind swept the door again. There was no way to relax with the noise, so I had to go down to the barn and stop it.

I walked barefoot down the old deck steps onto the dry dirt, something I had done my entire life. Quickly I remembered how Pine Barrens dirt looks clean, but turns your feet blacker than black. I took two steps before wondering if I should run back to grab my shoes, which were in the car on the other side of the house— too far away to get. Instead I continued my journey.

Using the new two-by-fours laid on the ground like a bridge over the dirt floor, I safely reached the middle. I carefully walked across the dirt, while thoughts of a snake jumping out at me freaked me out. I found it helpful to remind myself that I have been a child of this barn since I was born and have never been bitten by a snake inside of it. The barn protected me as a child and I knew it would protect me that day.

I grabbed the bottom half of the old, splintering door and pushed it closed. I attempted to latch the door and noticed that the hardware was missing from one side. Holding the bottom in place, I shut the top half and fought to attach them together. After I pushed the doors together, I latched them shut. I walked back through the barn, past the potential snake threat, hopped over the gigantic well hole, climbed back up the steps, and stared smiling at my old barn as I reassumed my sunbathing reading and journaling position on the deck.

Day by day, I journaled with Mom, played with the kids, and felt confident that all of our lives were going to get better. My confidence cracked when the doctors claimed Mom's cancer had overtaken her. She started to lose more and more weight. She was down to just seventy-six pounds.

The sight of her affected everyone in our family in different ways. Rory had silently avoided her for the past month because it scared her to watch her grandmother become significantly skinnier as she got significantly sicker. Rory often stood outside the door to talk, where she'd yell, "I love you, Nanny," from the hallway. I remember feeling very content when I heard her say it, relieved that she was still interacting with Mom and knowing the two of them had their own peace. Mom never seemed to be upset about Rory's inability to come closer. She understood even more than I ever could have (at the time), how my daughter was feeling about her illness. My father, son, and I allowed the two of them to design their new relationship and tried diligently to understand how these changes would make them both feel.

Nolan, the first blood-born grandson, loved visiting with Nanny. He would lay with her, hold her close, and watch movies with her. They could chat forever. On this particular day, Mom insisted on taking a photo with Nolan. She asked for her lipstick and put it on eagerly. I grabbed her camera off of the dresser and took the photograph reluctantly, knowing how sick she looked. I hesitated, thinking I should talk her out of the idea but she was excited, so I did as she asked.

It broke my heart to see Mom this way. I fought back the tears and tried to act as though everything was normal. I often analyzed her face and touched her skin just so I could remember every detail in the future. I listened to everything she had to say, asked her to tell stories about our past, and hung on her every word. I memorized her stories, retold them in mother books, and learned everything I could in those last six months. I felt the hands of time clicking away in every part of my being.

Two o'clock in the afternoon on August 13, 2014 I walked into Mom and Dad's room with my fourteen-year-old son, Nolan, and my newly nine-year-old daughter, Rory, in tow. Today we would celebrate my daughter's birthday as a family, before she and I headed out to the "real" party with Rory's friends.

I remember feeling proud of Rory when she bravely walked into Mom's room, over to her Nanny and opened, what would be, the last Nanny birthday gift ever. My daughter was so excited to open her new gift—a mandolin. She had wanted a mandolin for a long time and now it was hers. She hugged Nanny and told her she loved her. They agreed they would see each other tomorrow. Rory walked out of that room a happy little girl.

Mom was thrilled to be a part of another birthday for Rory. Every day that she woke up was a good day. Unfortunately, her cancer left her bedridden over the last two months of her life. We all knew this would be the last party she would attend for her granddaughter and that she wouldn't be going anywhere from this point on. In less than six months, Mom went from walking on her own to needing a walker to being pushed in a wheelchair to remaining in bed.

This birthday was the hardest gathering my family had yet to manage. On this day, after both of the kids walked out of the room, I went over and hugged Mom again. I pet her hair back and kissed her forehead, as I had repeatedly for six months. She held my hand as we talked for a few moments about how much she loved me and how much I loved her. Mom told me how proud she was of me as a mom and a daughter. She reminded me again of how she never thought I would be the one here for her. She never believed I would be "someone" who stepped up and took on a caregiver role. Given our past, this made sense and I laughed and agreed that this was not where I thought I would be either. These were conversations my mother and I had often these last few months of her life.

"I'm sorry I wasn't always there for you," Mom said in her last days.

I wished I could say "No Mom. You were there for me." But I couldn't. Just as she couldn't say I was there for her. Instead I held her tighter and said, "It's fine Mom. We are really fine."

I apologized for not understanding the sicknesses she'd endured most of my life. I got it. I was bitter and angry. "I'm sorry Mom. I was immature. I wish I could have understood," I said with tears in my eyes, praying for her forgiveness.

"You were just a kid," she said. She was right. I was just a kid back then, and it pained me to realize I was still just a kid—her kid.

Mom laughed, remembering how we pushed each other's buttons like nobody else could. "I hope your daughter is ten times worse than you ever were!" she joked.

221

I came back with, "I can handle the challenge!" She knew I could. Laughter and forgiveness became our new normal. I turned my back to walk out of the room, "And don't forget to find yourself a good man!" Mom said as she smacked my butt, laughing.

For the first time since I was nine, we were best friends again. I knew it, she knew it, and for the first time since I was a child, Dad knew it too.

I left the house feeling content and ready to take on a birthday party full of nine-year-old girls. Mom was excited that she had the night to herself with her husband, and the kids were all going to Seth's for a visitation after the party. I celebrated Rory's birthday with her friends, and then I dropped all three of the kids off and headed over to Matt's for a date. I felt content with our new life.

At 6:00 a.m., I received a phone call from my father "Danny, I need you to come home." The sound of Dad's voice was like no other sound I had ever heard. He seemed so far as he uttered these words on the other side of the phone. My eyes shot open as I stared at the ceiling fully awake. I hurried out of bed nauseous as I attempted to hold my emotions together.

I drove home down Jackson Road to Oak Shade Road in complete silence, zombie-like, holding onto the steering wheel tightly. The drive felt monotonous on most days but, today it was different. I was on auto pilot, barely able to catch my breath through each loud sob, while desperately trying to pay attention to the road. At six in the morning, the road was empty, and I was thankful.

I fought to recollect every word my mother said as I walked out of our home the prior night, during what I now realized was our last conversation. I pictured her face and what it felt like to kiss her skinny cheek as I said, "Goodbye, I will see you in the morning." I stepped away from her bed and felt her tiny hand grab onto mine. Smiling, she said something she had never said before "Danielle, I am so proud you are *my daughter,* and if given the chance I would have picked you as my friend."

I smiled back and chuckled, "I *know* Mom! I love you too."

I pulled up to the house and ran inside, crying hysterically, hugging my brother, and running to my father's side. I couldn't handle seeing her there, in the bed, where we had spoken so many times these last six months. I wanted her to wake up and put her arms around me one more time. I wanted her to tell me, "Don't worry. Everything is going to be all right and the cancer will go away, doodle bug." The reality was that I would never hear those words again.

My heart was breaking as I watched my father sob. He kept saying, "I fell asleep, I fell asleep, I didn't say good-bye, Danny."

Mom went peacefully in her sleep, and my father couldn't figure out why she wouldn't say good-bye to him. He wished that she woke him up. The pain I felt for my father was the most unbearable. It was like having my own heart ripped from my soul.

My mother liked to sleep naked. My father didn't want her to go to the funeral home naked. Someone had to dress my mother. My father couldn't do it. The sadness was too overwhelming. My brother didn't need that memory, so I volunteered. I knew it was the last thing I could do for my mother to show how much I appreciated her. She would have done the same for me. I went to the closet in her bedroom. I looked at all the clothes, knowing that not much still fit her. The closet of clothes seemed to engulf me for hours, yet only moments had passed. I picked out a red dress, one that I had never seen before. I knew it must belong to Aunt Marlene, my mother's sister.

I walked over to where Mom lay and picked up her tiny body, leaning her toward me like a sleeping baby. I put the beautiful red dress over her head, pushed her arms through the armholes, and pulled it down to her waist. I went into her drawer of underwear and picked out the best pair of Victoria Secret silk undies I could find. I placed them on her cold body and pulled the dress over her knees. I sat there for a moment grappling with how this would be my final memory.

My next step was to tell two beautiful children that they just lost their Nanny. I walked out of the room, hugged my brother, hugged my father, said hello to my mother's sisters, who had just arrived. I nodded at the strange man in the yellow pants who was waiting with a funeral home car. I got in my car and drove back to my kids, who were sleeping at the house I once shared with Seth.

The fifteen-minute drive from Tabernacle to Medford, one town over, seemed like another hour. I walked back into my old home, completely numb and indifferent to the changes in the house, and located my children. Overwhelmed with everything that was happening, I walked into Rory's room and lay with her on the bed. The boys came in after. Choked up, I told them "Nanny is gone." My eyes welled up with tears as I tried to fight them from rolling down my face. I was trying to be strong for the kids.

"No Mom. This isn't true," Nolan insisted. I reached out to hug him and he pulled away.

"No!" Rory started to cry, and Little felt the worst of all. Since the separation he hadn't seen his Nanny. He missed saying goodbye.

Nolan begged, "Please let me say goodbye. I want to go home." Knowing this wasn't the time for that because hospice was at the house collecting the medication and the funeral home was at the house picking Mom up, I said, "You can't see her kids." *I wished I didn't see her.* I wanted my children to remember their nanny talking, loving, and laughing. I didn't want them to remember a skeleton with no life in her.

We all said goodbye less than twenty-four hours before, and that was to be our last goodbye.

My children truly understood how sick their Nanny was even though none of us will ever understand why she had to go so young. When I finally calmed down and was ready to leave, Seth said, "Come home, we can make it all better."

I couldn't even breathe. I was in shock and feeling an emotion that I hadn't felt since I was nine-years-old. Grief had returned, and with it came depressing sadness.

I looked at Seth and heard my Mom's voice say, "You deserve a man that loves you."

"I don't believe I should make any serious decisions at this moment in time," I said and made my way to the front door.

Walking away from my marital home, I glanced back and heard my Mom, "Danielle, I am so proud you are *my daughter,* and if given the chance I would have picked you as my friend."

Epilogue:

Life moves on

It took me almost three years to complete this book. It was a painful journey reliving the past, understanding where I went wrong, and healing my internal relationship with Mom. I have grown through writing this memoir and I have come to peace with my life up to this moment.

By June 2016, I had the divorce Mom begged me to get. This was its own separate journey! (Possibly in BUTTERFLY 2 or SECRETS of the Butterfly!)

As I promised Mom, I still live with Dad, neither of us have cut our hair, and we take care of each other. We all struggled horribly in the beginning without her. Every member of my family suffered in a different way. Dad had to find his own life and happiness without Mom. This was a struggle the first year, but he seems better these days. He brought four kittens into the home and along with our four dogs, they keep him occupied. He still has never been on a single date and I don't believe that is in his future.

Two months after Mom passed; Dad gave us a scare and almost died in the hospital from Septic Shock after another stent operation. Watching Dad slow down has been very difficult for me. Walking up and down the steps a few times a day causes chest pains. The worst part about it is that he can't fix the problem. The doctors have determined that surgery is not an option. I struggle with the thought of losing another parent, but I know I can rely on the strength my life has instilled in me. Dad retired and now just lives his life happily at home with all of us as his company.

Nolan fought through his days knowing that he loved Nanny and she loved him back. Dad is teaching him to be an amazing young man, and at eighteen he couldn't have a better set of role models. As promised by Mom, Nolan was given her pickup truck. Sadly he had it one year and a car accident totaling the truck took another piece of mom away. We mourned the loss of the truck but took happiness in knowing Nolan walked away unscathed. He must have had an angel protecting him!

Rory still sometimes texts me, "I miss Nanny, Mom." I have no answer but "I know, darling. Me too." She wears her horseshoe ring daily as a reminder that she is there for her. The older Rory gets the more of her Nanny I see in her.

They both graduated schools this year—Rory's from eighth grade and Nolan from high school—knowing their Nanny knew they could succeed.

Little is doing great and is here all the time. He is graduating high school this year and joining the Navy in hopes of being a Navy Seal. Nanny always said, "That boy is gonna do just fine, Danny, no worries." I believe she will make sure to keep him safe.

The twins are doing well. They lost their dad Norman as I was working on this book. He didn't get the chance to read it but, he was cheering for me every time I ran into him.

Lauren is still one of my closest friends and we talk monthly at least. She is busy with her endeavors which include being Anarchy Girl, the largest Anarchy platform on Facebook. I know crazy, right! We still disagree a ton.

Aunt Barb is struggling now. We all are saddened because Uncle Joe was diagnosed with Cancer and we lived this nightmare again with another person we loved. I made sure to let him know his importance in my life before he passed away.

My brother Chad and I are still distant despite my attempt to live mom's dream of staying close for her. I know if I ever need him, he will be here.

Uncle George passed away in December of 2018. I will miss Uncle George forever. If it weren't for his kindness throughout my life, things would have never turned out the way they did.

We all still mourn mom in our own ways. I wear her ashes around my neck in a (vessel) and her ring daily as a reminder of how I am a product of her.

I wrote this book to find myself and to make sure I never forget Mom helped me become the woman I am today. I know in my heart Mom would be proud of all of us.

I struggled with the divorce and wished she was there to help, but her voice was always in my head. I promised her I would move on. I promised her I wouldn't settle and that I would find a nice man. I am so happy that she helped me make this choice. I can beyond a shadow of a doubt say that while Mom was nearing the end, I made her happy talking about Matt, the really amazing comedian. She knew I had absolutely no intentions of a relationship at the time but she would be proud that four years later I am still with Matt, happily recovered and in love.

Matt and I became engaged on July 11, 2017 and married on August 17th 2018 with our families surrounding us. Mom would be so proud that I chose a man who treats me like a Jewish American Princess. I wish I could tell her I found my happiness, almost as much as I wish I could have introduced him to Mom—this is my only regret. I know now that Mom's soul is free, and she surrounds me daily. Someday we will be reunited.

I never stop missing my mom. I think about her every day. I cried yesterday as I reread these pages. I cried because my mom isn't here. I cried because I really believed she'd survive. I truly believed the medicine would work. I believed in the doctors and the chemo and the radiation. I wanted to be with my mom longer, so I put all of my energy into willing it into the universe. Needless to say, my constant will was not heard. I wish I had more time to love my mom.

She's in every breath I take. I feel her beside me. She is a part of my personality, the words I use, my laugh and smile. My mom is never gone. Every time I see a Butterfly, I believe it is Mom assuring me that I am on the right path this time. Dad tells me daily that I am just like Mom. In the past this would have sent shivers down my spine, but now I am happy to be my mother's daughter.

Thank you for making me strong, Mom.

Your death brought me new life.

Butterfly: From Daughter to Mother

Made in the USA
Middletown, DE
12 March 2019